P9-EDR-580

Budgeting for
Not-for-Profit Organizations

WILEY NONPROFIT LAW, FINANCE, AND MANAGEMENT SERIES

The Art of Planned Giving: Understanding Donors and the Culture of Giving by Douglas E. White
Beyond Fund Raising: New Strategies for Nonprofit Investment and Innovation by Kay Grace
Budgeting for Not-for-Profit Organizations by David Maddox
Charity, Advocacy, and the Law by Bruce R. Hopkins
The *Complete Guide to Fund Raising Management* by Stanley Weinstein
The Complete Guide to Nonprofit Management by Smith, Bucklin & Associates
Critical Issues in Fund Raising edited by Dwight Burlingame
Developing Affordable Housing: A Practical Guide for Nonprofit Organizations, Second Edition by Bennett L. Hecht
Financial and Accounting Guide for Not-for-Profit Organizations, Fifth Edition by Malvern J. Gross, Jr., Richard F. Larkin, Roger S. Bruttomesso, John J. McNally, PricewaterhouseCoopers LLP
Financial Empowerment: More Money for More Mission by Peter C. Brinckerhoff
Financial Management for Nonprofit Organizations by Jo Ann Hankin, Alan Seidner and John Zietlow
Financial Planning for Nonprofit Organizations by Jody Blazek
The Fund Raiser's Guide to the Internet by Michael Johnston
Fund-Raising: Evaluating and Managing the Fund Development Process, Second Edition by James M. Greenfield
Fund-Raising Fundamentals: A Guide to Annual Giving for Professionals and Volunteers by James M. Greenfield
Fund-Raising Regulation: A State-by-State Handbook of Registration Forms, Requirements, and Procedures by Seth Perlman and Betsy Hills Bush
Grantseeker's Toolkit: A Comprehensive Guide to Finding Funding by Cheryl S. New and James Quick
High Performance Nonprofit Organizations: Managing Upstream for Greater Impact by Christine Letts, William Ryan, and Allen Grossman
Intermediate Sanctions: Curbing Nonprofit Abuse by Bruce R. Hopkins and D. Benson Tesdahl
International Fund Raising for Nonprofits by Thomas Harris
International Guide to Nonprofit Law by Lester A. Salamon and Stefan Toepler & Associates
The Law of Fund-Raising, Second Edition by Bruce R. Hopkins
The Law of Tax-Exempt Healthcare Organizations by Thomas K. Hyatt and Bruce R. Hopkins
The Law of Tax-Exempt Organizations, Sixth Edition by Bruce R. Hopkins
The Legal Answer Book for Nonprofit Organizations by Bruce R. Hopkins
A Legal Guide to Starting and Managing a Nonprofit Organization, Second Edition by Bruce R. Hopkins
Managing Affordable Housing: A Practical Guide to Creating Stable Communities by Bennett L. Hecht, Local Initiatives Support Corporation, and James Stockard
Managing Upstream: Creating High-Performance Nonprofit Organizations by Christine W. Letts, William P. Ryan, and Allan Grossman
Mission-Based Management: Leading Your Not-for-Profit Into the 21st Century by Peter C. Brinckerhoff
Mission-Based Marketing: How Your Not-for-Profit Can Succeed in a More Competitive World by Peter C. Brinckerhoff
Nonprofit Boards: Roles, Responsibilities, and Performance by Diane J. Duca
Nonprofit Compensation and Benefits Practices by Applied Research and Development Institute International, Inc.
The Nonprofit Counsel by Bruce R. Hopkins
The Nonprofit Guide to the Internet, Second Edition by Michael Johnston
Nonprofit Investment Policies: A Practical Guide to Creation and Implementation by Robert Fry, Jr.
The Nonprofit Law Dictionary by Bruce R. Hopkins
Nonprofit Compensation, Benefits, and Employment Law by David G. Samuels and Howard Pianko
Nonprofit Litigation: A Practical Guide with Forms and Checklists by Steven Bachmann
The Nonprofit Handbook, Second Edition: Volume I—Management by Tracy Daniel Connors
The Nonprofit Handbook, Second Edition: Volume II—Fund Raising by Jim Greenfield
The Nonprofit Manager's Resource Dictionary by Ronald A. Landskroner
Nonprofit Organizations' Business Forms: Disk Edition by John Wiley & Sons, Inc.
Partnerships and Joint Ventures Involving Tax-Exempt Organizations by Michael I. Sanders
Planned Giving: Management, Marketing, and Law by Ronald R. Jordan and Katelyn L. Quynn
Private Foundations: Tax Law and Compliance by Bruce R. Hopkins and Jody Blazek
Program Related Investments: A Technical Manual for Foundations by Christie I Baxter
Reengineering Your Nonprofit Organization: A Guide to Strategic Transformation by Alceste T. Pappas
Reinventing the University: Managing and Financing Institutions of Higher Education by Sandra L. Johnson and Sean C. Rusk, PricewaterhouseCoopers LLP
The Second Legal Answer Book for Nonprofit Organizations by Bruce R. Hopkins
Special Events: Proven Strategies for Nonprofit Fund Raising by Alan Wendroff
Strategic Communications for Nonprofit Organizations: Seven Steps to Creating a Successful Plan by Janel Radtke
Strategic Planning for Nonprofit Organizations: A Practical Guide and Workbook by Michael Allison and Jude Kaye, Support Center for Nonprofit Management
Streetsmart Financial Basics for Nonprofit Managers by Thomas A. McLaughlin
A Streetsmart Guide to Nonprofit Mergers and Networks by Thomas A. McLaughlin
Successful Marketing Strategies for Nonprofit Organizations by Barry J. McLeish
The Tax Law of Charitable Giving by Bruce R. Hopkins
The Tax Law of Colleges and Universities by Bertrand M. Harding
Tax Planning and Compliance for Tax-Exempt Organizations: Forms, Checklists, Procedures, Third Edition by Jody Blazek
The Universal Benefits of Volunteering: A Practical Workbook for Nonprofit Organizations, Volunteers and Corporations by Walter P. Pidgeon, Jr.
The Volunteer Management Handbook by Tracy Daniel Connors

Budgeting for Not-for-Profit Organizations

DAVID C. MADDOX

John Wiley & Sons, Inc.
New York • Chichester • Weinheim • Brisbane • Singapore • Toronto

This book is printed on acid-free paper. ♾

Published simultaneously in Canada.

Library of Congress Cataloging-in-Publication Data:

Maddox, David.
Budgeting for not-for-profit organizations / by David Maddox.
p. cm.—(Wiley nonprofit law, finance, and management series)
Includes bibliographical references and index.
ISBN 0-471-25397-9 (cl. : alk. paper)
1. Nonprofit organizations—Finance. I. Title. II. Series.
HG4027.65.M33 1999
658.15'9—dc21 99-12223

Printed in the United States of America.

10 9 8 7 6 5 4 3 2 1

SUBSCRIPTION NOTICE

This Wiley product is updated on a periodic basis with supplements to reflect important changes in the subject matter. If you purchased this product directly from John Wiley & Sons, Inc., we have already recorded your subscription for this update service.

If, however, you purchased this product from a bookstore and wish to receive future updates and revised or related volumes billed separately with a 30-day examination review, please send your name, company name (if applicable), address, and the title of the product to:

Supplement Department
John Wiley & Sons, Inc.
One Wiley Drive
Somerset, NJ 08875
1-800-225-5945

For customers outside the United States, please contact the Wiley office nearest you:

Professional & Reference Division
John Wiley & Sons Canada, Ltd.
22 Worcester Road
Rexdale, Ontario M9W 1L1
CANADA
(416) 675-3580
1-800-567-4797
FAX (416) 675-6599

Jacaranda Wiley Ltd.
PRT Division
P.O. Box 174
North Ryde, NSW 2113
AUSTRALIA
(02) 805-1100
FAX (02) 805-1597

John Wiley & Sons, Ltd.
Baffins Lane
Chichester
West Sussex, PO19 1UD
UNITED KINGDOM
(44) (243) 779777

John Wiley & Sons (SEA) Pte. Ltd.
37 Jalan Pemimpin
Block B # 05-04
Union Industrial Building
SINGAPORE 2057
(65) 258-1157

About the Author

David Maddox is a management consultant in KPMG's Higher Education Consulting practice. Mr. Maddox advises higher education and other nonprofit organizations on budgeting, finance, human resources, and administrative operations. His previous experience includes management positions in budgeting and human resources at Vanderbilt University and the University of Chicago. In addition, he has served as a board member for several nonprofit organizations in the arts and community service.

Mr. Maddox holds a bachelor's degree in music from Amherst College, a master's degree in the humanities from the University of Chicago, and an MBA from the Owen Graduate School of Management at Vanderbilt University.

About the Author

Acknowledgments

I have been the beneficiary of a number of generous teachers over the years who deserve credit for whatever is useful in this book: Alec McRae, formerly of Congressional Information Service, Inc.; from Vanderbilt University: H. Clint Davidson, Jr., Professors Thomas Mahoney and David Rados, Dean Martin Geisel, and Glen Clanton; from the University of Chicago: Henry S. Webber, Caren Skoulas, Lawrence Furnstahl, and Andrew Lyons; Laura Weathered, executive director of the Near NorthWest Arts Council; and from KPMG: Eileen McGinn, Hal Zeidman, and Roger Hardy. I owe deep thanks to Kathryn Behrens and David Hemingson at KPMG for their support, guidance, and the numerous opportunities they give me. Thanks also to Martha Cooley at John Wiley & Sons, who had the idea for this book.

Above all of these acknowledgments, I owe thanks to my wife Maria, who watches me run off to jobs and meetings with patience always, and encourages me in this project and many others. Beyond the obvious ways, this book would not be possible without my parents, Janet and Jerald Maddox, who in their work, teaching, and other pursuits gave me the example to follow and the introduction to the life behind these pages.

Contents

PART ONE

Introduction

CHAPTER ONE

Introduction

1.1 INTRODUCTION

The budget process can provoke very different and conflicting reactions. It may seem an obvious principle that budgeting is a critical discipline for bringing order to an organization. However, once inside an organization, the budget process may seem irrelevant and intrusive to effective management, even taking managers away from running departments and programs and tying them up in meetings and paperwork that have the same end result: admonitions to do more with less than is needed.

The frustrations with the budget process vary with the organization. A small organization may be very dependent on a few grants. If those grants come in, the money will be spent and programs will be offered; if not, the organization will scramble to find the cash each month to pay the rent and meet the payroll. Advanced financial planning and budgeting seem irrelevant. In larger organizations, money may be more accessible, but central officers who make decisions on who receives funding may prefer certain departments or programs or may be forced to fund certain operations.

In spite of objections to the process, budgeting is fundamental to management. It is one of the best tools available to focus and coordinate an organization. When the process is well designed and administered with political sensitivity, it provides an effective vehicle for decision making and communication. A process designed to fit the organization and its mission, strategy, and management principles will encourage everyone involved with the organization to stand behind the organization's resource allocation decisions. Rather than fostering resentment, the budget process should promote integration of the organization. In times of tight resources or organizational change, an organization needs the budget process as a guide. Few organizations can simply drift through the kinds of difficulties the nonprofit sector faces today.

1.2 PURPOSE OF THIS BOOK

The purpose of this book is to comprehensively review the budget process and to outline the principles of its design that improve the fit with an organization. On one level, the book provides a primer on budgeting. Anyone new to budgeting can use this book as a guide for installing or managing a budget system. For other nonprofit organization professionals, understanding the whole budget process will make it easier to operate effectively.

The book also tries to present principles and techniques that will allow an organization to make effective use of the budget process. Several chapters deal explicitly with these budget design issues and successful budgeting systems. Budgeting is an organizational development and leadership tool as well as a financial discipline. A good budgeting system enables an organization's leaders to mobilize the people in the organization and gives everyone from line managers to board members an appropriate way to get their comments heard and acted upon.

1.3 WHO SHOULD READ THIS BOOK

The book will move back and forth between three perspectives of key participants in the budget process. Each group has its own interests.

1. *The organization's leaders.* Their interest is in maintaining an efficient process for resolving the conflicting demands for resources, furthering what they see as the organization's primary objectives, and protecting the organization's financial position.
2. *Internal managers.* Typically, they are interested in getting resources for their program or area with a minimum of aggravation.

3. *External groups.* Boards and funders want the organization's budget to represent its true plans, to demonstrate that the organization is being run on sound financial principles, and to lay out a realistic plan to efficiently achieve its mission. Boards and funding agencies can be perceived as having two distinct perspectives. The board is more committed to the organization and its success. The funding agency is more concerned that specific program objectives are served by the allocation. Boards ensure stewardship of resources; funders often purchase services.

1.4 STRUCTURE OF THIS BOOK

This book is designed to provide an introduction to budgeting and financial planning, to outline principles of budget design, and to provide an in-depth discussion of topics related to managing an organization's finances and the budget process. The chapters are organized into five parts:

- *Part I: Introduction.* In addition to this introductory chapter, Chapter 2 presents some basic concepts about budgeting. These ideas will aid readers who need to install a budget system, which can take many forms or variations. These basic principles are important for others as well. Those trying to operate within an existing budget system will have more success if they understand the principles on which it was constructed or developed. Also, the rate of change in the nonprofit organizational environment is such that many organizations will need to reassess their budgeting practices on an almost continuous basis. Anyone tinkering with a budgeting system needs to keep these principles in mind.
- *Part II: The Budget Process.* Chapters 3 through 7 present step-by-step expositions of the budget cycle and its components: the operating, capital, and cash budgets.
- *Part III: Managing an Organization's Finances.* Chapters 8 through 15 move past the basic review of the budget process to discussions of how to manage an organization's finances through the budget process. There are in-depth discussions of key activities during each phase of the budget cycle and a review of management actions driven by the budget process, such as responses to surpluses and deficits and techniques for maintaining financial controls and reducing costs.

- *Part IV: Trends in Budgeting.* Chapters 16 and 17 address two of the major trends in budgeting: reallocation systems and responsibility center management. As future trends and approaches emerge, they will be covered in supplements to this volume.
- *Part V: Tools.* Chapters 18 and 19 return to discussions of the tools used in the budget process. The most fundamental are documents and forms, which have usually appeared in paper form but are increasingly being converted to electronic formats. Chapter 19 covers the various ways in which automation is used to support the budget process.

1.5 CASE STUDIES

In order to avoid reliance on abstractions and generalizations, examples are used wherever possible. Four sample organizations are presented that are based on organizations with which the author has worked as a board member, committee chairperson, manager, or consultant. These organizations represent some of the range of budgeting issues found in the nonprofit sector and the diversity of mission, financing, and organizational structure.

Thumbnail sketches of these organizations follow. Readers are advised to familiarize themselves with the general description of each organization. As examples are needed, the relevant information on the organization is presented.

(a) Organization 1: The University of Okoboji

The University of Okoboji is a midsized private university with an undergraduate liberal arts college and graduate programs in business, pharmacy, and social work. Most of its revenue comes from tuition, although private giving and endowments are also significant sources of support. It currently operates at a deficit, having found it faces new competition in some of its programs. See Exhibit 1.1.

(b) Organization 2: Victim Assistance Association

The Victim Assistance Association is a small organization that provides support to victims of crime in an urban neighborhood. Most of its support comes from a grant from the state attorney general's office, which has a program designed to support such neighborhood-based organizations. The group also receives a small gift and free rent from a local church. It

Exhibit 1.1 University of Okoboji Current Budget

	Unrestricted	*Auxiliaries*	*Total Current Unrestricted*	*Restricted*	*Plant*	*Total*
Tuition and fees	$52,000		$52,000			$52,000
Federal appropriations	2,000		2,000	4,300		6,300
State appropriations	1,100		1,100	4,200		5,300
Local appropriations	750		750			750
Grants and contracts	0		0	5,500		5,500
Private gifts	15,000		15,000	0	7,000	22,000
Endowment income used	8,050		8,050			8,050
Sales and services	500		500			500
Other sources	350		350		7,000	7,350
Auxiliary sales		34,000	34,000			34,000
Total revenue	**79,750**	**34,000**	**113,750**	**14,000**	**14,000**	**141,750**
E&G			0			0
Instruction	55,000		55,000	4,300		59,300
Research	6,700		6,700			6,700
Public services	2,500		2,500			2,500
Academic support	3,740		3,740			3,740
Student services	4,000		4,000			4,000
Institutional support	5,750		5,750			5,750
Operation and maintenance of plant	6,000		6,000		7,000	13,000
Scholarships	4,000		4,000	9,700		13,700
Mandatory transfer	1,560		1,560			1,560
Total E&G	89,250	0	89,250	14,000	7,000	110,250
Auxiliaries		30,920	30,920			30,920
Interest paid			0		210	210
Depreciation			0		700	700
Other costs			0		7,000	7,000
Total expenses	**89,250**	**30,920**	**120,170**	**14,000**	**14,910**	**149,080**
Net surplus/(deficit)	**($9,500)**	**$3,080**	**($6,420)**	**$0**	**($910)**	**($7,330)**

employs two people: a full-time director and a half-time staff assistant. See Exhibit 1.2.

(c) Organization 3: Community Arts Council

The Community Arts Council is a community-based organization that supports artists and the arts in a major city. It includes arts education programs, a gallery that runs shows curated by volunteers, and a newspaper for the arts community. The organization employs four people: a full-time director and an office assistant and two part-time education coordinators for its two main arts education programs. The group is funded heavily by several contracts and grants, the largest of which is a state arts seed grant that pays most of the director's salary. The Arts Council has watched cuts in arts funding warily and knows that it may need to rely more heavily on other sources of income in the future. See Exhibit 1.3.

Exhibit 1.2 Victim Assistance Association: Current Budget

Revenue	
State grant	$46,080
Plate collection	1,000
Contributions (rent)	12,000
Total revenue	**59,080**
Salaries	
Director	32,000
Office assistant (part-time)	10,000
Health insurance	2,400
Telephones	480
Rent	12,000
Supplies	225
Equipment	300
Events	400
Travel (clients)	250
Travel (staff)	250
Memberships	300
Publications	175
Total expenses	**58,780**
Net surplus/(deficit)	**$300**

Exhibit 1.3 Community Arts Council: Current Budget

Revenue	
Memberships	$ 2,000
Grants	70,000
Contracts	52,000
Rentals	4,500
Sales	1,200
Fund-raising	6,000
Advertising	4,000
Total revenue	**139,700**
Salaries	88,000
Benefits	3,300
Rent	12,000
Supplies	200
Telephones	600
Computer lease	2,400
Contract services	20,000
Exhibition costs	3,000
Insurance	1,000
Printing	7,000
Advertising	2,000
Total expenses	**139,500**
Net surplus/(deficit)	**$200**

(d) Organization 4: Presbyterian Church

This organization is a small, old church located in the downtown of a large city. It is supported from parishioner pledges and a $700,000 endowment. Mission activities consume 25 percent of the church's income and it employs a staff of six: a pastor, a part-time educational associate, a music director, a secretary, a building steward, and a cook. Due to its downtown location, the church struggles to maintain membership, since much of its historical congregational base has moved to the suburbs, and it feels driven to take a very active role in trying to alleviate suffering right outside its doors in the city. See Exhibit 1.4 for the church's budget.

1.6 CONCLUSION

This chapter is a roadmap for the entire book. The general purpose is to provide a comprehensive review of the budget process, outline its design

Exhibit 1.4 Presbyterian Church: Current Budget

Revenue	
Pledges	$181,000
Plate	20,000
Special offerings	12,000
Endowment	35,000
Rentals	10,000
Interest	3,000
Total revenue	**261,000**
Expenses	
Operations	
Salaries	140,000
Benefits	28,000
Supplies	1,200
Phones	1,200
Equipment	2,000
Utilities	5,000
Contract services	6,000
Mission	
Presbytery	20,000
Local mission	40,600
Ghana hospital	2,000
Church development, Brazil	3,000
Special offerings	12,000
Total expenses	**261,000**
Net surplus/(deficit)	**$0**

principles, and present techniques effectively using the budget process. We have recognized and attempted to balance the different needs of several key players in the budget process who might find this book useful: organization leaders, internal managers, and external groups such as boards. The book is divided into five major parts that move from the introduction and general overview material into more focused discussions that relate to managing an organization's finances, trends in budgeting, and tools used in the process. Before turning to the review of the budget process, several general concepts are presented in the next chapter.

CHAPTER TWO

General Concepts of Budgeting

2.1 INTRODUCTION

Anyone who wants to understand their organization's budget process or design and manage a budget process for an organization needs to keep in mind some basic concepts about budgeting. We will discuss many of these issues in depth later in the book, often at several points. We have identified five sets of key concepts that the reader should keep in mind in thinking about any aspect of budgeting:

1. The purposes of a budget
2. Types of budgeting systems and design
3. The difference between organizational and program budgeting
4. Leadership, accountability, and involvement in the process
5. Transparency and predictability as principles guiding budget process design

The reader may want to return to these sections after finishing later sections of the book that address details of the budget process and organizational financial management.

2.2 PURPOSES OF A BUDGET

Budgets have five general purposes:

1. They put business strategy into operation.
2. They allocate resources.
3. They provide incentives to managers.
4. They control spending.
5. They communicate plans and expectations.

(a) Business Strategy

An organization may set its strategy through a thorough planning process that involves many people creating mission statements, analyzing strengths, weaknesses, opportunities, and threats, prioritizing initiatives, and so forth. At the end, the planning group may produce a comprehensive strategic plan document. As anyone who has worked in an organization knows, all of this effort can mean next to nothing! To move strategic goals forward, the organization has to put its money where its mouth is and fund those things that advance its stated goals. The budget process provides the vehicle for operationalizing strategy by making decisions to allocate funds in line with the strategy.

Budgets inevitably reflect the organization's *real* strategy—whether that strategy is implicit or explicit, the product of conscious planning or circumstance. The budget shows what the organization thinks is going to happen and what initiatives it is going to take. Some aspects of a budget are less within the organization's ability to dictate—for example, if fuel costs are rising, the organization may have to devote significant additional resources to keeping its facility heated. Keeping the buildings warm may not be a primary strategic objective of the organization, but it may take precedence over more visionary expenditures. If enough of these types of costs hit a budget, although the organization may state a far-reaching strategic goal, its actual strategy for the time being is to keep the doors open. This situation is not very inspiring, but it is often the real world of nonprofit organizations.

In other cases, the budget is the place where funds are set aside for new programs, capital investments, and all types of enhanced resources. The budget may incorporate new goals for the organization, such as higher rates of fund-raising and memberships. The emphasis in a new budget may result from a conscious planning process or from the political struggles of various factions within the organization. The higher salary for the new dean of the medical school on some level means the medical school is receiving a higher profile in the university's financial future, even if the university feels it has little choice but to pay more to fill the position.

(b) Resource Allocation

Budgets presume resources are limited. There is not enough for everyone to have everything they want or even everything they need. Therefore, the organization has to decide how to distribute the funds it expects to have within the organization. The budget process forces the organization to take stock of its resources and to determine their limits. It must identify the sources of funds it can tap and how they will be used. An organization can structure its allocations on the basis of units or departments, programs, activities, or managers. In some cases, particular resources will be tied to particular units or programs, as in grants or restricted gifts. The budget process must distinguish those funds that are earmarked for specific purposes and then distribute the unrestricted funds at its disposal. In many cases, it will consider some programs to more or less stand on their own because of earmarked funds or their ability to bring in new resources, and other programs will be identified as most in need of organizational resources.

(c) Incentives

Every budget process is governed by rules, stated or unstated. These rules encourage certain behaviors on the part of people in the organization. The behaviors encouraged by the budget process benefit or harm the organization, depending in part on how well they were thought out, although unintended effects occur in even the most carefully designed system.

Let us take a classic example. Many budget systems give each unit an expense allocation for the year. This allocation should suffice to support the unit's annual operations. However, some units will spend a little more than their allocation, some a little less. Therefore, at the end of the year unused funds go back to the central administration so that it can cover units that ran deficits. Managers interpret this rule as "use it or lose it." If a manager succeeds in holding expenses below budget all year, he or she sees no reason to give the money back to cover deficits caused by someone who did not do as good a job of managing. In this environment of scarce resources, the manager sees that plenty of things are needed in his or her unit, so the staff is instructed to spend as much of the budget as possible in the last month of the fiscal year. This spending is not strictly necessary, but it is repeated across the organization. As a whole, the organization would be much better off without those purchases. It needs to design rules that provide incentives for managers to make more careful spending decisions throughout the year.

(d) Control

The traditional view of budgets considers them a tool for controlling spending. Departments receive budgets that tell them how much to spend, and central offices do not let them spend more than what appears in their budget. This approach to cost control is very simple to understand. It assumes that spending will tend to be unlimited if it is not cut off and that managers or departments need a lot of help in knowing when to cut back on spending. However, this approach has problems. It can be inflexible and costly to administer. It requires additional paperwork in the form of budget transfers to respond to changing conditions; it may require central staff to monitor departmental actions and to work with these departments when spending needs do not match the budget. The budget can become an obstacle to management, leading to substantial effort to work around it to achieve what the department needs to get done.

A newer approach to cost control emphasizes various forms of self-control rather than centrally administered control. In can be summarized with this statement: If goals are well stated, accepted, and internalized by well-chosen managers who are given decision-making power, those managers will make the most sensible spending decisions for the whole organization. The fundamental argument is that the organization should trust its managers as much as its central staff to make good financial decisions. The locus of control shifts to selection, training, communication, and evaluation of managers, and the budget becomes more important as a way to share information and set goals. Budget rules are designed to give managers strong incentives to make decisions in line with organizational goals. The organization achieves financial control through the entire system of procedure, rules, tools, and supervisory relationships.

(e) Communication

Budgets are critical vehicles for internal and external communications. The budget process allows leadership to describe its plans, goals, and assessment of economic conditions for the rest of the organization. In soliciting budget proposals, leadership can ask the various parts of the organization for their assessment of relevant conditions, thus providing new information about the organization's opportunities and threats and obtaining a reality check on leadership's vision. Once the budget is set, managers can take their marching orders from it.

External groups rely on budgets to understand the organization's plans and expectations. Funders want to see budgets that show how the organization intends to use the money it receives. The budget shows an organization's board what management thinks is going to happen in the coming year. The budget also allows the board and other external groups to assess management's ability to oversee finances, serve as a steward for resources, and achieve objectives. If the budget is unrealistic, it suggests that management does not have a plan for maintaining the organization's financial health. For example, if an organization plugs a deficit budget with a huge figure for one-time gifts well beyond the level of gifts achieved in the past, the board will question whether the organization has done everything it can to cut costs and align expenditures with revenues. The board may insist on seeing a concrete fund-raising plan to achieve this revenue objective or may introduce a cost-cutting campaign.

2.3 TYPES OF BUDGETING

Budget processes differ in their degree of centralization, emphasis on redistribution of resources, institutional focus, and time period coverage. Each of these dimensions of the budget process is described briefly.

(a) Centralized or Participatory Budgeting

In a heavily centralized budgeting system, a central office controls the budget process, makes decisions about how resources will be allocated, and controls expenditures once the budget is in place. Small organizations may have a centralized system where budgets are the responsibility of the organization's director, who takes care of this part of running the organization. In a larger organization, a centralized system will involve central budget or finance specialists and perhaps a separate budget office to assemble data, prepare analyses and reports, and supervise transactions. A centralized system typically focuses on maximizing the efficiency of distribution of resources between units. Each unit will keep its parochial interests in mind and insist it needs more resources. However, from an organization-wide perspective it may be clear that one organization needs more consideration than another, and a centralized system can redistribute resources as needed.

Participatory systems heavily involve units or program managers in developing budgets and controlling spending. In a participatory system, more of the information on revenue projections and expense requirements will flow from the bottom of the organization up. In this environment, the central staff focuses primarily on setting guidelines, coordinating the process, and compiling information. Participatory systems are generally believed to provide better information about the organization's finances, increase the sense of ownership and commitment to the budget, and maximize efficient use of resources.

A participatory system may reduce or eliminate the need for central budget staff, lowering costs and reducing administrative burdens. However, it is more difficult to reallocate resources between units in a participatory system. All of the participants will argue passionately for retaining the resources they currently receive, adding more political complexity to what is already a complicated analytical problem of determining the best application of resources.

(b) Incremental or Redistributive Budgeting

Incremental budgeting refers to systems that base future allocations on current allocations and the new budget is created by increasing or decreasing the current budget by certain amounts or percentages. Each department might receive a 3 percent increase in salaries and 1 percent on other expenses, calculated on the basis of its current allocation in those categories.

Incremental budgeting is easy to administer. The organization arrives at increase amounts through a fairly simple calculation and minimizes political conflicts since everyone is treated the same. Incremental budgeting implicitly assumes that current allocations are roughly correct if all departments have more or less been able to survive. Only in cases of disastrous budget performance on a unit level does the organization need to revisit the fundamental allocation pattern.

However, incremental budgeting has no mechanism for making significant adjustments to allocations between units. A unit that has a generous budget will only get better off relative to other units—its "extra" budget grows as it receives increases on that budget excess, whereas another unit treads water as essential funding is increased just (or not) enough to keep pace with cost increases.

Redistributive budget systems revisit the allocation at least in part, and may go so far as to reassess all allocations from scratch each year. By considering redistributing resources between units, the budget process can improve the relationship between allocations and the contributions and needs of units, take into consideration changing conditions, and create stronger links between resources and strategic objectives.

Redistribution is much more difficult to manage. The organization either needs to go through a process to build consensus for its decisions or must be prepared to weather the conflict from those who give up resources. The political issues related to budget redistribution have led to highly complicated processes to rationalize and bureaucratize these decisions.

(c) Institutional or Center-Based Budgets

An organization may view its budget on an institution-wide basis, meaning that the budget focuses on the organization as a whole in the way it organizes data, assigns management accountability, and handles resources. An institutional focus assumes that all resources are pooled. Small organizations obviously will view their budgets in total and not fracture them into smaller parts. Even large organizations may view the budgets primarily from an institutional perspective. A university does so when it views tuition income separately from instructional costs. Tuition revenue is seen as unrestricted revenue available to support all organizations. Instructional units receive a budget composed of the expenses they manage. In this case, the university sees its budget from an institutional perspective, made up of different pools of costs and revenues managed by different people. The organization's budget will work only if all of those pools work together.

By contrast, an organization can take a center-based approach in which it divides its budget into parts that stand on their own, more or less. The budget can be divided into departments, programs, business units, or responsibility centers. A strongly center-based approach assumes that the parts of the organization are financially independent in an operational if not a legal sense, and that they are responsible for generating their own revenues and/or controlling their own expenditures. A center-based approach suggests a looser organizational form, more like a confederation.

(d) Single or Multiyear Periods

While most organizations will have annual budgets, budget policies can give the budget more of a multiyear character. In traditional budget systems, the budget is strictly an annual event. The budget holds for one year, and at the end of the year surplus funds are returned to the central administration so that central administrators can work with managers to cover deficits. In the new year, the department starts from scratch with a new budget, and revenues and expenses are reset to zero.

Some budgets are set for more than one year. Governmental funds may be appropriated on a multiyear basis. In these cases, the organization may receive its entire funding at the beginning of the year, or in installments that correspond to annual or more frequent appropriations. The organization usually still has a year-by-year spending plan or budget, because if it gets too far ahead of its resources it has to wait a long time for new funds to arrive.

An annual budget can take on a multiyear character if departments carry forward surpluses and deficits. This situation encourages the manager to make financial plans that consider future events as well as the current year. A manager can hold back on spending in one year in anticipation of future expenses or for protection against future problems. A manager who runs a deficit has to start making longer-term plans to reverse the deficit and pay it back. The surplus or deficit may be recorded in a formal fund balance on the organization's general ledger, or it may be recorded outside of the accounting system in budget documentation. Some organizations charge internal interest on fund balances, giving an incentive to reduce fund balance deficits but also exacerbating the future challenges a unit faces in trying to get itself "out of the hole."

Multiyear approaches to budgeting encourage managers to save money and make long-term decisions that can strengthen their programs. However, this approach limits the flexibility and control of central administration. Once it commits to allow managers future use of surpluses, it cannot take those funds later to fix problems elsewhere without damaging the credibility of the process and managers' trust in the administration.

2.4 ORGANIZATIONAL VS. PROGRAM BUDGETS

The word *budget* encompasses two types: the organizational budget and the program budget. The organizational budget is an organizations' detailed funding plan for a period, usually a year (two-year biennial budgets are common for organizations funded largely from state appropriations). It specifies what funds are anticipated from what sources, and how those funds will be allocated between departments, accounts, and types of spending. To a varying extent, the budget then determines spending in the period it covers. The organizational budget is a tool used by the organization's leadership to communicate to its board so that the board can exercise its oversight role over leadership actions, and to the organization itself so that managers, staff, volunteers, and members can align themselves with the organization's financial management needs.

Program budgets are proposals prepared for specific fund sources that request a certain level of funding and identify how the organization will use those funds. The funding request is often paired with a service budget that shows the types and volume of service the organization will provide with the resources funded from the request. This process allows the funding agency to make a sort of market decision in buying a certain number of units of service. Implicitly, program budgets form a portion of the organization's overall budget, although due to timing differences or policy decisions, program budgeting and organizational budgeting may occur on separate tracks.

This book focuses on organizational budgeting because it has the deepest implications for organizational management. The author is interested in showing how organizations use budgeting to increase organizational effectiveness.

2.5 LEADERSHIP, ACCOUNTABILITY, AND INVOLVEMENT

The roles of participants in the budget process from a crucial element of any budget process design. The role of leadership in designing and running the budget process is a true first principle of budgeting. While leaderships' role is fairly consistent in a healthy budget process, the degree to which accountability and involvement extend to others in the process varies a great deal. Decisions on increasing involvement and delegating accountability must consider a few principles that govern these aspects of organization and budget design.

(a) Leadership

The budget process occurs fundamentally at the executive level. It is a tool for leadership to achieve its objectives. Therefore, leadership needs to take an active role in designing the process and setting rules. The highest level of the organization's leadership must participate in the process and guide it.

The staff of an organization may not like the budget process in place, but trying to force a budget process on leadership is not the answer. For example, finance staff may feel that the best budget process will involve lots of participation and consensus building through a budget committee structure. If the director of the organization does not trust the financial competence of the organization's managers, he or she will continue to make unilateral decisions. Managers will learn that it does not matter what recommendation the budget committee makes because the director makes the call. Managers will go directly to the director, circumventing the carefully designed process. It is critical that the design start from leadership's style and preferences, and work from there to the best solution for the organization.

In the most successful budget systems, the organization's leader or leaders will make clear their expectations and needs, and how they contribute to a vision of success for the organization. To bring their budget goals into effect, the leaders will endorse a process that gives them the "right" amount of opportunity for influence as it goes forward. An organization's leader may choose to participate actively in the budget process at every stage possibly due to difficulty articulating goals because of environmental complexity or rate of change in conditions, a very hands-on orientation, or inexperience or weakness among subordinates. In such a situation, the leader should insist that the process contain ample opportunity for him or her to provide input and make decisions as the process moves along. In contrast, a leader who is very comfortable with the management ability of subordinates and with the degree of shared understanding of the organization's requirements may be quite comfortable with less involvement in the process. At its most extreme, the leader may want a budget process in which he or she articulates goals for the budget to the organization's management team, delegates to them the task of constructing a budget that meets those goals, and waits until their work is complete to review and approve it. This hands-off approach allows a leader to focus on other issues, such as continued development of long-range strategies, cultivation of key relationships, and coaching and development of key staff.

(b) Accountability

Accountability is the basic mechanism through which people beyond leadership become involved in managing budgets. Once budgets have been created, someone is responsible for fulfilling them, or else the organization is free to drift financially and budgeting has been a pointless exercise. However, accountability is more than assigning a set of budget figures to someone.

The manager assigned a budget must have real control over resources that take the form of decision-making authority, information, and skills. A manager cannot be responsible for a budget in which she does not have the authority to approve expenditures. Also, she cannot exercise effective control if she cannot get information on financial transactions and other factors that influence the budget. Finally, she must have the skill to understand financial statements and make projections and assessments, or she must have access to people with these skills. For some kinds of organizations, the technical skills involved with managing a budget are not trivial. For example, an organization that delivers health care services needs to project clinical activity and billings, which are a complicated function of number of visits, negotiated prices for service, and collection rates. Without the ability to project clinical revenues, a health care enterprise would never know whether it had a chance of meeting its budget.

Distributed accountability may sound like a laudable goal, and certainly much management theory pushes for it. However, it will not be appropriate for all organizations. Leadership may be uncomfortable delegating authority, or the organization may be too small or interdependent. Therefore, when accountability is assigned to a manager, the organization needs to be sure that it really will allow that manager to be accountable. If not, it should redefine the degree of accountability.

(c) Involvement

Every organization needs to decide how broadly it will involve members of the organization in the budget development process and on what terms. High levels of involvement tend to improve the quality of information and decisions, the accuracy of the budget, and the level of acceptance of the budget as a valid guide for actions. However, it can also consume lots of staff time. The organization may decide to limit involvement in the budget process to core staff and leave other staff to focus on their primary missions. The organization also needs to decide whether to extend involvement in providing information or in making decisions. Involving more people in decision making will increase acceptance of those decisions, but it makes the decision-making process more cumbersome.

The optimal degree of involvement depends on the significance of the budget. A budget process that does little more than apply incremental increases to existing budget allocations rarely merits a complicated procedure that involves lots of people. However, if the budget process provides the forum for making significant financial decisions that will shape the organization's strategic direction, extensive involvement can prove beneficial to the organization and to participants.

2.6 TRANSPARENCY AND PREDICTABILITY

Underlying the decisions on budget process design, including levels of accountability and involvement, are fundamental concerns about the nature of financial information and financial management within an organization and about how organizations of varying degrees of complexity can get enough information about finances to make reasonable decisions. Transparency and predictability of information have an impact on decisions ranging from the timeline of the budget process to the assignment of accountability and the structure of incentives. Each organization handles these issues somewhat differently, through a unique mix of features in its budget process design. Usually these issues are implicit to the process design, not articulated explicitly and discussed. However, the difficulty of getting the right level of explanation and of reaching a sufficient degree of comfort with predictions forms some of the psychological underpinnings of the budget process.

(a) Transparency

Transparency is the degree to which a person working with a financial statement can understand the operating factors underlying the figures. This factor drives aspects of budget process design. For example, in a large organization it is difficult for any person to look at the organization's staff salary budget and understand what underlies it—how many people work there, how much they get paid, and, most importantly, what they do and how that contributes to the organization's achievement of its objectives. To evaluate the budget, it is necessary to know whether it includes a reasonable staff salary figure. To understand that, someone must break down the number to a level at which managers can look at part of the figure and explain what work gets done with the portion of the salary dollars expended. This level of knowledge must enter the budget process at all stages: development, monitoring, and analysis.

Transparency is not a function of the size of the figure. A large dollar amount may be very simple to analyze, for example, the organization's insurance premiums or utility costs. Even in staff costs, a large amount may be easy to explain: For example, custodial salaries are $400,000. The organization has 25 custodians, paid $16,000 each, who can each cover 20,000 square feet, and 500,000 square feet of buildings must be cleaned. In a human resources department, analyzing a $400,000 salary budget would be more complicated and might need to be broken down into subfunctions such as recruitment, benefits, and training before the nature of the costs can be clearly explained.

In small organizations, most costs are transparent to those involved with running the organization. The board can look at each part of the budget and understand it. Costs in large organizations can be comprehended through careful analysis and reporting, and through technology such as on-line analytical processing (OLAP) tools that allow organizations to "drill down" into costs. Large organizations may hire staff to analyze costs and explain them, or may establish reporting protocols so that this knowledge works its way up into the organization's leadership.

Budgeting, analysis, and control must reach a level of information and management at which costs are transparent. The budget should get translated into salaries for specific individuals and specific expenditures. Financial control also has to occur at this level, to make sure that budgets are spent on legitimate items and that staff members are paid correctly. Analysis must reach this level of detail (which is not to say that all analyses must be subjected to the smallest level of detail, only that capacity must exist to get to that level if questions require it). Central staff should do research to understand and monitor costs at this level, or the managers closest to the costs should be involved in the process.

(b) Predictability

The act of creating a budget assumes that revenues and costs can be predicted well enough to establish a target for them in advance. If revenues and costs are completely unpredictable, managers will feel powerless to comply with budgets and will pay no attention to the budget. Understanding financial phenomena does not just happen—someone in the organization has to do the work to understand the behavior of costs and revenues and the factors driving them well enough to make reasonable predictions of financial outcomes that will shape the budget process.

Some figures are easier to predict than others. Salaries of full-time staff in an environment of minimal to moderate turnover (and with hiring guidelines in place) can be predicted by simple math. Expenses that can be controlled by managers, such as most office supplies, can be predicted if managers can be counted on to follow their budgets. Other types of revenues or expenses are difficult to predict, such as large health care claims on a health plan with a small risk pool. In most years, no one will have extraordinary claims, but every so often a participant will experience a severe health problem and incur hundreds of thousands of dollars in health care costs.

More volatile financial streams require more intimate knowledge to enhance predictability. To reduce the uncertainty surrounding these aspects of the organization's finances, it is necessary to identify or bring in specialists who will feed their knowledge into the process of developing, monitoring, and analyzing budgets. The need for professional expertise to increase the predictability of finances is one factor that drives the establishment of central resources to support and manage the budget process.

All of these efforts must support an effort to provide managers with budgets that they can meet through their own efforts. Finances will never be completely predictable, but the organization should make an effort to reduce unpredictability where possible.

2.7 CONCLUSION

In this chapter we have presented several general concepts about budgeting. These concepts may strike some readers as abstractions, but as experience is gained as a participant in the budget process, these concepts are useful. We may need to understand the process in order to help design or redesign a budget system, or in order to operate more effectively within it. Keep these concepts in mind as we turn to our review of the budget process.

PART TWO

The Budget Process

CHAPTER THREE

Budget Cycle

3.1 INTRODUCTION

There are obvious differences between organizations—size, type of mission, number of programs, to name just a few factors. Across the variety, the budget process maintains a remarkably consistent shape from place to place. Generally, the budget process consists of three basic phases:

1. Budget development
2. Budget monitoring, tracking, and adjustments
3. Analysis of final results

These phases cross years: Budget development takes place before the budget year in question starts; monitoring and adjustment occur throughout the budget year; final results are analyzed after the year ends. (In theory, budgeting could be on a less-than-annual basis, say quarterly, but this is very rare.) The lack of a multiyear structure in the budget process usually signifies problems with the organization's financial management. To cite a common example, when an organization develops its budget after the year has already started, there is a strong indication that little financial planning occurs here. The best the organization can hope for is that the budget will record the results of discrete plans and deals that have been made to keep the organization running.

In most healthy organizations, one of these three phases is in progress at any given time, and the phases from different years feed back to each other. This chapter describes the budget cycle in terms of a "typical" process. Every organization will have its own variations on these procedures, and we try to reflect some of the major variations through references to our case organizations.

3.2 BUDGET DEVELOPMENT

The budget process should start with a set of activities to lay the ground for the next year's budget. Managers of the organization should start the process by evaluating its financial position and reviewing the organization's strategies.

Managers usually begin by looking at the results from the year that has just ended. Although another complete year—the one currently under way—will occur between the period covered by those results and the year for which they are preparing a budget, this information is the best they have at the time, as it covers the most recent complete year.

(a) Planning Step One: Committee Budget Planning

In most organizations other than the smallest ones, there is some group responsible for budget planning. It may include the leader of the organization, officers, staff, board members, or others. (In Section 10.3 we discuss roles within the budget process.)

(i) Analyze Most Recent Fiscal Year. The budget planning group—in whatever form it takes—should examine the previous year's financial results in relation to absolute standards and to the budget that was in effect for that year. Some of the questions to ask are as follows:

- Did the organization make or lose money?
- Did the programs cover their costs?
- How did the organization do relative to its budget?
- What were the sources of variances (good or bad) from the budget?
- How did the organization do in its major sources of revenue and major expense categories?
- What factors drove variances?
- How do these results reflect on the assumptions underlying the current year budget and the future?

Both absolute results and budget variances are important. In the Community Arts Council, results for the previous year show that the gallery program and the newspaper both lost money. (See Exhibit 3.1.) This loss was offset by a surplus in general operations. A different picture emerges when these results are compared to the budget: It turns out that the newspaper had unexpectedly strong advertising revenue and covered more of its costs than expected. The gallery, on the other hand, fell short of its sales target by one third.

In a large organization, budget planners can only answer the questions listed above if staff have prepared analytical materials in advance. The organization should also consider results for the current year to date if significant events have already occurred. In an educational institution, early indications of tuition revenue for the first session of the year may be available from enrollment services. If the budget process starts toward the middle of the current year or later (e.g., if budget planning starts in January at an organization with a June 30 year end), managers can make reasonable projections of current year results to factor into budget deliberations. However, projections remain uncertain, and the organization will want to include an assessment of the concrete results for the most recent completed year.

(ii) Analyze Multiple Years. For some factors, it may be useful to include multiple years of results in the data set under review. Certain kinds of economic factors require multiyear analysis:

- *Factors subject to long-term trends.* Demand for a service such as education or training may follow a more or less predictable trend. A single good year could provide the basis for faulty assumptions about the coming year. In the context of a multiyear graph, it could be apparent that the organization should prepare for a reduction. See Exhibits 3.2 and 3.3 for examples related to individual membership revenue in the Community Arts Council.
- *Volatile factors.* Certain expenses and revenues include large, irregular events, such as a multimillion-dollar gift or large claims in a health care benefits risk pool. For volatile phenomena, planners need to look at multiple years of data to determine a base budget level for planning purposes and to assess strategies to deal with large events. See Exhibit 3.4 for an example for the University of Okoboji's major gifts campaign.

(iii) Reviewing Strategy. In addition to reviewing financial results, the budget planning group will want to review the organization's strategy. Many organizations link the budget process to a formal strategy de-

Exhibit 3.1 Community Arts Council: Results for Year Ended September 30

	General	*State Arts Seed Grant*	*Art in the Schools*	*Summer Art Camp*	*Gallery Program*	*Newspaper*
Revenue						
Memberships	$2,400					
Grants	40,000	30,000				
Contracts			25,000	27,000		
Rentals	5,500					
Sales					800	
Fund-raising	5,000					
Advertising						5,400
Total revenue	**52,900**	**30,000**	**25,000**	**27,000**	**800**	**5,400**
Salaries	27,200	30,000	16,600	14,200		
Benefits	3,100					
Rent	12,000					
Supplies	300					
Telephones	610					
Computer lease	2,600					
Contract services			8,000	12,000		
Exhibition costs					3,300	
Insurance	975					
Printing	600		400	800		5,800
Advertising	2,300					
Total expense	**49,685**	**30,000**	**25,000**	**27,000**	**3,300**	**5,800**
Net surplus/ (deficit)	**$3,215**	**$0**	**$0**	**$0**	**($2,500)**	**($400)**

Variance in Arts Council Gallery and Newspaper Programs

	Gallery Program			*Newspaper*		
	Budget	*Actual*	*Variance*	*Budget*	*Actual*	*Variance*
Rentals	$1,200	$800	($400)			
Advertising				4,000	5,400	1,400
Total revenue	**1,200**	**800**	**(400)**	**4,000**	**5,400**	**1,400**
Exhibition costs	3,000	3,300	(300)			
Printing				5,500	5,800	(300)
Total expense	**3,000**	**3,300**	**(300)**	**5,500**	**5,800**	**(300)**
Net surplus/ (deficit)	**($1,800)**	**($2,500)**	**($700)**	**($1,500)**	**($400)**	**$1,100**

Exhibit 3.2 Community Arts Council: Membership Revenues

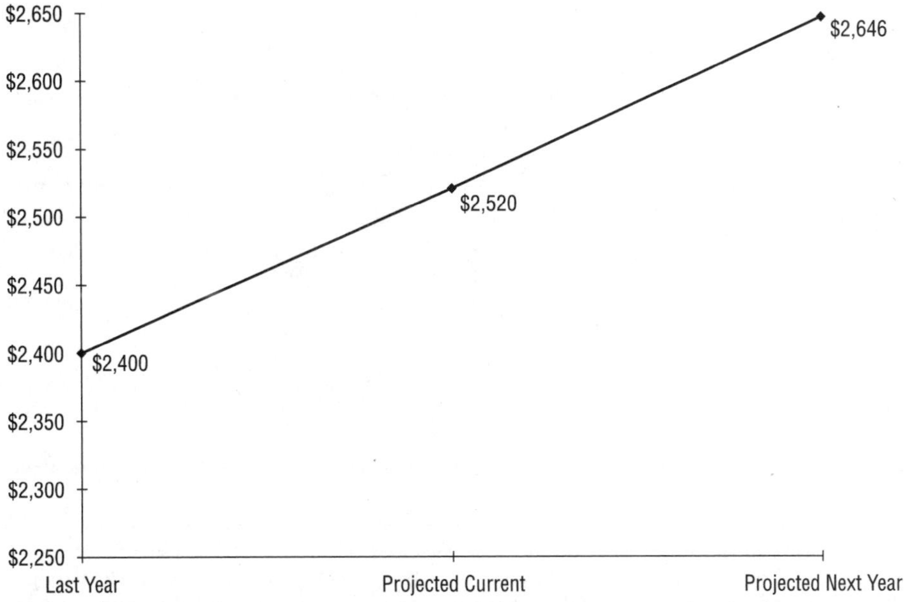

The Community Arts Council's revenue from memberships was $2,400 in the most recent year. Looking only at this data point, the organization might reasonably forecast 5 percent growth over two years to come up with a budget for the coming year.

velopment process. A typical method is to start the process with a meeting of the organization's board or leaders in which the organization's strategy is reviewed, significant factors about the organization's operations, markets, environment, clients, or funders are discussed, and major initiatives are identified.

Financial results need to be reviewed in light of strategy. You can only go so far analytically without a strategic view. The major variances emerge from the mathematical calculations, and sources may be revealed through supporting detail. The organization's leaders then need to discuss the options for improving negative performance in the coming year and for taking advantage of opportunities. Poor performance in a program might suggest that managers need to find ways to shore up that program. However, in the strategy development process, the organization may decide that demand for this program is drying up; therefore, the organization will look for the least traumatic way to back out of the program.

In the Community Arts Council, the overall strategy must be understood to know whether the gallery program is a critical portion of the organization's mission currently and in the future. If so, the budget process should assess whether it is realistic to push for higher levels of sales, or

Exhibit 3.3 Community Arts Council: Membership Revenues (4 years)

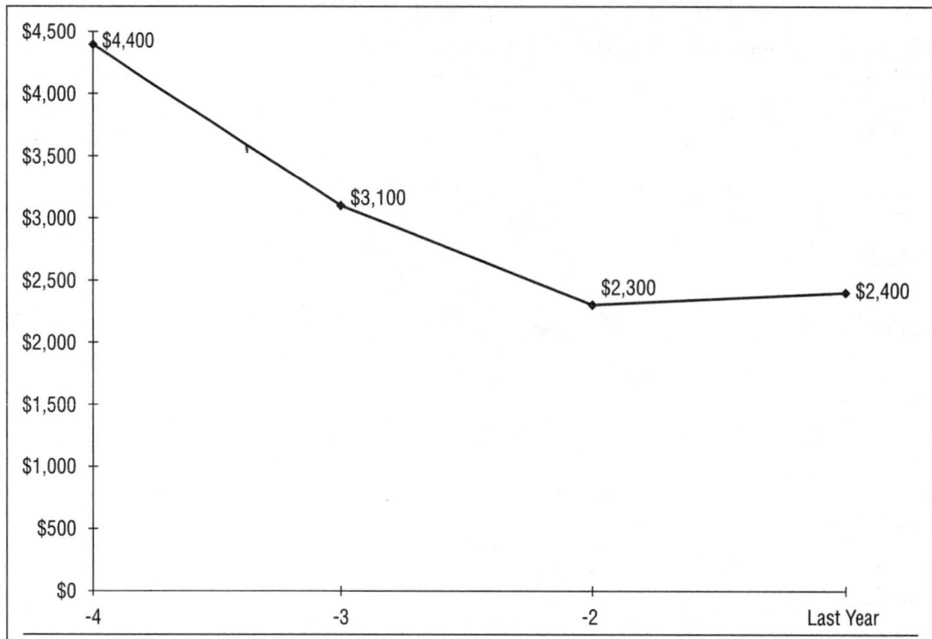

Review of several previous years show that memberships have been subject to a significant downward trend. The last year results were a slight reversal of a strong multiyear trend. The multiple run of data is necessary to ask the right questions in the budget process: Was last year an interruption in a long-term trend or is the tide turning?

whether the budget should be structured with a larger subsidy for the gallery from general operations. A related question would be whether the strong advertising results for the newspaper can be sustained or improved. On the other hand, it may not be clear that the organization should try to be an exhibitor as well as a hands-on educator. Perhaps the space would be better used for more education programs.

The discussion of strategy allows those planning the budget process to know whether significant initiatives are under way that may have an impact on financial performance. The upswing in membership revenues shown in Exhibit 3.3. may be a lucky break, but it might also be the first fruits of a major campaign to retain members and to contact former members to get them to renew their ties to the organization, or it may be the result of strong professional employment growth in the area that started 18 months ago and is shown by Chamber of Commerce statistics to be accelerating. The organization may have bought the improvement through increased spending on a part-time staff member to run this project, so the budget process would also need to recognize the dependency between that spending and the improvement in this revenue source. It may turn out that the expected improvement in memberships is not big enough to justify the expenditure to expand memberships.

Exhibit 3.4 University of Okoboji: Major Gifts

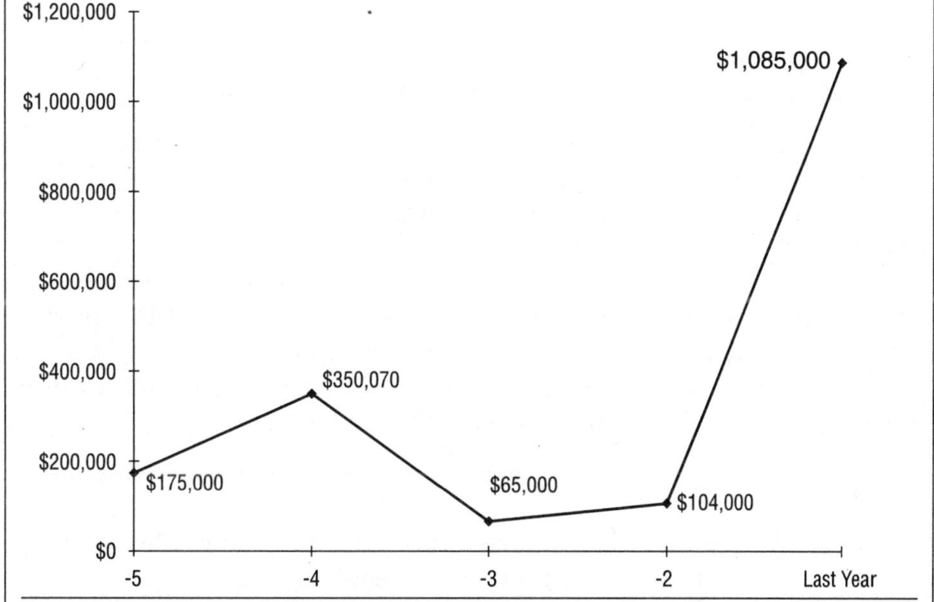

Major gifts to a college are highly volatile. In the last year, the University of Okoboji received an unusual $1 million gift. Although the college should strive to bring in a $1 million gift every year, a more realistic assessment might budget major gifts close to its historical range, which has hovered below $400,000 a year.

(iv) Reviewing General Parameters. The budget planning process also involves the identification and setting of major factors driving the budget. These general parameters include:

- Inflation adjustments for goods, services, wages, and benefits
- Programmed reductions in funding from major sources, such as an across-the-board percentage reduction for all state appropriations

Budget variances, trends in major elements of the budget, organizational strategies, and general parameters allow those planning the budget process to establish the initial guidelines for the budget, including considerations for increasing or decreasing certain types of revenue and expense. In a large organization, the parameters will typically be developed based on financial modeling that covers the whole institution. The financial model integrates all of the factors identified by management to determine the guidelines that would bring the organization to its budget goals. In many cases, the goal is to create a realistic budget that balances to zero: Revenues equal expenses. In other cases, a deficit budget may be planned as part of a multiyear investment or recovery cycle, or surpluses may be mandated to build capital for future investments.

(b) Planning Step Two: Staff Budget Planning

Once the groundwork has been established, budget development begins in earnest and in detail. At this point a broader set of staff get involved in the process. In a small organization, many of these steps and the budget groundwork are compressed.

In a medium or large organization, the process moves from the province of a small group of senior leaders and central staff to a broader set of managers and staff who prepare detailed budgets for individual departments. The central budget planners need to communicate to those preparing departmental budgets, who need to know:

- Their budget base
- Guidelines for developing proposals, including allowable increases (if any) for categories of expenses
- Deadlines and instructions for submissions
- Rationale for guidelines and the organizational financial picture within which the budget process fits

Organizations often neglect the last item, at some peril. Departmental staff are quick to assume budget guidelines and rules are capricious and unfair. Lacking an understanding of the reasons behind the guidelines, they resist the budget process in any way they can and criticize the central staff.

(i) The Budget Base. The budget base provides the starting point for the departmental budget. The budget might be zero based, meaning that each department is assumed to start with no funding and then prepares a request and justification for as much funding as is needed. If leaders agree with the rationale and the funds are available, they will approve the request. However rational this approach may appear, administering it is difficult because it constantly requires management to make tough trade-off decisions between units.

Therefore, most organizations use some sort of incremental approach, in which the funding level in the budget is based on the previous year's budget subject to some sort of increase or decrease factor. The organization and the department need to agree on the starting point. The most common starting point is the current year budget, which may have to be adjusted to back out one-time allocations or other special considerations.

Therefore, in a large organization the central staff sort out these issues, clean up the budget base, and then distribute a version of the budget base that the department should use.

(ii) Instructions and Guidelines. Along with documentation of the budget base, central staff send instructions on the guidelines to follow in preparing the request, which might look like the following:

Budget Guidelines

Salaries	3% increase. Individual salary proposals to follow in June based on annual evaluation
Supplies*	1% increase
Computer hardware*	Provide detailed listing of proposed computer purchases
Equipment*	3%

*Budget base and increase may be transferred between these categories, as long as the total equals that for the base plus increases. Budget base and increases may not be transferred between salary and nonsalary lines without permission of the Budget Committee.

The budget base and guidelines must go out with instructions and deadlines. The staff who prepare departmental budgets need to know what format to use in returning budget proposals: Should they write in changes on the hard copies provided, input them on a spreadsheet available on the network, or submit them in a departmentally formatted spreadsheet? They need to know what process to follow for requesting exceptions to the guidelines or for unusual or one-time allocations. And, of course, the managers need to know when the proposals are due, and to whom, for review. The managers may be responsibile for seeing that budgets are input into the organization's accounting system, which may take place at the time the proposals are submitted or after approval has been granted.

(iii) The Personnel Budget. Personnel budgets often receive unique handling. Personnel costs are different than other types of operating expenses in that they must be specified on an item-by-item basis—that is, a salary is assigned to each person who will receive a paycheck. Each department needs to know its overall personnel budget and how much of this budget will be allocated to each person. This requires person-by-person documentation. Also, specific increases may be based on the staff member's performance, so assignment of individual increases may happen very late in the year so that the evaluation can encompass as much activity as possible. In medium or large organizations, the board can approve the overall personnel budget earlier since it will not be signing off on individual increases (in a small organization, individual pay rates are often a concern of the board since it is the immediate driver for the organization's financial performance).

(iv) Preparation of Final Departmental Budget Proposals. With this information in hand, departments start preparing budgets for the accounts under their control. The complexity of this activity depends on the process design and organization structure. Small departments that have responsibility for managing expenses but not for generating revenues usually go through a simple process to develop a budget: applying the guideline rates of increase, making a few switches of budgets between specific items or object codes, and sending the budget back through the chain of command for review or approval.

By contrast, some departments may have budgets that are complicated and extensive enough to require a development process that echoes some of the activities involved in setting the organizational groundwork: reviewing departmental strategy, assessing the performance and trends of previous years, identifying major opportunities and strategies for reversing negative trends. If a department has responsibility for revenues and expenses, its budgeting will look much more like that of an independent entity. It may have the freedom to pursue new sources of revenue to supplement its resources. It may be large enough to consider significant reconfigurations of its expenses. If an organization has large subdivisions that operate with this degree of independence, it will need to allow time in the budget process for those units to fully develop their budgets internally before submitting them for compilation and review on an organization-wide basis.

In most medium or large organizations, preparation of budgets will start at the level of major expense and revenue categories (such as Supplies and Services) and major programs or units (such as the Law School) and then move to assigning budgets to specific accounts and object codes as defined in the organization's accounting system. Supplies and Services for the Law School might be broken down to Photocopies, Office Supplies, Subscriptions, Consulting Services, and so forth for the Law Clinic, the Dean's Office, Instructional Staff, and so on. While the budget may even be modeled on the basis of this level of detail, leadership is unlikely to specify guidelines at this level. Budget processes that involve too much account-level detail in the initial planning are likely to be too intricate to allow an effective focus on strategic issues. Exhibit 3.5 shows the object code detail for the University of Okoboji's budget.

At the departmental level, decisions are made on how many accounts to set up to record activity (should the Arts Council have one account for the gallery program or a separate account for each exhibit) and which line items to budget (the organization may have modeled and set a guideline for supplies, but the accounting system provides multiple object

Exhibit 3.5 University of Okoboji Current Year Unrestricted Budget Breakout by Division ($000s)

Object Code	*Description*	*Sciences*	*Arts and Business*	*Pharmacy*	*Social Work*	*Student Services*	*Administration*	*Development*	*Institutional Accounts*	*Total*
1000	Fall tuition	$13,000	$7,800	$2,600	$2,600					$26,000
1001	Spring tuition	11,700	7,020	2,340	2,340					23,400
1002	Summer session	1,040	624	208	208					2,080
1004	Fees	260	156	52	52					520
1100	Federal IDC's[1]								2,000	2,000
1200	State IDC's[1]								1,100	1,100
1300	Local IDC's[1]								750	750
1400	Private gifts	1,500			1,500				12,000	15,000
1520	Endowment spending account income								8,050	8,050
1600	Sales and services		375			125				500
1610	Other revenue					350				350
2100	Fall room					7,905				7,905
2105	Spring room					5,355				5,355
2200	Fall board					7,395				7,395
2205	Spring board					4,845				4,845
2400	Bookstore sales						8,500			8,500
3000	Faculty salaries	19,560	6,520	3,260	3,260					32,600
3100	Professional salaries	1,445	1,445	401	241	3,639	3,757	401	562	11,891
3200	Biweekly payroll	1,051	1,051	292	175	3,595	4,770	292	409	11,634
3250	Overtime	131	131	36	22	15	306	36	51	730
3400	Benefits pool charge	5,547	2,287	997	924	2,392	1,919	182	255	14,504
4000	Fall financial aid	1,700	40	120	140					2,000
4100	Spring financial aid	1,530	36	108	126					1,800
4200	Summer session financial aid	170	4	12	14					200

Exhibit 3.5 Continued

5000	Office supplies	525	315	263	105	2,333	386	315	2,308	6,550
5050	Lab supplies		525							525
5100	Computer software	525	315	263	105		386			1,594
5200	Postage	525	315	263	105	27		105	1,847	3,187
5250	Photocopying and duplicating	525	315	263	105	27	386	105	2,770	4,496
5300	Equipment lease payments						772			772
5400	Telephone—access	394	210	197	79	14	386	158	923	2,360
5410	Telephone—long distance	131	105	66	26			105	462	895
5500	Shop supplies						2,701			2,701
5600	Custodial supplies						1,543			1,543
5700	Cost of goods sold						4,638			4,638
6000	Contractual services					11,622		210		11,832
6500	Consulting					27	1,157	53	923	2,160
9000	Mandatory transfers								1,560	1,560
9500	Nonmandatory transfers									

[1]IDC is an abbreviation for indirect cost recoveries. It is the portion of a grant or contact designated to support incorrect costs of the project or program, such as a share of general administrative costs.

codes in this category—office supplies, photocopier supplies, art supplies, tools, paper, lab supplies, glassware, etc.). Exhibit 3.6 shows how the University of Okoboji's Business School breaks its budget into specific object codes and accounts.

(v) Reviewing and Approving Departmental Budgets. Once departments have completed their budget proposals, the proposals must be reviewed and approved. The levels of approval are largely a function of the size of the organization and complexity of its structure. Many medium and large organizations have a budget process that includes multiple layers of review, reaching an organization-wide level. It is typical in these organizations for central staff in a budget, accounting, or planning office to receive and consolidate the various proposals. The staff should check the proposals for arithmetic accuracy and compliance with guidelines, bring mistakes to the attention of the preparers, and see that they are corrected. The central staff consolidates these proposals into decision packages that can be reviewed by central leadership. Roles in the budget process are discussed in more depth in Chapter 10, but in any organization, regardless of size, some group (e.g., a budget committee), groups (the budget committee plus the faculty senate), or individual (the executive director) plays the role of reviewing budget proposals on behalf of the institution. A very good practice is for the central reviewers to meet separately with the leadership of each department submitting budgets to discuss the proposals and major assumptions, and to identify and negotiate changes.

If the net impact of the submitted proposals results in a budget that does not reach the goals set when the groundwork was laid, then the leaders of the process need to develop strategies to meet those goals. For example:

- The organization's budget leadership may ask department managers to make changes in proposals for their areas.
- Central staff may look for general elements to change (e.g., increase endowment payout, reduce the budget for central contingencies, use less conservative market assumptions).
- Leadership or central staff may develop a formula to apply to all budgets.

This process is often iterative, going back and forth until an acceptable organization-wide budget is reached.

(c) Reviewing and Approving the Final Budget

Once complete, the organization's budget is submitted to its board or its funding agency for approval. The board or funding agency frequently sets

Exhibit 3.6 University of Okoboji School of Business ($000s)

Current Year Budget by Category ($000s)		*Current Year Unrestricted Budget by Account/Object Code ($000s)*						
				1-22100	*1-22200*	*1-22201*	*1-22000*	
		Object Code	*Description*	*MBA*	*Exec*	*On-Site Programs*	*General*	*Total*
Tuition and fees	$15,600	1000	Fall tuition	$5,000	$2,400	$400		$7,800
		1001	Spring tuition	4,700	2,000	320		7,020
		1002	Summer session	624				624
		1004	Fees				156	156
Sales and services	375							
Restricted revenue	700	1600	Sales and services				375	375
Total revenue	**16,675**							
UR[1] Faculty salaries	6,520							
UR[1] staff salaries	2,627							
UR[1] Benefits	2,286							
Total UR[1] compensation	11,433	3000	Faculty salaries	4,890	1,630			6,520

Exhibit 3.6 Continued

		3100	Professional salaries	100	100	500	745	1,445
UR[1] financial aid	80	3200	Biweekly payroll				1,051	1,051
Other UR[1] operating costs	2,100	3250	Overtime				131	131
		3400	Benefits pool charge	1,248	433	125	482	2,288
Total UR[1] E&G[2]	13,613							
		4000	Fall financial aid	40				40
		4100	Spring financial aid	36				36
		4200	Summer session financial aid	4				4
Total rest expense	700							
		5000	Office supplies	82	68		45	195
		5050	Lab supplies	315	210			525
Total expenses	**14,313**	5100	Computer hardware				275	275
		5200	Postage	177	75		53	305
Net surplus/(deficit)	**$2,362**	5250	Photocopying and duplicating	80	65	30	40	215
		5400	Telephone—access				205	205
		5410	Telephone—long distance	28	25	2	25	80

[1]Unrestricted
[2]Educational and General

a deadline for receipt of the organization's budget. The organization builds its entire budget development process timeline by working backward from that established due date.

In some cases, multiple points of external review are scheduled: The board may review a long-range projection early in the process to get an understanding of basic assumptions, then the Finance Committee may review an early draft of the budget, and the final draft may go to the Finance Committee before it receives full board review. These additional review points further drive the budget development timeline. Every organization and every board sets up its own review procedure.

The relationship between organizations and external bodies generally fits one of the following:

- The external body expects management to present a reasonable plan for acquiring and spending resources for the next year. Management drives this process, its job being to get the board to agree that its plans are sound and to approve them. Private nonprofits tend to fit in this category.
- The external body provides the funds, and it will decide how much to give the organization based on the proposal submitted. Management drives the process less in this case, with its job being to try to get as much funding as it can from the external body. Public organizations and individual programs tend to fit this model.

Organizations in the former category usually have more ability to predict the outcome of the final review and can start communicating internally early on about expectations for next year. Those in the latter category have less capacity to anticipate the external body's decisions. Once the decision comes back (often at the last possible minute), the organization needs to assess how it did, finding the gaps between what it requested and what it received. Unanticipated large gaps can occur, which require the organization to revisit its budgets.

Once the budget for the next year is finalized, it should be communicated to managers and staff to confirm that their final proposal was accepted or to indicate modifications. Ideally, central staff have maintained communications with departmental staff throughout the process, letting them know how their proposals stand. Ongoing communications constitute one of the weakest areas in many budget processes. It is human nature for budget staff to worry about the problems immediately in front of them, so once in receipt of the budget proposal they may turn their attention to consolidating the proposals and making them work in aggregate. To the department managers who submitted proposals, the intervening months between submission of the proposal and word on final approval may seem like a "black box": Proposals are submitted, they hear nothing for months, and at the end a budget comes out that varies from the proposal with no explanation. To avoid this situation, central staff should look for appropriate and meaningful ways to communicate on an ongoing basis.

(d) Loading Budgets into the Accounting System

As the final step in the budget development process, budgets are loaded into the accounting system. Most accounting systems include a field for the current year budget as well as a field that records the cumulative impact of transactions booked to that account/object code combination. This method allows the accounting system to provide reports on the percentage of the budget consumed throughout the year, a fundamental tool for monitoring budget performance. The account/object code budgets need to be input into the accounting system once final approval has been received. As the new year starts, the new budgets replace the old budgets, and the current year activity field is reset to zero.

The requirements for this step depend on the organization's systems and policies. If the budget preparation materials are integrated with the accounting system, the files used to report, compile, and review budgets contain the data needed for the accounting system. In a more automated environment, central staff can transfer the data to the accounting system from the material they have worked with in reviewing and preparing the budgets for approvals. In other systems, the new budget must be manually input, either by a central office or by the departments, which receive access to the organizational system to make these entries.

The smaller the organization, the less need for a complicated process during any stage of budget development. Assessment of the funding environment may be tantamount to establishing the budget for major sources of grant funding. There is obviously no need to prepare instructions and communicate them to a second, third, and fourth level of budget preparers/reviewers. The salary budget consists of so few salaries that the only reasonable way to set it is to start with individual salary proposals (rather than a pool). Once the organization can make the budget work (i.e., it looks as if the organization will be able to keep its doors open) and can get to the board, the process has been completed.

(e) Conclusion

Even with small organizations, it is important to acknowledge the groups that have an interest in the budget and to communicate with them. The board must review the budget to adequately exercise its fiduciary responsibilities. Members deserve to have some information on the organization's financial plans. The organization's charter may require that the members review and vote on the budget.

3.3 BUDGET MONITORING, TRACKING, AND ADJUSTMENTS

From the point of view of line managers, activity related to monitoring and tracking the current year budget usually consumes more time than budget development. The first task in managing the current year budget is to make sure that spending stays within limits and that revenue goals are achieved. A better way of viewing this job is probably to say that someone in the organization needs to determine that the correct relationship between revenues and expenses is being maintained. If revenues exceed plan, increased spending may be acceptable or necessary. In face of revenue shortfalls, it does not do the organization any good to meet its expense budgets.

(a) Monitoring Results and Activity

Let us describe the monitoring process by first assuming the simplest case, where the organization has a fixed revenue base. In this situation, it has a simple goal: Do not spend more than the budget. If expenses fall evenly throughout the year, or the manager can control the timing of expenditures, then it is adequate to judge the budget situation by assuming that one twelfth of the annual budget is consumed each month. If the fiscal year starts in July and expenditures have consumed half the budget at the end of December, the manager has stayed on budget. If expenditures exceeded 50% of the budget, the manager must find ways to slow spending.

This situation may sound overly simple, but it will apply to organizations with a budget based on fixed reliable allocations from an outside funding source, or for departments within a larger organization that have fixed expense budgets and do not have the flexibility and risk that comes with departmental revenue budgets. One of the key housekeeping tasks each month is to make sure that transactions against this budget have been properly recorded. Have all of the purchases been recorded? Have revenues been received and credited correctly? For a department within a larger organization, the monthly process will involve reconciling the transactions reported by the central accounting system to make sure they match the department's records—that the department did not get charged the wrong amount, in the wrong category, and so forth. A certain portion of the time, one department will get charged for another department's transactions. For an organization without significant internal subdivisions, the same can happen when the bank receives checks and deposits.

Few organizations operate in a world so simple that dividing by 12 is all that is analytically necessary. In most cases, the manager will need to assess activity to date against specific expectations he or she has for the rest of the budget period:

- Has the department planned a major purchase but not processed it yet?
- Do any major expenses tend to hit late in the year (i.e., there is a predictable seasonality to expenses)?
- How likely is it that an as-yet-unknown significant expense might hit (i.e., volatility in expenses)?

In any of these cases, 50 percent expenditure of budget halfway throughout the year indicates trouble. If expenses follow a seasonal pattern, the manager can use a simple calculation to determine how much of the budget should be expended at each point throughout the year (see Exhibit 3.7). Also, the manager will feel that he can anticipate more about

Exhibit 3.7 Seasonality of Expenditures: Example

	Year 1		*Year 2*		
	Dollars	*Percent*	*Dollars*	*Percent*	*Average Percent*
Total actual	$158,500		$177,400		
Jan	18,000	11.4	18,500	10.4	10.9
Feb	15,000	9.5	17,000	9.6	9.5
March	24,000	15.1	30,000	16.9	16.0
April	14,000	8.8	19,400	10.9	9.9
May	11,500	7.3	16,000	9.0	8.1
June	8,000	5.0	8,500	4.8	4.9
July	6,500	4.1	6,300	3.6	3.8
Aug	7,000	4.4	6,700	3.8	4.1
Sept	8,000	5.0	8,000	4.5	4.8
Oct	13,500	8.5	12,000	6.8	7.6
Nov	14,000	8.8	15,500	8.7	8.8
Dec	$19,000	12.0	$19,500	11.0	11.5

For this organization, expenditures have followed a fairly consistent distribution over two years; on average, 60 percent of the budget is expended in the first half of the year, spending slows in the third quarter, and it picks up again in the last three months. In predicting the monthly distribution of expenses in the future, the manager of this organization could take the average of the last two years as a guide for the future. In doing this calculation, it is important to take expenditures as a percent of actuals as opposed to the percentage of the budget. This way, the effect of seasonality will be captured, not flaws in budgeting or other causes of variance between budget and plan. More sophisticated methods of calculating seasonality have been developed, but most organizations would not need to use them in this sort of situation. For more information on adjustments to time series data, see any standard textbook on forecasting (two are cited in the Bibliography).

the year the further he gets into it. Therefore, he will hold expenditures as late as possible to make sure he does not need the funds to cover an unplanned expense.

In some cases, seasonality of expenditures and revenues is such a significant aspect of the organization's finances that the organization will prepare a monthly revenue and expense budget as part of the budget development process. Reports of financial activity will then express the budget as a budget-to-date figure, comparable to the activity-to-date figure. Expenses to date will equal the budget to date if the organization stays on budget. Surpluses and deficits can be expressed in monthly terms. The Presbyterian Church has also stated its budget on a monthly basis because of its dependence on pledges and plate collections, a highly seasonal revenue stream (see Exhibit 3.8). If the year starts out slow or collections in the summer come in unusually low, the church's session (the governing board of a Presbyterian congregation) will have to start making adjustments in expenditures or making special appeals to the congregation to honor or exceed pledges.

(b) Frequency and Timing of Reviews

Seasonality also drives one of the other factors to consider when reviewing budgets: frequency and timing of reviews. While it is advisable to keep up with the accuracy of transactions on a very regular basis, typically monthly, it may not be worthwhile to assess the status of a budget every month. The frequency of review can depend on one or more of several factors:

- Requirements set by external bodies
- Enough activity occurring since the beginning of the year or since the last review to provide new information
- Major events and transactions occurring, and hitting financial records

The most common driver of review and reporting is that it is required by the board, finance committee, or funding agency or there is an internal meeting scheduled at which interim results traditionally are presented. In some cases, the organization has thought out the timing of these reviews to spur management to assess the organization's financial performance at appropriate times. In other cases, the call for review has evolved in a less systematic way, and the preparation of budget status reports assumes a life of its own that has little value for management. A prime example of the latter is when the first review comes too early in the year to be meaningful.

Exhibit 3.8 Presbyterian Church Monthly Budget Fiscal Year Ended December 31

	Total	*Jan*	*Feb*	*Mar*	*April*	*May*	*June*	*July*	*Aug*	*Sept*	*Oct*	*Nov*	*Dec*
Revenue													
Pledges	$181,000	$19,000	$14,000	$20,000	$22,000	$14,000	$5,000	$5,000	$5,000	$10,000	$12,000	$20,000	$35,000
Plate	20,000	2,000	1,500	2,000	3,500	500	500	500	500	1,500	2,000	2,000	3,500
Special offerings	12,000	600	700	2,500	2,000	200	200	150	150	500	1,500	1,500	2,000
Endowment	35,000	8,750			8,750			8,750			8,750		
Rentals	10,000	375	375	375	1,500	2,000	2,000	1,500	375	375	375	375	375
Interest	3,000	250	250	250	250	250	250	250	250	250	250	250	250
Total revenues	**261,000**	**30,975**	**16,825**	**25,125**	**38,000**	**16,950**	**7,950**	**16,150**	**6,275**	**12,625**	**24,875**	**24,125**	**41,125**
Expenses													
Operations													
Salaries	140,000	11,667	11,667	11,667	11,667	11,667	11,667	11,667	11,667	11,667	11,667	11,667	11,667
Benefits	28,000	2,333	2,333	2,333	2,333	2,333	2,333	2,333	2,333	2,333	2,333	2,333	2,333
Supplies	1,200	100	100	100	100	100	100	100	100	100	100	100	100
Phones	1,200	100	100	100	100	100	100	100	100	100	100	100	100
Equipment	2,000	167	167	167	167	167	167	167	167	167	167	167	167
Utilities	5,000	275	250	150	125	550	750	825	875	600	150	200	250
Contract services	6,000	500	500	500	500	500	500	500	500	500	500	500	500
Mission													
Presbytery	20,000	5,000			5,000			5,000			5,000		
Local mission	40,600	3,175	3,175	3,175	3,175	3,175	3,175	3,175	3,175	3,175	3,175	3,175	5,675
Ghana hospital	2,000						1,000						1,000
Church development, Brazil	3,000				1,500						1,500		
Special offerings	12,000	600	700	2,500	2,000	200	200	150	150	500	1,500	1,500	2,000
Total expenses	**261,000**	**23,917**	**18,992**	**20,692**	**26,667**	**18,792**	**19,992**	**24,017**	**19,067**	**19,142**	**26,192**	**19,742**	**23,792**
Net surplus/(deficit)	**$0**	**$7,058**	**($2,167)**	**$4,433**	**$11,333**	**($1,842)**	**($12,042)**	**($7,867)**	**($12,792)**	**($6,517)**	**($1,317)**	**$4,383**	**$17,333**

The principle of allowing enough activity to occur to make the review worthwhile underlies quarterly review cycles. Usually not enough happens in any single month to merit review. This situation suggests waiting until a few months into the year, even until the halfway point, to conduct the first major review, and then allowing multiple months to pass between reviews. Before and between reviews, managers should keep an eye out for major problems.

Another strategy is to time budget reviews in relation to major events in the organization's calendar. Colleges generally review results sometime after final tuition numbers are in for the fall term of the academic year, again after the second term in a semester system, and again as the institution approaches the end of its fiscal year (college and university fiscal years commonly end on June 30). A dance company that gives a performance of the *Nutcracker* during December and then has its regular season in the spring would want to review results in January, after it has recorded expenses and revenues for the *Nutcracker*, and frequently during the spring as it prepares and presents its regular season performances.

(c) Year-End Projections

Once the manager is satisfied that the transactions attributed to his accounts are correct, the task of budget review fundamentally involves projecting year-end results based on results so far and any other relevant information. The "simple case" approach of shooting for 50 percent consumption of resources by the halfway mark in the year presumes a projection: Spending falls evenly throughout the year, and the rate of spending so far will continue into the future. All of the more involved issues in assessing budget status arise from more complicated projection problems.

Multiyear histories can provide important information for assessing current year results. Extrapolating from fall enrollment levels to enrollment levels and tuition receipts for the whole year requires an estimate of student retention and midyear arrivals. The best place to start that analysis is with historical records of fall to spring retention.

It is also important to recognize new initiatives or programs that may be affecting the budget, driving results for the remainder of the year that will vary from previous history. It is also likely to be the case that those who approved the initiative will want to know how much impact it had.

(d) Budget Adjustments and Management Responses

In concrete terms, current year budget reviews and projections can have two primary areas of impact on the organization:

1. Drive changes in current year activities to conform to conditions that differ from budget assumptions.
2. Inform the process of developing the budget for the next year.

Minor projected deviations from budget may cause managers to request adjustments to their budgets, such as transfers between accounts or between object codes. Organizational policies determine the necessity of making budget adjustments and the restrictions on doing so. The frequency of budget adjustments depends on the ways in which the organization uses budgets to control spending.

An organization can exercise tight control over spending by holding managers to the amounts budgeted for each line item. One way of doing this is to use an accounting system that rejects transactions if they would cause the current year activity field to exceed the budget for any account/object code combination. If the University of Okoboji enacted this policy, the Business School (see Exhibit 3.9) would need to make an adjustment to the office supplies line for the Executive Program if $67,800 had been spent in that object code and it still needed to spend $300 on binders. The Business School could buy those binders if it transferred $100 from any other line still underspent, such as photocopying. The Business School could also make the transfer from another program.

Obviously this degree of control on an object code level necessitates a large number of budget adjustments. In this example, the budget adjustment of $100 will only provide temporary relief if any other expenses hit the Office Supplies object code, necessitating further budget adjustments or a larger adjustment at this point while estimating the remaining activity in this object code for the year. Many organizations

Exhibit 3.9 Budget Adjustment to (Over Proposed Transaction)

	Budget	*YTD Activity*	*Proposed Transaction*	*Budget Adjustment*	*Revised Budget*
Fall tuition	$4,000,000	$4,000,000			$4,000,000
Spring tuition	2,000,000	2,000,000			2,000,000
Faculty salaries	1,630,000	1,230,000			1,630,000
Professional salaries	100,000	75,000			100,000
Benefits pool charge	433,000	320,000			433,000
Office supplies	68,000	67,800	300	100	68,100
Lab supplies	210,000	180,000			210,000
Postage	75,000	72,000			75,000
Photocopying	65,000	44,000		(100)	64,900
Telephones—long distance	$25,000	$18,000			$25,000

avoid this situation by classifying object codes in groups and controlling expenditures on the level of that grouping, so a department can offset overages in one object code by underspending others without generating a separate adjustment transaction. These rules may further depend on the fund type involved. In the Business School example, the Financial Data Services is classified in a separate fund group, 2 as opposed to 1, which indicates it is considered an auxiliary operation. The university's accounting policies will give the manager of that account more leeway, and it does not matter whether any object code or group goes over as long as the account breaks even.

Another variable in budget adjustments is the level of managerial discretion in making transfers. Often common sense rules apply, such as a manager can approve any adjustment between and within accounts over which she has control, as long as the adjustment nets to zero. The organization requires higher levels of approval, understandably, if the adjustment would increase the overall level of funding, or would transfer resources from one manager to another.

Organizations may place some restrictions on transfers between certain categories. Many organizations discourage transfers between salary and nonsalary lines and subject them to more constraints. Even if the organization has an employment-at-will relationship with its staff, most in the nonprofit sector consider salaries more of a long-term commitment. Funding between salaries and nonsalaries is not considered fungible. Similar restrictions may apply to equipment purchases or capital spending.

Budget adjustments are primarily a bureaucratic procedure that occurs in large organizations. The more significant impact of midyear budget review in all organizations comes when it reveals sufficiently large variances from expectations relative to the organization's overall resource base to necessitate major changes in operations or finances. Budget deficits are discussed in more depth in Chapter 13. Let us just acknowledge here that one purpose of the budget status review is to alert managers and external groups to any financial crisis that will require them to turn some of their attention from their planned activities and develop a strategy for responding to the crisis. The budget review can also indicate a windfall, but it seems that windfalls occur less frequently than crises and in most cases the organization can take its time to decide how to respond to a windfall—in other words, how to spend the extra money.

We must note that budget status review should be a routine matter. If the organization has done a good job of assessing its environment, anticipating events, and planning its finances, it should rarely encounter severe midyear crises, and budget reviews should seldom be the first place where indications of trouble emerge. It is very easy to say that an organization is facing problems due to conditions out of its control, but most often organizations can easily see those conditions in advance if leadership acknowledges its situation, avoids the temptation to explain away worrisome conditions, and discusses them openly. The worst organizational financial crises come when managers build a budget that depends too heavily on unreliable income sources and lacks the flexibility to scale back spending when feared but predictable events finally come to pass.

Midyear budget analysis can inform the budget development process in constructive ways. A few months into the new year may give a pretty good indication of the future for trend-driven revenue or expense factors such as tuition or patient visits. The new year may shed light on the extent of a new initiative's impact, such as an image advertising campaign. Budget development may also need to factor in negative trends, the failure of an initiative, or the loss of key personnel. However, current year feedback to the development process has to stop somewhere. There will always be more information coming in and there will always be uncertainty about the future. At some point, management needs to settle on its assumptions and plans for the next year so that the proposal can be pulled together and approved. Constantly going back to those who prepare budgets and asking them to make adjustments in light of the most up-to-date information does not justify the time consumed and the protraction of the decision process.

3.4 ANALYSIS OF FINAL RESULTS

(a) Introduction

When the year has ended and the final results are tallied, the budget process has come full cycle. Only with final results can the organization judge whether its budgeting process has succeeded or failed.

- Did the process succeed in anticipating events this year?
- Did the process help the organization identify and respond to conditions as they changed during the year?
- What do the final results tell us that we need to take into consideration for our planning for next year, and do they suggest any adjustments we need to make in our plans, goals, or actions during the year that just got started?

In large organizations, the fiscal year-end kicks off a formal and time-consuming process in which staff compile and analyze the results. Smaller organizations may not spend much time pondering results, but most take a look at how the year came out to see whether they gained or lost ground. Busy leaders of small organizations may be tempted to settle for a cursory review of results, but that can leave the organization open to being blindsided.

(b) Reporting Results

Most organizations are required to report results in some form to their board or other external governing bodies. Boards should insist that management provide a thorough analysis of budget results, even in a small organization.

The first step in year-end reporting is to finalize the financial data. For a small organization, this can be as simple as specifying some date parameters in Quicken (a bookkeeping software program) and running a report. Larger organizations will need to finalize accrual transactions, depreciation entries, capitalization sweeps, reserve adjustments, and so forth. This process can take some time, although too much time may indicate poor management of the accounting function in the comptroller's office or in departments that feed transactions to the comptroller's office.

Reporting results relative to budget should not be confused with financial reports prepared by external auditors. Auditors' reports provide a statement of the organization's financial position according to industry-standard rules and formats, with a comparison to its position a year earlier. Some of the key differences between an auditor's report and a budget include:

- The audited financial reports are not analytical. They do not report variances, let alone attempt to explain them. Internal managers have the predominant responsibility for this sort of analysis. The role of the external auditors is to ensure the correct reporting of basic financial data and to confirm that adequate controls and accounting procedures are in place.
- The reports follow audit conventions that may not respond to the concerns of the managers and the board. For example, the Financial Accounting Standards Board Statement of Financial Accounting Standards Number 117 specifies that the audited financial reports report the excess of gifts over spending as income in the period in which the gift is received. In many cases, the board and management have a specific purpose in mind for those funds and

want to treat them as restricted, essentially committed to expenditure in a future period and therefore not to be treated as revenue available in the current period.

The distinction between audited financial reports and the results of year-end budget analysis points to an important point about budget reporting: The format and content of budget reports are largely an internal matter, and are not governing by formal external standards. As an aspect of their fiduciary responsibility, management and governing bodies must develop budget reports that satisfy their needs for managing the institution's resources to achieve its objectives.

(c) Reporting Variances

Variance analysis constitutes the fundamental discipline of evaluating budgetary performance. Analysts pursue several dimensions of variance to reach an understanding of what drove financial performance. Results for the year just ended are compared to:

- *Budget for the year just ended.* The budget represents what management thought would happen, so this variance shows whether results differed from expectations as they stood more than a year ago.
- *Previous year's results.* This variance shows how this year differed from previous years, or how it conformed to long-term trends.
- *Budget for the current year.* The current year budget contains the most recent assumptions, and this variance can show whether the results support current expectations.

Each set of variances needs to be calculated on an organization-wide basis. Variances for major operating units should be calculated as a matter of course. The largest variances, in terms of absolute dollars or percentage, become candidates for further analysis. Additional analytical steps may include:

- Break the variance down into smaller levels of organization, isolating the variance to a particular organizational unit or account. If the University of Okoboji found it had a significant shortfall in tuition, the first level of variance might point to the Business School as the source. Further analysis might show that most of that variance came from the Executive program.

- "Decompose" the variance into its key drivers. Tuition changes from year to year are a function of absolute enrollment, price changes, and changes in the mix of students between programs (which carry different prices). Enrollment itself varies with changes in the number of entering students and changes in retention. The results can vary on all of these dimensions both from previous years and from the assumptions about number, price, mix, enrollment, and retention implicit in last year's or the current year's budget assumptions.

Theoretically, all variances can be attributed to basic drivers, but it may not be feasible to derive them from centrally managed information sources such as the financial system or the patient registration system. In that case, central staff will need to ask the managers most directly responsible for the element or for the area exhibiting the variance to provide the explanation. In a more distributed budgeting system, leadership assumes that all managers will conduct detailed analyses of variances in their area and report them up and across the organization. Of course, the organization will still need to take a centralized look at variances in case the effects are too broadly diffused across departments to emerge from their individual analytical efforts.

Trend-driven aspects of the organization's activities and support will need to be put into a multiyear context for review and analysis of trends. Trends can be viewed as a kind of multiyear variance, but the reporting and analysis take a different form than variances, which focus on differences between pairs of data points.

In our University of Okoboji example (Exhibit 3.10), the university did somewhat worse that expected: It ran a deficit of over $5 million when it anticipated a $4.5 million shortfall. To understand the causes of this deficit, the university will have to view certain variances together. Tuition and aid together came in $2.5 million ahead of budget, which made up for negative variances in auxiliaries, which on a net basis (revenue and expense) ran a deficit of $1.5 million from plan; instead of netting a surplus of $400,000 as budgeted, the auxiliaries lost $1.1 million. Both the absolute loss and the lost surplus are relevant, because the budget assumed a positive contribution from auxiliaries.

Some variances can be taken in isolation—unrestricted staff salaries going over budget by $4 million has significance by itself. Others make the most sense in tandem—restricted revenues went over by $500,000, as did expenses, resulting in a net effect of zero unless the restricted funds were supposed to pay for expenses (such as staff salaries) that appeared as unrestricted costs but which could have been transferred to restricted funds if more had come in. These variances can be summarized as follows:

Budgeted deficit 1996–97 ($000s)	($4,550)
Higher net tuition	2,500
Higher gifts	1,500
Lower unrestricted expenses	2,660
Higher staff salaries	(4,032)
Higher benefits	(1,262)
Worse returns from auxiliaries	(1,500)
Lower government appropriations	(500)
All other, net	74
Actual deficit 1996–97	($5,110)

For an organization of this size, this level of detail does not provide much insight on the organization's performance, but it does point toward areas of further analysis:

- What units generated higher staff salaries? Did the higher salaries come from permanent additions to the staff this year, or was the budget unrealistically low?
- Which programs produced the higher net tuition, and will it continue?
- Which auxiliaries ran deficits?

Comparing the results to the current budget leads to questions about current assumptions.

The questions this comparison raises are as follows:

Actual deficit 1996–97 ($000s)	($5,110)
Better net tuition	2,700
Lower staff salaries	4,440
Better auxiliaries	4,180
Lower benefits	464
Lower gifts	(1,500)
Higher faculty salaries	(2,584)
Higher unrestricted expense	(8,920)
Lower endowment income	(990)
All other, net	(10)
Budgeted deficit 1997–98	($7,330)

Exhibit 3.10 University of Okoboji Variance Between Actual and Budget ($000s)

	1996–97 Budget	*1996–97 Actual*	*Variance*
Tuition and fees	$46,000	$49,000	$3,000
Governmental appropriations	4,000	3,500	(500)
Private gifts	15,000	16,500	1,500
Endowment income used	9,000	9,040	40
Sales and services	500	400	(100)
Other sources	350	400	50
Auxiliaries	30,000	29,000	(1,000)
Restricted revenue	13,000	13,500	500
Plant revenue	6,000	7,500	1,500
Total revenue	**123,850**	**128,840**	**4,990**
Unrestricted faculty salaries	30,000	30,016	(16)
Unrestricted staff salaries	15,000	19,032	(4,032)
Unrestricted benefits	11,000	12,262	(1,262)
Total unrestricted compensation	56,000	61,310	(5,310)
Unrestricted financial aid	3,200	3,700	(500)
Other unrestricted operating costs	20,000	17,340	2,660
Total unrestricted E&G[1]	79,200	82,350	(3,150)
Auxiliaries	29,600	30,100	(500)
Total rest expense	13,000	13,500	(500)
Total plant expense	6,600	8,000	(1,400)
Total expenses	**128,400**	**133,950**	**(5,550)**
Net surplus/(deficit)	**($4,550)**	**($5,110)**	**($560)**

[1]Educational and general.

- The net tuition budget for this year calls for an improvement over last year's net tuition. How much of the improvement in last year's actuals was factored into the budget for improved revenue?
- Will the higher staff salaries continue, and will lower unrestricted expense continue? What assumptions underlie the increase in unrestricted expenses budgeted for this year?
- Where does the anticipated improvement in auxiliary performance come from, and do last year's results put it in a new light?

(d) Final Analysis

As should be apparent from these examples, variance analysis spits out tons of data. The process of sorting and grouping these figures and drilling down produces many individual comparisons between pairs of numbers. The analyst must possess the ability to filter all of these data to focus on the most important comparisons. Boards and senior managers of large organizations cannot take the time to absorb all of the data the analyst has waded through. There are no rules to provide direction for the analysis. At times, the decision on the analytical focus may seem arbitrary and capricious. At the risk of making overblown claims for financial analysis, variance analysis starts to move the financial analyst from the realm of science to that of art.

Management and governing bodies will use this (focused) analysis to:

- Assess the organization's success in the previous year.
- Adjust strategic thinking forward.
- Assess managerial performance, from the most senior officers through individual managers.
- Establish initial assumptions for the budget planning process.
- Make adjustments to budgets and actions for the current year.

Exhibit 3.11 The Overlapping Cycles of Budgeting

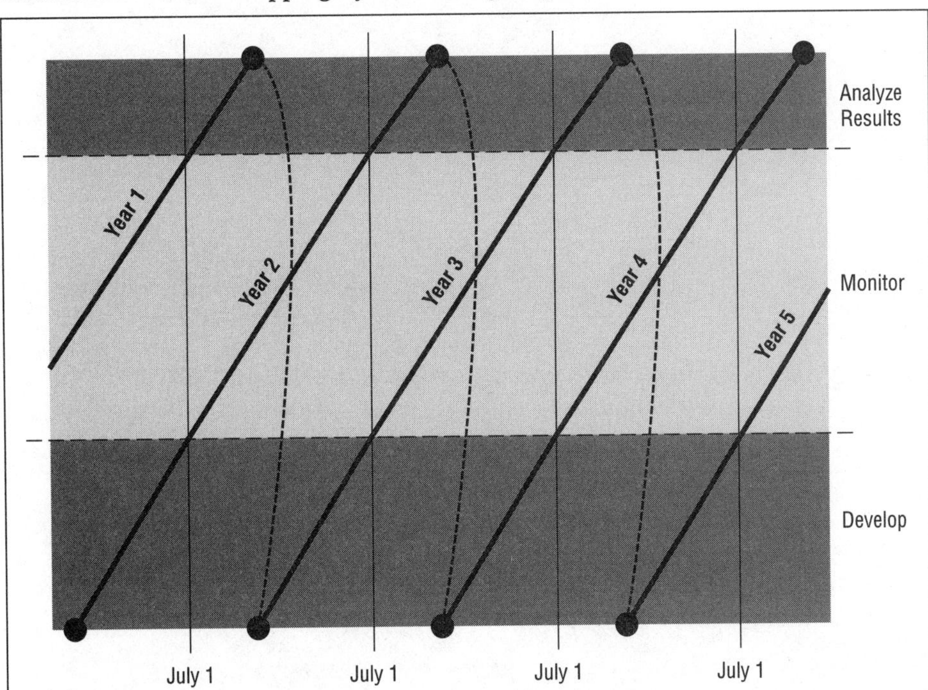

3.5 CONCLUSION

The broad outlines of budget cycle are remarkably consistent from organization to organization. Most budgets are managed in three major phases: (1) developing the budget for the next year: (2) monitoring, tracking, and adjusting the budget for the current year; and (3) analyzing results for the year just ended. In almost every organization that takes financial management seriously, the budget process is experienced as a set of overlapping cycles that constantly roll from one of these stages to the next. See Exhibit 3.11.

CHAPTER FOUR

Components of a Budget

4.1 INTRODUCTION

Most organizations have three primary budgets:

1. Operating
2. Capital
3. Cash

These reflect the three fundamental statements of financial accounting—income statement, balance sheet, and statement of cash flows—that together form the standard financial portrait of an organization. An organization may supplement these budgets with other budgets and schedules, such as service or fund-raising budgets.

Some small organizations reduce budgeting to an operating budget. They treat all capital purchases as current period, or operating, expenses. The director monitors cash by reviewing account statements from the bank. However, all organizations need to understand and report their asset base, and it is important to be in a position to anticipate cash flow, particularly in a small organization, which can run immediate risks of running out of cash with few options for response available other than skipping a payroll or closing the organization. In this chapter and Chapters 5, 6, and 7, we will assume that all organizations maintain the three basic budgets. We need to define a few terms first.

(a) Operating Activity

Operating activity is revenue received and expenses incurred in the current period from which the organization expects to receive the full benefit in the current period. Operating expenses may include cash and noncash items: For example, once an organization issues a bill for services to be rendered in the current period, it counts as current period revenue whether payment is received in the period or not. Once the bill is issued, it is assumed that payment will be collected. The difference between what is billed and what is expected to be collected is recorded as write-offs of bad debts.

(b) Capital Activity

Capital activity is transactions related to "any project that involves the use of spending power in return for an anticipated flow of future benefits for a long period, generally more than one year."[1] Capital projects include construction and building projects, purchases of equipment, major computer software, books and works of art, and stage sets. Capital is considered to be consumed through use; the operational cost of capital is represented through depreciation charges, costs that are calculated based on items' values and useful lives, and which are charged to the organization's annual operations.

(c) Cash Flow

Cash flow includes all receipts and disbursements of cash during the year. The net effect of cash flow results in the organization's ending cash balance. The cash balance and cash flow do not differentiate between cash flows related to capital projects and operations, and they do not take into consideration future claims on or benefits from cash received or disbursed during the period (e.g., an accrued payroll liability mid–pay cycle for hours that staff members have worked but for which they have not yet been paid).

4.2 OPERATING BUDGET

Most people think of the operating budget when they think of a budget (if they do at all). It shows all of the organization's revenues, all of the expenses, and the difference between the two shows whether the organization expects to make or lose money. While nonprofit organizations do not

[1]Surendra Singhvi, "The Capital Investment Budgeting Process," 19-2, in *Handbook of Budgeting*, 3rd ed., Rachlin and Sweeny.

make profits, their operations can drain or build up assets such as cash reserves or endowments.

The operating budget can be thought of as flowing out of revenues. The organization determines how much money it will have in the coming year and then it knows how much it can spend. Of course, there is a more complicated relationship between revenues and expenses—in many cases, the decisions on how to spend money drive the revenues that can be expected: "You have to spend money to make money."

Most organizations have several sources of revenue, each of which must be projected using a different method.

- If an organization receives several major grants, it may predict those revenues by reviewing the status of each grant and assessing its probability of renewal, increase, or decrease.
- Some revenue factors follow trends, such as memberships or donations to the annual fund. Revenue budgets may be derived from projections of those trends.
- Some revenue sources are a function of identified drivers, such as tuition revenues from students. The number of students can be estimated based on assumptions about the retention of current students and application trends for new students, and tuition revenue can be derived from that base.

Organizations with a single source of revenue are easier to budget but carry much greater risk of losing their financial lifeblood. The Victim Assistance program depends on a single grant. If a new state's attorney is elected, that person will have new priorities and may decide to end or restructure this program. The Victim Assistance program's leadership and board need to monitor developments in the state capitol and start exploring strategies for diversifying the funding base.

Revenue budgets may constitute goals as well as projections. An organization may set a target for fund raising and establish that as the budget. The fund-raising budget may now represent a departure from trends. From that point forward, the budget becomes the goal for the fund-raising staff, who are asked to redouble their efforts to achieve that goal. It may be the case that the organization has no choice but to try to achieve this level of fund raising, or the organization may have decided it can and should do better.

Expense budgets can be structured in different ways:

- *Type of expense or type of activity*. The Arts Council uses a mixture of both expense type and type of activity or program, as can be seen in Exhibit 4.1. Telephones are a type of expense that may support

Exhibit 4.1 Arts Council Nonsalary Expenses

Expense Group	*Type*
Rent	Expense
Supplies	Expense
Telephones	Expense
Computer lease	Expense
Contract services	Expense
Exhibition costs	Activity
Insurance	Expense
Printing	Expense
Advertising	Expense

any number of activities—general administration, calls to solicit advertisers for the newspaper, contacts with arts education program students. Exhibition costs relate to a type of activity—installing exhibitions—that may cover many types of expenses. Installing the exhibit may require building supplies such as lumber, paint, and plaster. There will be costs for wine, beer, and food at the opening. The organization may include as part of exhibition costs some printing and photocopying costs for gallery labels and artists' statements of purpose, which could also be classified under the printing. In theory it is preferable to use a consistent method of organizing expenses, but in practice it is often easier to use a mixture.

- *Degree of specificity.* The organization may budget its expenses according to broader classes of expenses as opposed to the specific expense types or object codes that it uses to record them in the accounting system. A large organization will have hundreds of object codes, making it impractical to prepare budgets that display all of them. A well-run large organization will structure its chart of accounts to organize object codes into logical groupings. These groupings or classes may provide a better basis for leadership to make its resource allocation decisions than a budget broken down into every detailed object code. Exhibit 4.2 shows how the "other unrestricted expense" budget for the university's School of Arts and Sciences translates into specific object codes.

Organization of expense budgets is a less troublesome matter for small organizations. Even so, information can easily get confused. If the budget for exhibition expenses includes printing, it may be difficult at the end of the year to reconcile the bill from printers with the organization's

Exhibit 4.2 University of Okoboji School of Arts and Sciences ($000s)

	Budget
Tuition and fees	$26,000
Private gifts	1,500
Restricted revenue	8,400
Total revenue	35,900
UR[1] faculty salaries	19,560
UR[1] staff salaries	2,627
UR[1] benefits	5,546
Total UR[1] compensation	27,733
UR[1] financial aid	3,400
Other UR[1] operating costs	2,626
	6,026
Total UR[1] E&G[2]	33,759
Total rest expense	8,400
Total expenses	42,159
Net surplus/(deficit)	($6,259)

Detail for "Other Unrestricted Expenses"

Object Code	Description	Budget
5000	Office supplies	$525
5100	Computer software	525
5200	Postage	525
5250	Photocopying and duplicating	525
5400	Telephones—access	394
5410	Telephones—long distance	131
	Total for category	2,625

[1]Unrestricted
[2]Educational and general

budget and financial records. Anyone reviewing the records will want to make sure a printing bill did not get double counted—once as a printing expense and once as an exhibition expense. If too many object codes are used or they are used inconsistently, it may be difficult to determine against which budget line expenses should be reviewed. Some charges may be found under an object code called "printing," others under one called "photocopying services." Should those be added together to get the total for printing? Should the photocopying services be grouped with some other budgets, or do they represent an unanticipated area of expenditure intended to be offset by underspending in another area? None of these questions should cause a problem if the group's financial transactions are well organized and well documented, but few small organizations have the staff time or depth of volunteer support to spend a lot of time on financial record keeping, increasing the risk of missing, duplicating, or misclassifying a transaction.

Most organizations should subdivide the operating budget along one or more lines.

- *Program.* The Arts Council organizes its budget along these lines. See Exhibit 4.3. Program organization recognizes that different

Exhibit 4.3 Arts Council Budget Programs

Program	*Revenue*	*Expense*	*Net*
General and state arts seed grant	$82,500	$79,500	$3,500
Art in the schools	25,000	25,000	0
Summer art camp	27,000	27,000	0
Gallery	1,200	3,000	(1,800)
Newspaper	4,000	5,500	(1,500)
Total	$139,700	$139,500	$200

programs may have different sources of funds, different management and staff, discrete expenses, and outcome measures specific to that program.

- *Organization.* A large organization divides itself into units that focus on certain aspects of operations or certain programs, each of which has its own manager. The organization is structured in a hierarchy of managers reporting to other managers, each of whom bears some responsibility for managing the finances of the activities that fall under them. In some cases, organizations divide along programmatic lines, with separate managers given responsibility for different programs.

- *Fund type.* Budgets may need to reflect the types of funds being budgeted, and organizations may apply different rules to different fund types. Frequently, organizations distinguish between restricted and unrestricted funds. Restricted funds carry donor restrictions on their use, and therefore the organization must track them separately. The budgets for these funds may be derived from program budgets submitted to get the funds. The nonprofit accounting profession has developed detailed standards for classifying revenues and expenses, known as fund accounting. Exhibit 4.4 provides an example of a multiple fund budget, which breaks the University of Okoboji's budget into various fund groups. Exhibit 4.5 shows how even a small organization such as the Victim Assistance Association recognizes the distinction between fund types in its budgeting, maintaining one budget, essentially a program budget, that accounts for the use of funds received from the State Attorney's Office, and another that shows the additional impact of the small "unrestricted" support the organization receives from the church that serves as its landlord.

In a large organization, multiple levels of subdivision often occur. The organization divides its budgets as needed to show the portion of the

Exhibit 4.4 University of Okoboji Current Year Budget Breakout by Division ($000s)

	Arts and Sciences	*Business*	*Pharmacy*	*Social Work*	*Total Academic*	*Student Services*	*Administration*	*Development*	*Institutional*	*Total*
Tuition and fees	$26,000	$15,600	$5,200	$5,200	$52,000					$52,000
Governmental appropriations					0				3,850	3,850
Private gifts	1,500			1,500	3,000				12,000	15,000
Endowment income used					0				8,050	8,050
Sales and services		375			375	125				500
Other sources					0	350				350
Auxiliaries					0	25,500	8,500			34,000
Restricted revenue	8,400	700	1,400	3,500	14,000					14,000
Plant revenue					0				7,000	7,000
Total revenue	**35,900**	**16,675**	**6,600**	**10,200**	**69,375**	**25,975**	**8,500**	**0**	**30,900**	**134,750**
UR[1] faculty salaries	19,560	6,520	3,260	3,260	32,600					32,600
UR[1] staff salaries	2,627	2,627	730	438	6,420	292	6,129	730	1,022	14,592
UR[1] benefits	5,546	2,286	997	924	9,755	73	1,532	182	255	11,798
Total UR[1] compensation	27,733	11,433	4,987	4,622	48,776	365	7,661	912	1,277	58,990
UR[1] financial aid	3,400	80	240	280	4,000					4,000
Other UR[1] operating costs	2,626	2100.8	1,313	525	6,565	135	7,716	1,050	10,793	26,260
Total UR[1] E&G[2] expenses	33,759	13,614	6,540	5,427	59,341	500	15,377	1,962	12,070	89,250
Auxiliaries					0	23,190	7,730			30,920
Total rest expense	8,400	700	1,400	3,500	14,000					14,000
Total plant expense					0				7,910	7,910
Total expenses	**42,159**	**14,314**	**7,940**	**8,927**	**73,341**	**23,690**	**23,107**	**1,962**	**19,980**	**142,080**
Net surplus/(deficit)	**($6,259)**	**$2,361**	**($1,340)**	**1,273**	**($3,966)**	**$2,285**	**($14,607)**	**($1,962)**	**$10,920**	**($7,330)**

[1]Unrestricted
[2]Educational and general

Exhibit 4.5 Victim Assistance Association

Budget (for state grant application)		*Full budget*	
Salaries		Revenues	
Director	$32,000	State grant	$46,080
Office assistant (part-time)	10,000	Plate collection	1,000
Health insurance	2,400	Contributions (rent)	12,000
Telephones	480	Total revenues	59,080
Supplies	225		
Travel (clients)	250		
Travel (staff)	250	Salaries	
Memberships	300	Director	32,000
Publications	175	Office assistant (part-time)	10,000
Total budget	$46,080	Health insurance	2,400
		Telephones	480
		Rent	12,000
		Supplies	225
		Equipment	300
		Events	400
		Travel (clients)	250
		Travel (staff)	250
		Memberships	300
		Publications	175
		Total expense	58,780
		Net surplus/(deficit)	$300

budget that applies to particular managers. Portions may be expressed it in terms of multiple funds to track the interaction of restricted and unrestricted funds and to encourage managers to look at all fund types to achieve the best overall results.

The operating budget may include subsidiary budgets developed in almost as much detail and reviewed as an integral part of the budget development process. Examples could include personnel budgets, which might include details on numbers of FTE (full-time equivalent) in particular staff categories, or budgets keyed to particular revenue sources such as tuition and financial aid, which might show enrollments, retention figures, and average financial aid packages as part of the budget proposal and display. Variances in the nonfinancial drivers will explain much of the financial variance.

4.3 CAPITAL BUDGET

We briefly defined capital activity above. *Capital* is the organization's assets, the things that it can either use to fulfill its mission or sell. Capital assets have exchange value, and the organization would try to sell them if it had to close its doors and raise cash. Capital items have lasting value that can also serve as collateral for borrowing. Some of the typical capital items are:

- Land
- Buildings
- Improvements to buildings
- Furniture
- Fixtures
- Computers
- Major computer software (including costs related to installing it)
- Equipment
- Works of art
- Musical instruments
- Stage sets and costumes
- Books

Capital projects are the projects the organization undertakes to acquire these items, through purchase, construction, or other means. Some personnel costs can be included if they form an integral cost of acquiring the item—the cost for systems specialists to install computer software, or for the wages of craftspeople to install a new roof.

Capital projects differ from operating expenses in that they involve both expenditures and a source of funds. Capital projects may simply be funded from operating cash balances, but the organization may have other options as well—for example, borrowing or bond financing, gifts, or government grants. The impetus for the project may have been the availability of funding for a certain kind of undertaking. Each capital project has its own budget that identifies the amount and timing of expenditures and the source of funds. Capital projects often cross fiscal years from initiation to completion.

The capital budget covers all of the activity the organization anticipates for the year related to acquisition or disposal of capital assets, including the portion of capital project financing and expenditure that will occur during the year. The capital budget draws heavily on the budgets for approved capital projects. The focus in the capital budgeting cycle is on reviewing and approving major projects.

In Exhibit 4.6, the capital budget separates costs that represent the projected costs of capital projects already under way from new projects and smaller capital costs such as small alterations projects and equipment and furniture purchases. The organization would focus in particular upon deciding whether to approve the new projects, the largest of which—the new dormitory—would have its biggest impact in future years, since the first year in which the project would be planned and designed involves lower costs than the construction phase of the project. The committee might question some of the figures for the ongoing projects, particularly whether the proposed budget for the administration building renovation is a realistic figure, or whether it was just "plugged" to match the total budget. If it is expected to go over budget, the organization needs to reconsider its other expenditures.

Most larger organizations have some sort of defined process for developing, reviewing, and approving capital projects that is distinct from the process for developing the operating budget. It may involve a separate capital projects committee, or it may be supported by staff in the Facilities area rather than the Budget Office.

Major capital projects are reviewed on a project-by-project basis, unlike operating expenses, which tend to be reviewed by categories of ex-

Exhibit 4.6 Proposed FY99 Capital Budget

	Completion Target	*FY98 Budget*	*Proposed FY99 Budget*	*Previous Spending*	*Remaining Cost*	*Total Budget*
Continuing projects						
Fiber optics installation	2001	$500,000	$500,000	$445,000	$1,055,000	$2,500,000
Library addition	2000	850,000	1,000,000	225,000	225,000	2,300,000
Administration building renovation	1999	600,000	25,000	275,000	0	900,000
New projects						
New dormitory	2001	0	120,000	0	2,880,000	3,000,000
Resurface football field	1999	0	600,000	0	0	600,000
Biology lab renovation	1999	0	800,000	0	0	800,000
Replace roof, Business School	1999	0	700,000	0	0	700,000
Small projects		450,000	625,000			
Equipment and furniture		300,000	320,000			
Total proposed FY99 capital budget			$4,690,000			

pense and revenue. In other words, while it may make perfect sense to review the contracted services line across the operating budget, it makes no sense to review the contracted services line across capital projects. Therefore, the process involves the preparation of detailed documentation on the proposed projects. Project documentation must include a project timeline, and the approval given to the project may affect the organization's budget for several years in the future.

Because of their magnitude, capital projects have to be designed with the source of funds in mind. The organization may carry cash balances from operations sufficient to fund some capital projects. In some cases, the funding drives the decision to make the capital investment. Certain gifts or grants are available only for capital projects or for a particular capital project, so the organization decides to take advantage of funds that would be lost to it otherwise. This approach to capital budgeting is clearly less than optimal. In an ideal world, organizations would assess their strategic aims, analyze the capital requirements to achieve them, and develop plans to fund the required investments. Leadership would pass over projects that deviate from this plan because it would distract the organization's time and attention from its aims. An organization can only successfully manage a limited number of major projects at one time. That is the ideal world. In reality, resources are scarce enough that organizations have to combine opportunistic actions with strategic planning.

4.4 CASH BUDGET

As noted earlier, the cash budget is the one most likely to be neglected. A small organization may be too busy living from hand to mouth to worry about future cash availability, or the small stream of funds available may be very predictable. Larger organizations may be confident that enough cash will be available as long as operating results stay in balance and management limits the amount of capital projects funded from unrestricted sources.

However, the experience of other organizations points to the need to track cash separately. The Presbyterian Church in our example predicts on a monthly basis its cash receipts in the form of pledges and plate collections received. The church always runs a current fund deficit in the summer, but if it builds up enough of a cash reserve early in the year it can ride through the summer without bouncing or delaying paychecks. The current cash budget (see Exhibit 4.7) shows the church just breaking even through the summer. If the reserves are low, the chair of the session's stewardship committee will send a letter to the congregation pleading for members to keep up with their pledges and make advance payments. If the church has anemic receipts during the summer,

Exhibit 4.7 Presbyterian Church Cash Budget

	Receipts	*Uses*	*Net*	*Balance*
Starting cash balance				$22,000
Monthly activity				
January	30,975	(23,917)	7,058	29,058
February	16,825	(18,992)	(2,167)	26,892
March	25,125	(20,692)	4,433	31,325
April	38,000	(26,667)	11,333	42,658
May	16,950	(18,792)	(1,842)	40,817
June	7,950	(19,992)	(12,042)	28,775
July	16,150	(24,017)	(7,867)	20,908
August	6,275	(19,067)	(12,792)	8,117
September	12,625	(19,142)	(6,517)	1,600
October	24,875	(26,192)	(1,317)	283
November	24,125	(19,742)	4,383	4,667
December	41,125	(23,792)	17,333	22,000
Ending cash balance				$22,000

the beleaguered stewardship chair may make calls throughout the congregation, or ask for a loan from one of the congregation's wealthier members to tide them through. As a last resort, the church could temporarily liquidate some of its endowment, but sound management and the endowment's rules might make that difficult.

4.5 CONCLUSION

The organizational budget has three dimensions: operating results, capital acquisition or disposal, and cash flow. In a simple organization, these dimensions may be combined into a single budget, but most organizations of any size or complexity will need to develop each dimension separately. Even a small organization that expenses items with a life longer than one year (and therefore avoids creation of a separate capital budget) may include significant noncash items on its operating statement, such as in-kind contributions, requiring that it assess cash flows independently of its total operations. For all organizations, it is useful to understand the conceptual distinctions between operations, cash, and capital. In the remainder of Part II, we will examine budgeting techniques for each of the components.

CHAPTER FIVE

Operating Budget

5.1 INTRODUCTION

Most organizations do not evaluate the design of their operating budget each year. The structure is handed down from year to year, possibly specified by the Board. However, the structure implicitly answers a set of design questions. The organization may revisit some of these questions frequently and refine the format of its operating budget. A new organization would need to address the following questions and others in designing its operating budget practices:

Expense and Revenue Categories

- Will we submit budgets for each line item found in the chart of accounts, or will we combine object codes in some way to make it easier to construct and review the budgets?
- If we combine object codes, will we follow groupings recognized in the chart of accounts, or design a unique or variant set of groupings for the purposes of budgeting?
- Are there particular object codes that need to be budgeted and reviewed separately?

Organizational or Programmatic Budgets

- Will we subdivide the budget into organizational or programmatic groups or only review an organization-wide budget?
- Do we have recognized groupings that should be followed, or do we need to customize the groupings of accounts?

Fund types

- Do we budget restricted funds and auxiliaries?
- Do we include these funds in budgets for organizations or programs?

The organization will address these principles when making minor modifications to its budgeting practices or wholesale changes. This chapter examines the principles underlying all parts of the operating budget.

5.2 BUDGETING REVENUES

Whether revenues drive expenses ("this is how much we will get, so this is how much we can spend") or respond to expenses ("we have to find this much revenue to support our basic expenses"), the process of budgeting revenues should encompass three key elements.

1. *Identify all primary sources of revenue.* The primary revenue sources usually align with the revenue categories used in the budget statements that feed from and to the chart of accounts, but there may be cases where some revenue elements are broken out from these categories. The Arts Council starts with its basic revenue categories, but treats one of the key grants as a separate source because of its criticality in supporting general operations. (See Exhibit 5.1.) Other grants and contracts support specific programs—the council will incur the expenses related to those programs only if the grant or contract comes in. The seed grant covers much of the director's salary; if the state denies or cuts it, the council will have to go to lengths to find substitute sources of revenue.
2. *Determine how to establish the budget for each primary source.* Sources of revenue will fall into categories that require different techniques for projection and budgeting. In addition to classifying the revenues by type of budgeting technique, a large organization will

Exhibit 5.1 Identifying Sources of Revenue

Major Revenue Sources	*Current Year*
Memberships	$ 2,400
State arts seed grant	30,000
Other grants	40,000
Arts education contracts	52,000
Rentals	4,500
Gallery sales	1,200
Fund raising	6,000
Advertising	4,000

need to identify the department or individual responsible for information on some revenue items—for example, the financial analyst in the physician billing office will provide projections for clinical billings based on a model she maintains.

Revenue items tend to fall into one of the following categories:

- Large items
- Revenue from sales of services or goods
- Discrete items that are hard to predict
- Revenue pools
- Rates of return
- Items driven by other items

(a) Large Items

The best example of this category is a grant. The organization may know the amount of the grant in advance, maybe with some degree of uncertainty. The budgeting exercise in these cases is to identify the source for each grant, gift, or other item in this category and compile the amounts expected during the year. During this exercise, the organization should note the amount of risk of the item failing to come through or coming through at a different level. Grantors or donors may reduce or eliminate giving programs due to financial disappointments or internal issues such as leadership change. In some cases, notification of an award may not arrive before the budget is prepared, so someone has to take a guess as to the size of the award.

A large organization may have many items in this category, making the task of compiling revenue estimates difficult. Smaller organizations should have more ability to develop a detailed budget for these items. The organization may expect a handful of major items on which it should focus. For example, an organization may typically get three major grants that provide a majority of its funding for the year. The revenue budget would be built up by reviewing each grant, its likely size and timing, and compiling the amounts.

(b) Revenue from Sales of Services or Goods

Many organizations will derive some portion of their revenue from sales in some shape or form. Sales revenue is a function of units sold and the price received per unit. This basic calculation covers many types of revenue sources: receipts from providing health care services, tuition for classes taken, sales of artworks, memberships. These sources usually lend themselves to modeling as a basis for budgeting.

A simple technique for modeling sales revenue bases a future projection on historical data. The Arts Council may budget its revenue from memberships using this sort of model. Council records show the following recent history in its two categories of memberships:

	1995	*1996*	*1997*	*1998*
Corporate memberships ($100 level)	12	8	12	11
Individual memberships ($25 level)	128	92	44	54
Revenue	$4,400	$3,100	$2,300	$2,450

Because the council has kept membership prices constant and plans to continue to do so, it is only necessary to predict the number of memberships in each category:

- Corporate memberships show no clear trend, so the best prediction for this class might be the average of the last four years, or 11.
- Individual memberships show a strong downward trend with an upturn in the last year. A simple trend calculation based on all four years worth of data continues the downward line established in the first three years into the future and generates a prediction of 10. However, the council should understand the causes for the reversal in this trend and determine whether it suggests a higher level of individual memberships.

In the sample budget, the board opted for caution and assumed a slightly lower number of corporate memberships and a return to the 1997 level of individual memberships. If the 1998 trends continue in 1999, the board will consider it a windfall and will think about more optimistic budgeting for 2000.

	1995	*1996*	*1997*	*1998*	*Budget*
Corp. memberships ($100 level)	12	8	12	11	10
Ind. memberships ($25 level)	128	92	44	54	40
Revenue	$4,400	$3,100	$2,300	$2,450	$2,000

This example is a single factor sales model: Revenue is completely a function of one factor, number of sales. The Arts Council would need a more complicated model if the board wanted to consider changing the price of memberships. Price changes might have an effect on the number of memberships sold. The director would need to set up a dual-factor—price and quantity—model to test the possible effects and interactions of changes in prices and quantities. This model will lead into murky territory: the possible effect of price changes on the number of memberships sold. Will a lower price attract more people, leading to a net gain? Will higher prices lead enough people to cancel their memberships to cost more than is gained? These questions can only be answered with probabilities, although historical information on price increases or market research can shed much light on likely responses. Unfortunately, the Arts Council does not have any experience with price changes it can use as a basis for that prediction, and it cannot afford market research. The organization may be able to get some help from other organizations or associations sharing their experience.

We have discussed two basic models: single factor (number of units) and double factor (unit/price). Many organizations will need to use a more complicated model, such as a units/price/mix model. This model is used in cases where the purchasers can choose between various levels of service and price, and may move between those levels. An example would be student housing, where a certain number of students will need housing, but they can choose between various types of rooms. Each type of room will have a different price. Room choice may be partially a function of the demographics of the student pool—if the school has separate dormitories for freshmen and upperclassmen, the mix of the student body will drive some of the choices. However, the school needs a model that can account for elements of choice between singles, doubles, and triples, rooms in recently renovated buildings, rooms closer to the central campus, and rooms with air conditioning.

Multifactor revenue models are also important in health care, where revenue is a function of the units of service provided, the types of service, the price received for the unit of service, and the percent collected. Health care providers face an array of payers with whom they negotiate different prices and who have different patterns of failure to pay. They need to hire staff (or consultants) who can develop models that take these factors into consideration.

(c) Discrete Items

This category covers revenues such as major gifts that come from a small number of sources in relatively large amounts and can be hard to predict. Major gifts can experience dramatic year-to-year changes because of a single donor. The organization usually must budget gifts at some level, but large gifts may not be so unusual when viewed over multiple years. One approach is to look at the history for the revenue category and determine whether there is any reliable trend or basic level of giving. In the following example, 1997 stands out as an anomaly. Upon further investigation, it turns out that 1997 saw a one-time gift of $30,000 from the estate of a long-time supporter. Leaving out that single gift, 1997 falls in line with other years at $11,000. The adjusted average of the four years is $10,500, as opposed to $18,000 unadjusted: $10,500 would be a reasonable, conservative figure to budget; however, if the organization ran these data further back and found similar very large gifts falling every four years or so, the unadjusted average of $18,000 might be more appropriate. The years in which large gifts fall would offset the years that come in below average.

	1995	*1996*	*1997*	*1998*
Major gifts	$10,000	$12,000	$41,000	$9,000

At the Arts Council, it may turn out that gallery sales also fall into this category. Most of the shows are of emerging artists who offer their work at relatively low prices and generate few and low commissions. The budget of $1,200 may be based on a year in which there was an unusually successful show of more expensive works, one of which sold for $3,500. The council's 30% commission came to $1,050. The council should look at the history for this revenue category to see how common and significant single major sales have been in the past.

(d) Revenue Pools

Revenue pools cover types of revenue that are too complicated to permit examination of each contributing item on a case-by-case basis and cannot be reduced to a simple sales model (of one or more factors). At the Arts Council, rentals of the facility and advertising fall into this category. The facility is rented frequently for rehearsals, performances, parties, and receptions, usually several times a week. The organization has some guidelines for rates, but usually the director negotiates each rental individually depending on length of use, disruption to other activities, purpose of the event, and ability to pay. The best way to predict this revenue source is to look at the level of rental income received in the previous year and ask the director if she thinks rentals will go up or down.

Advertising in the newspaper falls into the same category. The editor maintains a complicated schedule of prices, so the revenues are a function of how many ads are placed and the size. It would be difficult to build a model that could predict the number and size of ads because the variety of options results in small numbers at any size–price combination. Small numbers are harder to predict on a trend basis. The editor of the newspaper sells the ads, and he works better if he is given a revenue target and just scrambles to meet that. Therefore, the Arts Council sets its advertising budget by reviewing previous years for trends but primarily by basing the revenue budget on the amount of increased revenue needed to support anticipated increases in costs of production.

As an organization gets bigger, more items are either treated as revenue pools or central budget staff compile the budgets from the detailed work of people deeper in the organization. At a research university, central staff cannot review the status of each grant. Therefore, they may review historical data on grants to determine the rate of change in the overall level and review published reports on funding trends in Congress to make their own prediction. Each department may engage in a more detailed analysis of the grants in its area and may feed the results of that analysis up the chain of command for inclusion in the budget.

(e) Rates of Return

Certain revenue sources will be driven by the rate of return on investments. An obvious example is an organization's endowment funds, which it invests in stocks, bonds, and so forth. Predictions of future returns from those funds will depend on assumptions about interest rates and stock performance. Such predictions are very difficult given the volatility of the stock market and keep many people on Wall Street employed and well compensated. Thus, many organizations establish endowment spending policies that limit spending to a portion of the average value of the funds for some period in the past, rather than relying on predictions about future returns.

A better example may be returns from interest on cash balances, which typically get invested in short-term instruments such as certificates of deposit, money market funds, and even simple interest-bearing bank accounts. The budget needs to assume whether rates of return will increase or decrease in the coming year.

(f) Items Driven by Other Items

The issue of returns from cash balances raises the point that some sources of revenue depend on other items. For example, federal government research grants include a provision for administrative costs that indirectly support the grant, such as payroll or accounting services. Indirect cost recoveries are based on a rate that is developed by the school and negotiated with the federal government. For every dollar of money received for the direct costs of performing the research funded by the grant, the institution will receive an additional amount to cover indirect costs of the research. Once the rate has been negotiated, the amount of indirect cost recoveries is driven by the value of the federal grants received by the institution's researchers.

Returns from cash balances provide another example. In addition to dependence on rates of return, interest revenue from cash depends on the level of cash balances. Cash balances are a function of all cash inflows and expenditures expected for the year, including restricted funds received in advance of expenditures, proceeds from construction loans, and expenditures on capital. Predicting cash balances will require construction of a working model of all other elements of the budget.

3. *Compile the revenues.* After having developed a budget for each major revenue source, all of the items need to be brought together into a single, comprehensive view of revenues in the new budget. As seen in Exhibit 5.2, the Arts Council's revenue budget consists of eight primary sources, with a variety of budgeting methods required. In total the Arts Council expects $139,700 in revenue.

   The compiled revenue projections and targets will give the organization starting parameters for expense budgets. In most cases, revenue budgets are subject to revision in light of operating needs. As expense budgeting goes forward, revenues may move from being constraints to being goals as the organization identifies its legitimate needs for resources and determines the best opportunities to stretch beyond what is predicted into what can be achieved.

Exhibit 5.2 Budget for All Primary Sources

Major Revenue Source	*Budget*	*Type*	*Budgeting Method*
Memberships	$2,000	Unit/price	Membership model
State arts seed grant	30,000	Large item	Review grant status
Other grants	40,000	Large items	Review grant status
Arts education contracts	52,000	Large items	Review program status
Rentals	4,500	Revenue pool	Set growth factor
Gallery sales	1,200	Unit/price	Sales model
Fund raising	6,000	Discrete items	Average of historical level
Advertising	4,000	Revenue pool	Set growth factor
Total	$139,700		

5.3 BUDGETING EXPENSES

In many organizations, expense budgeting is a paradox: While it requires the most time from line managers (central staff predict, budget and control many revenues), it also seems perfunctory. Large organizations often engage in some form of incremental expense budgeting; well-reasoned proposals for additional expenses fall on deaf ears. Small organizations key their expense budget to the availability of revenue. The real effort goes into determining revenue availability.

However, to understand how the expense budget works, you need to approach it as if you were starting from zero and building up each element. Such an understanding forms the foundation for variances and for making cuts or reallocations when required or permissible.

(a) Cost Drivers

Costs are driven by the one or more factors:

- Inflation
- Activity
- Negotiations and contracts
- Revenue

(i) Inflation. Inflation is the most obvious driver of expenses. Everyone knows that prices have a tendency to go up, and during some periods inflation constitutes a central fact of economic life (such as the period of double-digit inflation in the 1970s). The question is how the organization will respond to the pressure on costs. In the ideal world, the same inflationary pressures drive revenues, so the organization can allow inflationary adjustments in expense budgets. While perhaps we live in the best of all possible worlds, it is hardly ideal.

Inflation is a concept based on the average increase in prices of a basket of goods, which means some items in the basket experience greater rates of increase. Organizations often find the particular sources of increases more problematic. Recently, paper costs exhibited severe price increases due to reduced capacity. Costs of printing skyrocketed, well beyond rates of increase in revenues for most organizations. Organizations had to respond to these costs by reducing the amount of printing performed, reducing costs through use of lower-quality paper or less sophisticated printing processes, or shifting resources from other uses. A similar budgeting scramble is required whenever the U.S. Postal Service increases mail rates.

Organizations may face certain types of inflation to which they must respond. During periods of economic growth, wages will tend to rise. Up to a point, a nonprofit organization may choose to resist these wage increases, even if it means losing a few people or sustaining some internal salary inequities as the organization matches offers for some staff. However, the rate of attrition or salary inequity eventually will reach a point where it threatens the functioning of the organization and the organization has no choice but to go along with those increases. A situation may be created in which expenses drive revenues, as the organization starts looking for ways to boost revenues to support the higher salaries required to stay in business.

Closely related to inflation is the cost of living. Cost-of-living adjustments (COLAs) are made to sustain the purchasing power of the staff's paychecks. Cost of living is related to consumer inflation although it might also reflect adjustments in consumption patterns in response to price changes, whereas the Consumer Price Index (CPI) measures only changes in prices. Cost of living is not related to wage or compensation inflation, which is driven by the demand for workers. Wages may increase at a rate greater than consumer inflation in a strong economy.

(ii) Activity. Some costs are directly related to the volume of certain activities. Program budgets are founded on the basis of the activity that they are supporting. The program budget is built up by determining how much of each expense category is required to support the proposed activities, from office supplies to telephones, cost of renting or renovating space, and personnel. The budget for the Victim Assistance program (see Exhibit 5.3) is built up largely by activity.

Budget items such as client and staff travel are based on the presumed number of rides needed for court escorts, a division between cabs and buses, and the cost for each. Similarly, a standard cost has been set for

Exhibit 5.3 Activity-Based Costs

Item	*Budget*	*Derivation*
Director's salary	$32,000	Previous base $30,000 with $2,000 merit increase
Office assistant (part-time)	10,000	$1,000 a month for 10 months
Health insurance	2,400	$120 a month premiums
Telephones	480	$40 a month for basic service
Rent	12,000	$1,000 a month in-kind contribution
Supplies	225	$15–20 a month incidentals
Equipment	300	New typewriter and fax machine
Events	400	4 neighborhood symposia at $100 each
Travel (clients)	250	20 cab rides at $10 each, 50 bus fares $1 each
Travel (staff)	250	20 cab rides at $10 each, 50 bus fares $1 each
Memberships	300	Chamber of Commerce $100, National Organization $200
Publications	175	Total subscription cost for 3 publications
Total	$58,780	

the neighborhood symposia, and the budget is based on the number anticipated for the coming year.

Organizations that produce goods for sale (e.g., a printing operation or a carpentry workshop) or acquire goods for resale (e.g., a bookstore or a museum store) incur costs for the material they will use in production or resale, known as costs of goods sold. Costs of goods sold have an obvious link to activity: With more sales, more costs are incurred.

In theory, all of the expenses in an organization should be traceable to some activity that it supports, which is the theory behind zero-based budgeting and activity-based budgeting, discussed in Chapter 16. It is often a useful exercise to examine all of the organization's costs from this light. What does the $700 incurred by the Arts Council for photocopying support? Should the organization include part of it in next year's grant renewal request? Should part of it be eliminated?

However, at the level of general operations it becomes very difficult to trace costs to specific programs. People and costs interact in complicated ways to form the organization.

(iii) Negotiated, Contracted, or Fixed Prices. Negotiated costs will drive some of the expense elements. In Exhibit 5.3, the director negotiated a starting salary of $30,000, with an understanding that merit adjustments would be forthcoming. Health insurance costs are based on the best price the director could find and negotiate for that coverage. The organization has little choice but to include those in the budget. The budget in this case is a document of the results of negotiated or contracted prices. The negotiated or contracted prices should be reliable, and the price is what controls spending here, not the budget. The budget process should identify those items that are governed by contracts and work around them.

Dues or support of a national organization are often fixed and imposed on the organization. The Presbyterian Church may have its apportionment to the Presbytery based on a census of its membership on a certain date.

(iv) Revenue. In some cases, revenue can drive a cost element. The Presbyterian Church has a policy that at least 25% of its revenues will go to outreach and mission. Therefore, it calculates the expense item "local mission" by taking 25 percent of budgeted revenues (less special offerings, for which the church feels it only plays a "pass-through" role, making sure the gifts get to the organizations for which they were solicited), removing the amounts earmarked for the Presbytery and the church's commitments in Ghana and Brazil. The remainder becomes the budget for local mission, which will be distributed by the church's mission committee. If the revenue projections change in the budget process, this expense item will change as well. If at the end of the budget process the church projects a surplus, it often rolls the surplus into the local mission budget, which was the case in Exhibit 5.4 where the final mission budget exceeds the 25% calculation.

(b) Types of Expenses

The behavior of different expense types determines the required analytical techniques, whatever the type of expense. While expense types vary widely from organization to organization, there are some common types that we should discuss in detail:

- Personnel
- Other required or fixed costs

Exhibit 5.4 Construction of Mission Budget

Total budgeted revenues	$261,000
Less special offerings	12,000
Remainder	249,000
25% for mission	62,250
Earmarked	
Presbytery	20,000
Ghana hospital	2,000
Church development, Brazil	3,000
Remainder for local mission	37,250
Final mission budget	$40,600

- Variable or discretionary costs
- Depreciation
- Contingencies

(i) Personnel. Personnel costs form the largest expense item of most nonprofit organization budgets, often reaching 80 percent or 90 percent of the total. For that reason, and because of ethical considerations for the employees, this area deserves the most focus in the budget process. Personnel costs consist of wages and the cost of staff benefits; wages and benefits together are referred to as compensation. We will cover the following issues related to budgeting personnel costs:

- Adding positions
- Salary increases
- Special considerations: unions, temporaries, contract workers, outsourcing
- Budgeting techniques
- Benefits

Adding Positions. The first tough budget decision an organization faces is whether to add people to its paid staff. A small organization often starts with volunteer staff only, enabling it to absorb disruptions to revenue painlessly. At some point, most will consider adding full-time staff, perhaps bringing higher professionalism to its operations, probably a more continuous focus on its mission. They have to have confidence in the stability of their revenue streams to make this commitment and surrender some of the flexibility they enjoyed as an all-volunteer organization. These concerns continue as the organization grows. In a larger organization, staffing decisions may be easier. There are staff departures as well as new hires, and the budget is big enough to absorb shortfalls in revenue in the short term. In any case, there may be certain key staff whose appointment constitutes a strategic allocation of resources, such as faculty at a university.

Any decision to add people to the budget involves some degree of longer-term commitment of the organization's current and future resources. Laws of economics would suggest that personnel costs are a variable cost of production—you buy the hours you need to produce the units you can sell. In the nonprofit sector, personnel costs take on more character of fixed costs—the payroll consists of a certain number of people whose salary is fixed for the year, regardless of output or level of activity. Some corporations are coming to view their line workforce in this manner as well, as an investment in productive capacity.

Why don't organizations just fire staff if they cannot afford to pay them or activity levels fluctuate downward? It comes down to law, ethics, and policy. Many states operate under the concept of employment at will. Employers and employees are presumed to be in a mutually voluntary relationship without contractual binds, which may be terminated by either side without cause. In some states, there are more protections assumed. However, the point is that in many states organizations formally have the right to hire and fire at will, but organizations in those states seldom act as if that were the case. Other considerations constrain these organizations.

Federal labor law gives workers certain protections. Many staff fall into classes protected by various federal laws—minorities, women, people over 40, people with disabilities. All of these groups have legal recourse in case their dismissal was motivated by an act of discrimination. The legal process can be costly, even if the employer wins, so most nonprofit employers are careful to fire for a specific cause or in cases of severe financial exigency so as to minimize exposure to legal costs.

Many nonprofits operate within an ethic that values fairness. It seems unfair to fire someone at the first signs of financial trouble if he has been doing a good job. It seems fairer—more ethical—for the organization to stick by the person once they have made a commitment to each other.

In recognition of legal and ethical considerations, many organizations adopt policies that specify the grounds for dismissal. In many cases, the primary reason permitted for dismissal is poor performance, which must be documented (this will be useful to the organization if legal proceedings ensue). As long as the employee does a good job, he has some expectation of continued employment and becomes more like a fixed cost to the organization.

Following upon the decision to hire is the decision on how much to pay someone. We discuss compensation issues in more depth in Chapter 15. The underlying forces behind pay rates are one of those mysteries of economics. Adam Smith thought he had it figured out as being related to the degree of sacrifice the person was willing to endure, including hard physical conditions and the effort required to gain the education necessary. In the intervening two centuries, this simple formulation has not held up too well. We will not try to reveal the reasons for pay rates, but will discuss four primary considerations in setting pay levels:

1. The organization's ability to pay
2. Prevailing wages for similar people and positions
3. Motivation
4. Equity between the organization's employees

Ability to pay may be where an organization starts. It would like to have the part-time volunteer coordinator, who already works long hours, work full-time. The board determines how much money can be pulled together for a salary and asks the coordinator if he would serve in a full-time capacity for that salary. The coordinator may say yes because something is better than nothing and he is already dedicated to the organization's mission.

In this scenario, the organization's ability to pay is a reasonable and successful determinant of salary. The ability to pay often defines the salary range an organization will offer, but it frequently runs into another reality, that of prevailing wages. For any job, there is a labor market of qualified individuals. Markets may be local, regional, or national, depending upon the degree of specialization of the position. For example, an organization took will look in town for candidates for a receptionist position. However, they may recruit across the state for teachers and will advertise in some national outlets for the director. Within the relevant market, there are typical ranges of wages for each type of position. If there is a greater demand for people with certain skills, there will be continuing upward pressure on wages for those people. Organizations will have an easier time hiring someone looking for a job in that market if they pay the prevailing wage, paying higher in the range for a more desirable candidate.

An organization determines the prevailing wage by asking other employers what they are paying for a position. The staff can do this informally by asking its board and their colleagues, or they can conduct a formal survey or purchase survey results from professional organizations or consulting groups.

Organizations frequently use pay rates to reward and motivate employees. There is some controversy as to the true effectiveness of using pay to promote performance. However, most organizations find that it makes sense to pay more to recognize good performance. Performance recognition will be one consideration in budgeting personnel costs. In a small organization, it will take the form of considering an increase above inflation. Larger organizations may set aside a pool of salary increase funds for merit increases.

The final determinant can be equity within the organization. People who do similar types of work expect to get paid at similar levels. Older employees, all other things being equal, expect to earn more or at least as much as newer hires. Equity is hard to express in objective terms—similarity of work is a matter of interpretation, and it is hard to know how much weight to give seniority or new skills. Larger organizations often establish formal classification systems for measuring the relative value of jobs and then assigning them to pay ranges that reflect classification relationships. Job markets may require a departure from formal equity and from these classification-driven pay relationships, as rates of pay accelerate for a particular job classification, exceeding any differential that can be justified under the organization's classification system. However, the organization has to go along with those rates of pay to have the position filled.

Just because an organization has created a position does not mean that there will be a cost to the organization. Once a position has been created, it only costs money when it is filled. The organization may choose to delay hiring in order to preserve funds, or it may have difficulty finding the right person and inadvertently save money. Of course, the next full year will see the full impact of the salary. In a small organization, the difference between approving and filling positions provides only a short-term effect. However, in larger organizations, unfilled positions have a continuous impact as some jobs get filled but new ones go vacant.

A large organization that wants to know its expected payroll costs cannot just tally the salaries of all budgeted positions. It must factor in the number of positions vacant at any given time, which may be approximated by basing the payroll cost projection on a "snapshot" of all current employees—this list would leave off the current vacancies. Snapshots always carry the risk of bearing seasonal bias; the date of the data may be one on which staffing levels are typically at a high or low level. Like any seasonal phenomenon, historical data can reveal patterns that can be applied as a seasonal adjustment.

In budgeting, organizations face a choice on how to approach the effect of vacancies. If budgets are very tight, the organization may want to budget only its true expected payroll costs, which requires some sort of adjustment for expected vacancies. In other cases, the salary budget includes the funds for all approved positions. The organization assumes that salary costs will always come in under budget; salary savings can offset overruns in other areas or feed budget surpluses to increase the organization's fund balance. The difference between salary budgets and expected salary costs may end up providing departments with discretionary funds.

Salary Increases. After deciding whether to add and fill positions, the organization also needs to decide on salary increases for the continuing positions in the organization. Salary increases are driven by:

- Cost of living
- Motivation and performance
- Job markets
- Equity

First of all, the employees will want to avoid seeing their purchasing power diminish in the face of inflation for the things they have to buy. Many employees expect an annual adjustment to keep them whole relative to the cost of living. For this reason, the organization may decide to give an across-the-board increase pegged to recent increases in consumer prices. A standard benchmark for changes in consumer prices is the Consumer Price Index (CPI), issued by the U.S. Department of Commerce's Bureau of Labor Statistics. In addition to the national CPI the BLS issues CPIs for the four Bureau of Census regions and many local areas.

Organizations have tended to move away from across-the-board increases in favor of distributing salary increases based on performance. Salary is one of the most important incentives available to the organization; keying salary increases to performance gives both positive and negative incentives: Good performance will earn an increase at or above the change in the cost of living, and low performance will cause the employee to lose ground to inflation. Across-the-board increases give no incentive for stronger performers and no disincentive to lackluster performers.

The theory of merit-based performance runs into some organizational realities. If the organization has limited resources available, it has a limited ability to offer extraordinary increases for extraordinary performance. Also, in an organization generally staffed with strong people, it can be hard to go beyond the cost-of-living increase for anyone.

As discussed earlier in regard to starting salaries, job markets can drive pay increases. In an active labor market, employers that offer pay increases lower than others run the risk of employees jumping to those other organizations. Differential rates of pay will create the most obvious attraction to leave, but differential rates of pay increases can have an effect as well, signaling that one organization wants to do more for its employees than others. Employers may have to keep pace with both the level and the rate of increase.

Finally, equity considerations can drive pay increase policies. Across-the-board increases may seem fair to the staff, as can a system of differential increases based on documented performance or productivity.

Benefits. The other portion of compensation, in addition to salary, is benefits. Benefits programs are any nonsalary compensation received from the employer or through the employer. Some benefits are mandatory, such as employer contributions to Social Security and Unemployment Compensation. Other programs are optional, at the discretion of the employer or negotiated with employees. These may include:

- Health insurance
- Retirement benefits

- Life insurance
- Tuition reimbursement and other educational benefits

Many benefits may be paid for in whole or in part by the employer, or may be employee paid. Employers used to pay the full cost of employee premiums for health insurance, but have moved strongly to require employees to pay a share of this cost. In some cases, the benefit program is established to allow employees to take advantage of the employer's purchasing power to get good rates; many employers offer a nominal amount of life insurance and then allow employees to buy additional insurance at rates negotiated by the organization based on the risk profile of its employee base.

Not everyone paid by the organization will get benefits. Temporary employees and contractors typically do not receive benefits. Full-time and part-time employees may have different levels of coverage. The level of benefits is governed by the organization's policies and applicable laws such as the Employee Retirement Income Security Act (ERISA), which, among other things, regulates eligibility requirements for pension benefits.

Like many aspects of the budget, budgeting benefits is more complicated for larger organizations. The Arts Council provides health insurance for its two full-time employees: the director and the office assistant. The part-time education coordinators do not receive benefits. The budget is based on the director's assumptions about what price she will get for basic health coverage for herself and the office assistant on the market.

At the University of Okoboji, the benefits budget is based on information provided by the Office of Human Resources. (See Exhibit 5.5.) HR staff analysts prepare a thorough analysis of the benefits budget on a program-by-program basis. They base some portions on a percentage of salaries: for example, Social Security, life insurance, retirement. Others they base on assumed numbers of staff, enrollment levels, and prices negotiated with vendors: for example, health care. These projections are compiled to form the benefits budget for the university. Budget staff later spread these costs across departments using the benefits rate as an allocation method (cost allocation is discussed in more detail below).

Special Considerations: Unions, Temporaries, Contract Workers, Outsourcing. Organizations with unionized workers have an added level of complexity in setting their salary budgets. For unionized workers, the negotiated union contract (often one that covers several years) will determine salary increases. Depending on where you are in the contract cycle, the budgeting process can be very simple—insert the contractually specified increase—or complicated—guess the outcome of the bargaining

Exhibit 5.5 University of Okoboji Benefits Budget

Component	*Amount*	*Calculation Technique*
Social Security	$6,483,353	Federal employer tax rate applied to qualifying salaries
Retirement	1,814,725	Projected cash payments to retirees during the next year
Postretirement benefit obligation	1,200,000	Actuarially determined charge to fund reserve for future retirement obligations to retirees
Life insurance	810,358	Employer-paid coverage based on negotiated rate per $1,000 of salaries covered
Health insurance	4,700,000	Negotiated rates for different levels of coverage applied to projected enrollments
Tuition benefits	305,064	Projected based on previous utilization of benefit and tuition increases
Total	$15,363,500	

process or leave that portion blank so as to not give any hints about management's assumptions about contract outcomes. When considering adding positions, the organization will need to evaluate whether the new position will be in the bargaining unit. Decisions to eliminate positions may require consultation with the union.

All of the previous discussion on salary budgets has focused on permanent, regular positions that have a fixed nature. Other types of labor costs that are more variable include temporaries and various types of contract employees. Budget policies may give departments more flexibility in spending money on these categories of labor since they do not lock the organization into long-term costs. From an ethical point of view, the organization should expect less in the way of commitment from these employees in recognition of their more tenuous employment relationship. The organization should take care to avoid over-using or misusing temporary status.

Many organizations hire people on a contract basis for specific projects—that is, the organization hires them for specific services or a specific project as outlined in some sort of contractually binding document such as a letter or formal contract. The Arts Council uses contract employees to deliver instruction in its arts education programs. Each employee receives $1,000 for teaching one class in the program. Contract employees do not receive benefits and have no other obligations to the Arts Council beyond their teaching responsibilities in the programs.

Contractors give the organization more flexibility in budgeting, but can be more difficult to manage. As the level of activity gets higher and more constant, the organization will assess the advisability of combining some contract positions into a permanent or full-time position. Management is relieved of having to line up individual contractors and the organization can get the new employee involved in new projects while providing support to the other employees.

Some organizations differentiate between positions funded by grants ("soft money") and those backed by unrestricted resources. Soft money positions are often established with the understanding that the position will be discontinued if the funding ends. The Arts Council has established two education coordinator positions to manage its two contract programs. Those positions pay $13,000 and $12,000 a year, and are responsible for writing grants, promoting the programs, hiring and coordinating the teachers, and supervising the programs when they take place. The costs for these positions appear in the line "Salaries" under the columns for "Art in the Schools" and "Summer Arts Camp" (these columns also include a small portion of the salaries for the council's director and office assistant in recognition of the time they dedicate to supporting this program). The coordinators have been hired with the understanding that their positions will be eliminated if their grants end. In contrast, although the majority of the director's salary comes from a grant, the board has established that position as permanent and is committed to finding an alternate source of funding in case the State Arts Seed Grant ends. Exhibit 5.6 shows how the Arts Council salaries are funded by program.

In addition to deciding whether to use contract employees rather than full-time staff, more organizations are facing questions of whether to outsource some activities. Outsourcing refers to arrangements under which an organization hires another organization to provide services its own staff previously had performed or could perform. This practice is most prevalent in large organizations that have a history of providing many services themselves. The theory behind outsourcing is that an organization cannot be efficient at managing all kinds of activities; therefore,

Exhibit 5.6 Arts Council Salaries Funding by Program

	General Funds	*State Arts Seed Grant*	*Art in the Schools*	*Summer Art Camp*	*Total*
All salaries	27,200	$30,000	$16,600	$14,200	$88,000
Components					
Director	6,800	30,000	2,000	1,200	40,000
Office assistant	20,400		1,600	1,000	23,000
Education coordinator, schools program			13,000		13,000
Education coordinator, summer program				$12,000	$12,000

an external group that specializes in an area can do it cheaper and/or better and still make a profit. Organizations have outsourced functions such as food services, housekeeping, maintenance, printing services, security, and bookstores. As a result, in the budget, costs are converted from predominantly salaries to payments to contractors.

Budgeting Techniques. Given the complexities related to managing people and personnel costs, and the large financial impact of the payroll, many organizations adopt a different method for budgeting payroll than nonpayroll costs. In a small organization, the board may approve the salary for each regular position. Larger organizations often place more restrictions on departments' handling of payroll budgets. Typical restrictions include:

- Special approvals for any transfer of budget base between salary and nonsalary lines
- The budget pool for salaries handled separately from the rest of the budget pool
- Approvals required to add any position
- Salary budgets managed by central finance staff

Salary review in small organizations should be a very hands-on matter. The board is in a position to review and approve all salaries. In larger organizations, the distribution of salary increases needs to be delegated to department managers. Typically it is done by calculating a salary increase pool for each department based on current filled positions, establishing guidelines for distributing increases, and giving department managers the responsibility for making individual allocations of those increased funds to their staff. The manager's decisions may be reviewed by the person to whom he reports, and the overall set of proposals is often reviewed by central staff for compliance with guidelines.

(ii) Other Required or Fixed Costs. Once the organization has resolved its revenue personnel expenses, it can turn to what is likely to be the smaller portion of expenses. If an organization were building its budget from a baseline of zero, it would want to start by identifying required and fixed expenses.

Required costs are necessary to stay in business. They include the cost of providing space for operations, which could take the form of rent, and/or costs for maintaining and heating a building. Basic telephone service also falls into this category.

In a larger organization, more costs are required. A university has no choice but to provide security services, computer network support, printed course catalogs, and so forth. A smaller organization can do without more, or can solicit donated services or volunteers.

Many of these costs are fixed in the short run, but the organization has more flexibility when it takes a longer-term view of things. Once a lease is signed, rent is a fixed cost. However, the organization has the option of moving once the lease is up and may have the option of paying a penalty to break the lease, taking a one-time hit to move to more appropriate quarters.

All required costs deserve scrutiny. While there is no question that buildings need to be heated during the winter, there may be multiple sources for fuel purchases, and consumption could be controlled by management of building use patterns or energy conservation measures. In a large organization, specialists have the task of investigating these possibilities and making the best recommendations. Still, those people managing the process must make sure the questions are being asked. In a largely volunteer organization such as a church, the questions may not be asked regularly—the right people are needed on the building committee who will pursue deals with fuel brokers and can evaluate a proposed contract.

(iii) Variable or Discretionary Costs. Most organizations have several major categories of expenses that are variable, discretionary, or a function of program activity. The organization will want to identify those items and determine the most appropriate way to budget them.

In universities, student financial aid is often the second largest expenditure after compensation. Financial aid can be modeled based on the expected numbers of students, their relative level of financial need, and the price of tuition. In keeping with recent American Institute of Certified Public Accountants (AICPA) standards on financial reporting for colleges and universities, more schools are viewing financial aid as a discount from tuition and showing tuition net of aid payments. It is reasonable to integrate financial aid into the institution's model of enrollments and tuition.

Organizations that sell goods or services may have distinct costs of what they sell that are a function of sales levels. Receipts from beer and wine sales at gallery openings will be accompanied by their costs. A church organization may sell T-shirts as a fund raiser, and it will need to budget the costs of the shirts and the silk screening as well as budget sales.

Many costs are activity related. The Arts Council uses a standard cost of $1,000 for installation costs for an exhibit; three exhibits are planned this year, so the exhibition costs budget is $3,000. Printing costs per issue of the newspaper run $880 to $950, or an average of about $915; six issues are planned, which amounts to about $5,500. See Exhibit 5.7.

Exhibit 5.7 Arts Council Cost Budget

	General	*State Arts Seed Grant*	*Art in the Schools*	*Summer Art Camp*	*Gallery Program*	*News-paper*	*Total*
Revenues	$52,500	$30,000	$25,000	$27,000	$1,200	$4,000	$139,700
Salaries	27,200	30,000	16,600	14,200			88,000
Benefits	3,300						3,300
Rent	12,000						12,000
Supplies	200						200
Telephones	600						600
Computer lease	2,400						2,400
Contract services			8,000	12,000			20,000
Exhibition costs					3,000		3,000
Insurance	1,000						1,000
Printing	300		400	800		5,500	7,000
Advertising	2,000						2,000
Total expenses	49,000	30,000	25,000	27,000	3,000	5,500	139,500
Net	$3,500	$0	0	0	($1,800)	($1,500)	$200

An organization may require a certain activity to recoup its costs from separate revenue streams. To follow through on that requirement, the organization needs to go beyond the costs that are most directly activity related such as those mentioned in the previous paragraph. The Arts Council recognizes the printing costs of the newspaper in its budget structure, but does it capture all of the costs it incurs? What about the editor's use of the leased computers, the extra space required to house files and a workspace for this program, and telephone and incidental postage costs? If the board wanted the paper to be self-sufficient, it would need to examine the full range of associated costs. While it might be sufficiently helpful to the organization's finances for advertising revenues to cover printing costs, the council should explicitly recognize that it still subsidizes the paper from general funds.

The decision on budgeting the Arts Council newspaper provides a useful example of the ways strategic decisions emerge in the budget process. The newspaper may have been functioning unquestioned for a number of years. By considering whether advertising should cover more of the paper's costs, the board raises the question of the paper's importance to the council. In considering raising the advertising budget, does the council just want to find a convenient, more ambitious target for advertising revenues, or does the board want to eliminate the subsidy of the paper? If the board does not want to subsidize the paper from general funds, does it believe the paper is important enough to the council's activities to justify continuation of the program? The question of budgeting the newspaper's expenses and revenues forces the board to give at least passing consideration to fundamental questions about its role in the organization and may prompt a more in-depth inquiry.

(iv) Depreciation. Some of the largest expenditures in an organization will be for capital items: furniture, computers, improvements to the physical space, equipment. Capital expenditures usually appear as a cash expense in the year the item is received as the organization recognizes the payments made to vendors or contractors. If it has been a good year revenue-wise, it may be possible to catch up on some purchases that have been put on hold—buying an ergonomically sound chair and desk for the office assistant, a new scanner or fax machine. However, how can the organization reflect the fact that the fax machine it is buying this year will still be providing good service next year? Shouldn't part of the cost be allocated to next year when it will still be in service? Otherwise, the organization would be better off going to the local copy shop to send faxes at $1 per page, in terms of making a good showing to its board and funders.

The accounting profession has responded to this problem by developing accrual accounting, which is used by most medium and large organizations. Generally speaking, accrual accounting tries to represent the year's true activity from an economic point of view—value acquired less value consumed. By contrast, smaller organizations may use a cash accounting system that recognizes all cash transactions in the period they occur, regardless of future use.

In an accrual accounting system, this economic reality is recognized by capitalizing the item. After the cost for acquiring the item is entered into the organization's financial books, reducing cash, it is entered as an increase to physical assets, which offsets the cost on the operating statement and offsets the reduced cash on the balance sheet with increased physical assets. A piece of equipment is not like cash: It does not hold its value, but loses value through use. Accounting practices recognize that reality by depreciating the asset, or writing down its value a bit every year. The rate of depreciation is determined by how long it can be used before replacement is necessary and is known as the item's useful life. Rather than evaluate each item carefully for its individual useful life, standard rates of depreciation are applied: 3 years for items such as computers, which become outmoded quickly; 30 or 50 years for assets such as buildings, which can go a long time before they need to be replaced or substantially renovated (a major renovation can be the equivalent or more of replacing a building at its original value). See Exhibit 5.8 for a sample depreciation schedule.

In an accrual accounting system, depreciation is applied to all capital items—that is, all items that are expected to bring benefits for future periods. In not all cases does the notion of depreciation make sense intu-

Exhibit 5.8 Sample Depreciation Schedule as of Year End 1998

Item	*Original Cost*	*Date Acquired*	*Useful Life (years)*	*Annual Depreciation*	*Cumulative Depreciation*	*Net Value*
Headquarters building	$2,500,000	1984	50	$50,000	$750,000	$1,750,000
HVAC system	225,000	1994	15	15,000	75,000	150,000
Vehicle	18,000	1991	5	0	18,000	0
Personal computers	15,000	1997	3	5,000	10,000	5,000
Resurface parking lot	4,000	1996	10	400	1,200	2,800
Desks	3,000	1992	10	300	2,100	900
Folding chairs	1,500	1989	10	150	1,500	0
Printer	980	1997	5	196	392	588
Office chair (director)	650	1998	10	65	65	585
Photocopier	500	1996	5	100	300	200
Budgeted depreciation				$71,211		

itively—for example, library books. If the book is printed on high-acid paper, it might disintegrate and need to be replaced or subject to expensive preservation treatments. However, a book printed on acid-free paper will continue to be usable indefinitely and its value may increase if it achieves rare book status. However, the accounting profession has adopted depreciation as a uniform, simplified approach to capturing the complicated economic fact that most resources get depleted over time and lose their value. It would be completely unreasonable to ask organizations to evaluate the actual economic or market value of each asset on their books every year, and to ask anyone reviewing the organization's financial records to understand how this value was derived. Depreciation provides a common methodology that all organizations use to make an estimate of the value of assets.

(v) Contingencies. Everyone involved in the budget process will be painfully aware that many of the revenues and costs cannot be predicted and budgeted with certainty. Every year, things happen that no one could expect and that throw the departmental, program, and organizational budgets into disarray. To some people this situation proves that the budget process itself lacks credibility altogether. It is most likely a naive or disingenuous position.

The budget process should make some provision for the unexpected. Large organizations will set aside contingencies or reserves to respond to unforeseen situations of sufficient size. The contingencies may reside in special accounts designated for this purpose or in accounts with budgetary slack (systematically overbudgeted). Different levels of leadership may control contingency funds: Funds may exist for the president, vice presidents, and one level of directors. However, it is important not to overbudget contingencies, because the organization loses the planning and control advantages of budgeting when everything is allocated to discretionary funds without clearly defined purposes.

There is no standard formula an organization should use for setting contingency levels. It may base its contingencies on an analysis of the kinds of requests that come forward over a several-year period, or officers may hold traditional levels of contingency funds that periodically receive incremental increases.

Smaller organizations will not have that luxury. The best they may be able to do is recognize the likely risk for revenue shortfalls or large expenses, identify expenses that they could cut if necessary, and determine the capacity of board members and donors to make up shortfalls through loans or gifts. This planning process is akin to developing a disaster recovery plan in case of natural disasters or power failures—think of it as a financial disaster recovery plan. For many organizations, dependent on few sources of income, this sort of situation is a more immediate possibility than anyone will want to imagine.

(c) Incremental Budgeting

Much of the previous discussion of expense budgeting has assumed that the organization budgets from the ground up, assuming a budget of zero in each account as a starting point and allocating expense budgets according to demonstrated needs. As many readers may think while going through this section, "This has nothing to do with practices at my organization. Here, expense budgeting is simple: They take last year's budget, tell you how much you can add to each category (if anything), and let you make any shifts you want between categories. The overall amount you receive has nothing to do with what you need, what specific items cost, or what additional revenue you can achieve."

Although organizations are moving away from rigid incremental budgeting, this budgeting method is still common. It is very simple. The central budget staff builds a model of institutional revenues and expenses. They collect some initial assumptions about revenue and perhaps about some expense categories (if there is an agreement to increase salaries 3% a year, that will be factored in). Based on those calculations, they set a guideline for the level of expense increase they think the organization can afford in each of a few major categories, such as supplies and general expenses, equipment and furniture, and travel.

Departments receive a budget baseline, usually based on their current year budget, and these guidelines. Their total allocation for increased expenses is calculated by multiplying the appropriate guideline rate times the budgeted amount in each category. The budget may be submitted on the basis of expense categories or object codes. Exhibit 5.9 shows the budget for the University of Okoboji's Business School. In the first case, increase factors are identified for each object code and used to project a budget for each. The Business School then adjusts the guideline to move the funds where they are needed, with some restrictions—funds cannot be moved between salaries and other object codes. The university might choose to budget on the base of higher-level categories, since it usually applies the same increase factor to all object codes within a category. See Exhibit 5.10.

Under incremental budgeting, the budget manager has no responsibility for determining the overall size of the expense budget. Her job is to move budgeted funds between expense lines and accounts under her control as seems useful. Often the manager tries to fine tune the budget to achieve a better balance between budgets and actual expenses: One line may always go over budget, which causes unnecessary concern when it shows up as overexpended and which may require budget adjustments at year end. The manager will try to fix this situation by moving funds from a line or an account that typically comes in under budget.

(d) Allocating Expenses

Expense allocation refers to the practice of splitting an expense item or category and assigning shares of it to other departments. For example, the

Exhibit 5.9 University of Okoboji Business School Expense Budget (By Object Code)

Object Code	*Description*	*Base (Current Budget)*	*Increase Factor (%)*	*Guideline Projection*	*Proposed Budget*
3000	Faculty salaries	$6,520,000	4	$6,780,800	$6,780,800
3100	Professional salaries	1,444,608	3	1,487,946	1,552,946
3200	Biweekly payroll	1,050,624	3	1,082,143	1,017,143
3250	Overtime	131,328	0	131,328	131,328
Total, salaries		9,146,560		9,482,217	9,482,217
5000	Office supplies	315,000	0	315,000	350,000
5050	Lab supplies	525,000	0	525,000	475,000
5100	Computer hardware	315,000	5	330,750	315,750
5200	Postage	315,000	0	315,000	330,000
5250	Photocopying and duplicating	315,000	0	315,000	330,000
5400	Telephones–access	210,000	3	216,300	216,300
5410	Telephones–long distance	105,000	3	108,150	108,150
Total, other expenses		2,100,000		2,125,200	2,125,200
		Total		$11,607,417	$11,607,417

Exhibit 5.10 University of Okoboji Business School Expense Budget (By Expense Category)

Category		*Base (Current Budget)*	*Increase Factor (%)*	*Guideline Projection*	*Proposed Budget*
3000	Salaries	$9,146,560	3.66	$9,481,324	$9,481,324
5000/5200	Supplies	1,470,000	0	1,470,000	1,485,000
5100	Computers	315,000	5	330,750	315,750
5400	Telephones	315,000	3	324,450	324,450
Total		$11,246,560		$11,606,524	$11,606,524

Arts Council allocates part of its full-time salaries to the Summer Arts Camp and Art in the Schools program. The University of Okoboji allocates staff benefits to schools and departments through a mechanism called the benefits pool charge.

The first step in allocating expenses is to determine why the expense should be allocated. There are three basic reasons to allocate costs:

1. *Control consumption.* If a cost element is directly affected by the actions of managers across the organization, allocating the cost to them may cause them to limit their consumption of the resource or to find ways to fund increased costs. Also, if managers' budgeted revenues exceed expenses because not all expenses hit the budgets of revenue-generating units, the organization needs that department to do better than break even. Allocating costs to the unit may counter the manager's natural tendency to spend more if it looks like the budget is running a surplus.

2. *Receive payment from funders for the whole cost of a program.* In addition to its direct costs, a program may require resources such as the time of the organization's director and general staff. A methodical allocation of expenses can allow the organization to recover the whole cost of the program.

3. *Capture full unit cost.* An organization that thinks of each unit or program as a separate business unit may want to know if each program is carrying its weight, which means its direct costs and its share of overhead functions upon which all programs rely.

There are four good reasons not to allocate costs:

1. *Lack of managerial control.* If managers do not control the costs allocated to them, they will not feel responsible for the overall results of the unit because they exercise no influence over those cost elements.

2. *Administrative effort.* The more rigorous the allocation method, the more effort it requires to calculate and administer. In an effort to match allocation methodologies with accurate cost drivers, an organization can create an unwieldy edifice of allocations. An organization should question whether the information and effects provided by cost allocation justify the cost of constructing and maintaining the cost allocation system.

3. *Destructive incentives.* In some cases, cost allocations can lead to decisions that are suboptimal for the organization. If heating costs are allocated to departments, one department may choose to keep the buildings quite cold and turn the heat off over the weekend. The temperature of the classrooms results in bad feelings and higher attrition for students taking classes in that building, and the low weekend temperatures put strain on the building systems. In both cases, the negative effects of these decisions might not be felt until after the manager making the decisions has moved on to another job.

4. *False pictures of business.* Allocations can be hard to get right, and a false allocation can give a false sense that a program or unit has performed well or poorly.

The Arts Council decided to allocate some of its permanent salaries to the arts education programs because the regular staff inevitably ends up assisting those programs a great deal, and the organization could use the additional funding for those positions. In helping the coordinators prepare grant requests, the director figured that she and the office assistant spent about 15 days a year supporting the Art in the Schools program and 9 days supporting the Summer Arts Camp.

	Art in the Schools	*Summer Art Camp*
Total work days per year	260	260
Days dedicated to program	15	9
Percentage	5.8%	3.6%
Total salaries, director and office assistant	$63,000	$63,000
Portion assigned to program	$3,654	$2,268
Rounded down	$3,600	$2,200

This method is the most direct way of allocating costs—that is, figure out how much of a resource a particular program or office uses. The best way to make that assessment is often to ask the people who provide the service to make a guess or track their effort over some time period. Doing this on a wide scale can consume too much time and cause too much disruption. In some cases, statistics can provide a technique to track utilization, such as using the number of phone calls to determine telephone utilization and allocate monthly phone charges. Such statistics are often at best proxies for the effort required. The effort of the Payroll Office could be determined based on the number of checks issued by the home department, but that would not capture the significant effort that goes into resolving problems with paychecks and questions from employees. Even if a tally could be kept of the source of those questions, some questions require much more effort than others. Before long, we have come back to asking members of the department to track their effort.

Having explained the problems with formula-driven allocations, we need to recognize that there are cases in which this approach is useful and most feasible. The University of Okoboji allocates staff benefits costs as a way of encouraging caution in managers when making hiring decisions. In addition to funding the salary for increased positions, managers will need to fund the cost of benefits for the person. The allocation of benefits also means they get additional financial gain for their department from reducing positions or holding them vacant.

Allocating benefits by literal use would be complicated. Some employees use their benefits a lot, others little. Those who choose health maintenance organizations have a constant cost to the organization based on the negotiated rate per enrollee. Those who enroll in fee-for-service or preferred provider plans are more difficult to predict. In addition to the difficulty of keeping track of the benefits cost profile of each individual employee, the organization has no interest in creating incentives for managers to encourage certain benefits choices by their staff or to worry about events outside of their control such as large health care or life insurance claims. The university also believes employees should be free to select the plan that best suits them.

Therefore, the university just calculates two benefits rates, one for full-time and one for part-time employees, since they get very different benefits options. (See Exhibit 5.11.) The human resources staff calculates the total expected cost for both groups based on previous history, their research on industry trends, and their expectations about rate negotiations with providers.

Many cost allocation methodologies are designed to serve internal purposes such as controlling consumption and external purposes such as calculating budgets and charges for federal grants. Federal cost recovery drives many cost allocation efforts, and methodologies must often pass muster with the federal government. The method previously described for allocating benefits is based on techniques that have been approved by federal agencies responsible for administering research grants.

Full cost allocation involves a number of allocation techniques. Costs

Exhibit 5.11 Assessing Costs of Benefits

	Last Year Actual	*This Year Budget*	*Next Year Estimate*
Benefits for part-time staff	$ 798,400	$ 614,600	$ 627,300
Salaries for part-time staff	$ 6,266,600	$ 4,823,600	$ 4,920,100
Rate applied	13%	12.74%	
Calculated rate	12.74%		12.75%
Benefits for full-time staff	$15,169,800	$14,749,400	$15,426,600
Salaries for full-time staff	$56,399,700	$55,471,400	$57,135,500
Rate applied	28%	26.6%	
Calculated rate[1]	26.9%		27%
Total benefits	$15,698,200	$15,354,000	$16,053,900
Eligible salary	$61,956,300	$59,545,000	$61,268,100
Overall ratio (for information only)	25.77%	25.79%	26.20%

[1]In the previous year, a rate of 28% was budgeted for full-time staff, but actual experience showed the cost of benefits for this group came out at a lower rate. The applied rate for the current budget reflects this experience and other information.

may be allocated based on type (e.g., benefits or utilities) or by organizational unit (e.g., library, accounting office). Exhibit 5.12 provides a list of cost allocation drivers at a university. The university wants to create a full cost budget for each academic school; therefore, it will distribute all of the costs related to administrative departments and institutional expenses and revenues to the academic areas using a variety of allocation methods.

Note that in some cases there are revenues to be allocated, or a net profit. The institutional revenues include federal indirect cost recoveries, payout from the general endowment, and unrestricted gifts. Student Services, for example, runs a "profit" because of successful programs in housing, food services, and athletics, which the university has chosen to share among academic programs.

The calculations required to complete this allocation are not particularly straightforward. Purchasing includes some of the staff served by Human Resources, and that office issues some of the purchases supported by Purchasing. The portion of work performed by Purchasing for Human Resources and vice versa needs to be factored in when deciding how much cost to assign to academic areas.

As an example, let us look at a scaled-down version of the University of Okoboji allocation, where the only departments included are Purchasing, Human Resources, Arts and Science, and Business. The costs for Purchasing and Human Resources need to be assigned to the two academic units.

The percent of activity each department does for its own operations needs to be absorbed into that assigned out, so percentages are based on

Exhibit 5.12 Cost Allocation

	Expense	*Net*	*Method*
President's office	$2,300	$2,300	Percent of total expense budget
Institutional revenue		(23,900)	Percent of total expense budget
Development	1,962	1,962	Number of alumni
Utilities	6,996	6,996	Metered
Other plant unrestricted costs	12,500	5,500	Building square footage
Depreciation	910	910	Building square footage
Student services	23,690	(2,285)	Number of students
Human resources	1,600	1,600	Number of faculty and staff
Payroll	250	250	Number of faculty and staff
Finance	1,500	1,500	Percent of total expense budget
Purchasing	700	700	Percent of total purchases
Security	1,900	1,900	Number of students
Library	5,500	5,500	Number of faculty
Museum	1,200	1,200	Number of students
Auxiliaries	7,730	(770)	Percent of total expense base
Total	68,738	3,363	

the totals without employees in Human Resources and purchases on behalf of the Purchasing department. Not only do the original figures for Purchasing and Human Resources need to get assigned to the two academic units, the amounts allocated *between* Purchasing and Human Resources need to be further allocated to Arts and Sciences and Business.

The sequence of allocating the residual costs affects the final outcome. If we assign Purchasing first, Arts and Sciences will get a share of the portion of Purchasing assigned to Human Resources out of proportion with its smaller level of purchases relative to the Business School. If the University follows the opposite sequence, the Business School will get a larger share of the costs of Human Resources assigned to Purchasing. These costs result in discernible differences in the calculated full costs. The amounts may not seem severe to the reader, but the managers of those units might fiercely debate the assignments. Also, the effect could be much larger when all of the units are included or larger categories such as the library are at stake.

The most objective means of making this calculation is an iterative

	Expense ($000s)	*Purchases*	*Percent Total*	*Employees*	*Percent Total*
Purchasing	$ 700	33		14	5.7
Human Resources	1,600	105	11.3	35	
Arts and Science	42,159	345	37.3	144	58.5
Business	14,314	475	51.4	88	35.8
Total	$58,773	658		281	

calculation in which a new total is calculated for Human Resources and Purchasing as they receive their share of the other department's cost at the same time that their original costs are allocated away. The result is two lower figures for each department made up solely of their portion of costs allocated from the other unit. The allocation calculation is then repeated to allocate out the new lower costs for Human Resources and Purchasing. Again, there is a residual cost composed of each department's share of the allocated cost from the other. Repeat this process a few times, and the residual costs will approach close enough to zero to declare the cost fully allocated. This simple example required four iterations to arrive at costs in Purchasing and Human Resources close to zero. This method makes sense mathematically, but is more difficult to manage in a real-world situation with more departments to allocate.

	Purchasing Assigned First	*Human Resources Assigned First*	*Iterative*
Arts and Sciences ($000s)	$43,463	$43,429	$43,446
Business	15,310	15,345	15,328
	$58,773	$58,773	$58,773

Cost allocation methodologies are intellectually stimulating to cost analysts but difficult to put into practice. Organizations should use them only when they can make a clear business case for going to the trouble of allocating costs.

(e) Program Budgets

Discrete budgets are generally prepared for agencies that fund specific programs. If the grant is being provided for general organizational support or for a significant part of the organization's operations, the agency may require the organization to provide detail on its whole budget so that the agency can see where its funding fits into the organization's overall financing scheme.

Each funding agency or grant program will have its own format, time period, and timelines that must be followed. It is not uncommon for an agency to grant funds for a period that does not match the organization's own fiscal year. Many federal grants are issued on an October 1 to September 30 basis, whereas most organizations have fiscal years that end on December 31 or June 30. Thus, the organization must compile the figures for that grant on a different basis than the one used in the organizational budget and in the accounting system. (This situation leads some program directors to maintain off-line financial records that match their granting agency.) Staff preparing these budgets need to keep in mind the effect of fiscal year mismatches. If salary increases are given in July and the grant runs through September 30, salary figures need to include a provision for a July 1 increase.

Granting agencies not only ask that requests follow their format but also they usually will ask for reports on activity that follow the format and that can be backed up by an audit trail of supporting documentation. Therefore, costs must be tracked in line with that format, which can involve different definitions of expenses. The Victim Assistance program may track supplies as a single item that includes photocopies, whereas the State Attorney's Office wants to see two lines, one for photocopies and one for office supplies. In this case, the director will need to keep a separate record of photocopy costs in order to adjust the office supplies figure in quarterly reports. It is more likely that the Victim Assistance program will use the State Attorney's budget categories in managing its financial information given the predominant place of the State Attorney's Office grant in its finances.

One decision facing the organization is whether to include program budgets in its organizational budget. Larger organizations may decide to leave program budgets out of the institutional budget because the funds from the external source are earmarked for specific activities, budgeted separately, and tracked and monitored by the person managing the grant and the funding agency. As long as the funding agency is happy, the host organization does not need to worry about this budget. It focuses on budgeting the funds it really controls.

In a small organization, these sources of funds are too important to ignore in constructing the organization's budget. The Victim Assistance program offers an extreme example. The Arts Council is more typical. Funds from external agencies are critical to its survival—not only the seed grant that supports general operations but also the partial support for full-time salaries that comes from program grants. The $5,800 they receive from arts education grants to support general staff exceeds their $4,000 income from space rentals. Also, if costs exceed the budget in those programs, the organization will have to cover the overruns. Therefore, the Arts Council has little choice but to budget restricted and unrestricted funds together.

Large organizations may be tempted to leave restricted funds out of the budget, but they need to consider cross-fund effects. If a program can get more grants, it may be able to use those funds to cover salaries and other costs currently funded from unrestricted sources. Institutions have long taken an overly conservative view of donor restrictions and not looked creatively for ways of fulfilling the donor's wishes and using those funds to cover more expenses. It makes sense to present managers in a large organization with a budget and statements for all of their funds as a means of encouraging them to think creatively about the entire financing structure for their programs.

5.4 CONCLUSION

Most people think of the operating budget when they think of a budget, and it is the part of the budget that involves the largest number of people in most budgeting systems. Revenues and expenses break down into categories that require different approaches in order to reach a budget figure. The process of developing the operating budget is largely one of working through each type of revenue and expense, bringing them together, and then letting the overall results and interactions between categories guide subsequent refinements until the organization reaches an acceptable budget. The other component of the budget that also engages people throughout the organization is the capital budget, to which we turn our attention in the next chapter.

CHAPTER SIX

Capital Budgets

6.1 INTRODUCTION

As defined earlier, capital expenses are expenditures expected to bring benefits for a period longer than one year. They can include very large projects, but can also include smaller items with a long useful life. Furniture and fixtures are a capital investment—an organization hopes the director's desk will last longer than one year, and if the board must close the doors they will try to sell the desk at some price. However, not all capital expenditures are budgeted in a separate capital budgeting process. Smaller items are typically purchased from operating budgets, and accountants make adjustments after the fact to reflect the change in assets.

The capital budgeting process focuses on large projects. A small organization may never face the issue of capital budgeting because it never gets to the point of making major capital investments. Program delivery may depend on staff and volunteers working out of rented or borrowed space with little equipment required. The Victim Assistance program falls in that category. The university and the church both have considerable capital concerns.

There are two aspects to capital budgets:

1. Project budgets
2. The organization's capital spending plan for the year

6.2 PROJECT PLAN

Every major capital project starts with a project plan. This plan should include the following:

- A very clear statement of the project's purpose, including the benefits the organization will receive from the project
- A technical description of the project, including issues related to its construction or acquisition and operations. A project timeline is crucial for budgeting.
- Thorough financial analysis of the project, including a financing plan and an analysis of expected cash flows through the project's complete life.

Establishing program requirements and estimating costs both require some expert input. In the case of a building project, this could come from an architect, engineer, or construction manager on staff with the organization or from outside. This technical advisor will help determine appropriate space needs for the program, estimate the space requirements for each portion, and the cost for providing that space through construction, renovation, or acquisition or lease. The technical advisor will help identify cost elements that the project's sponsors might miss, such as land acquisition or parking. Even for non-construction projects, technical advice can be crucial—estimating the cost of acquiring and implementing a computer system is usually greatly enhanced by the work of information technology specialists, estimating the cost for a new telephone switch requires a telecommunications expert. The larger the project, the greater the challenge the organization faces in developing a realistic estimate and the greater risk that overlooked technical considerations will drive the project cost well past what is budgeted or make it difficult to achieve the full functionality anticipated from the capital acquisition. This concern applies for purchases of major systems and equipment as much as it applies to construction.

As an example, consider a case in which a department at the University of Okoboji wants to construct an addition to its existing facility. First, the university must articulate its reason for the capital project. In this case it is to accommodate targeted increases in enrollment. Its current facility already operates at capacity. To add an additional 200 students, the university must add 10 full-time faculty members, two seminar rooms, and one more small lecture room. Exhibit 6.1 demonstrates how these requirements are calculated.

The department decided to round down its request for additional classrooms and make up the rest from better utilization of existing facili-

Exhibit 6.1 Business School Building Addition Program Requirements

Additional students	200
Additional hours required per term	
Seminars (1.5 per student per term)	300
Lecture (1.5 per student per term)	300
Sections required	
Seminars (15 students per section)	20
Lectures (40 students per section)	7.5
Classrooms	
Seminars (8 sections per week)	2.5
Lectures (6 sections per week)	1.25
Faculty	
50% taught by full-time faculty	13.75 sections
1.5 sections per FT faculty member	9.17 faculty

ties. It decided to increase its request for office space in anticipation of utilization by visiting faculty.

Based on these calculations, the department works with the university's capital planning group to develop an estimated cost for the project. The estimate uses the university's standard figures for space requirements for each component of the program, and university standard estimates for the cost per square foot. These costs are based on a combination of the university's experience and standard rates for the Okoboji area. (See Exhibit 6.2.)

The steps described so far have only brought the project to the level of a rough estimate. This may be adequate in some organizations for se-

Exhibit 6.2 Capital Project Estimate

	SF Each	*Number*	*Cost/SF*	*Total SF*	*Total Cost*
Faculty Offices	150	10	$125	1,500	$187,500
Seminar Rooms	500	2	$150	1,000	150,000
Small Lecture Room	1,200	1	$175	1,200	210,000
Circulation, elevators, stairs, public space (30%)	1,110		$150	1,110	166,500
Subtotal, construction				4,810	714,000
Furnishings (20%)					142,800
Contingency (10%)					85,680
Total					$942,480

curing the funds or approval to proceed on a project. Other organizations at this point would appropriate a smaller amount of funds to develop a detailed program and budget, and would approve the full project on the basis of that work. In the detailed budgeting for our sample building addition, an architect or engineer would prepare designs for the project, specifying the details of configuration, construction, and materials. From these designs, the architect or engineer would specify the cost for fees and construction costs. Furthermore, the construction costs would be built up by analyzing the cost for each building system—foundation, roof, fire protection, plumbing, elevators, and so forth. The detailed project budget might resemble the example shown in Exhibit 6.3. As background to this budget the architect would have a detailed budget by building system for the $605,000 cost of construction for the facility. The equipment and furnishings line also has backup, since it has now been built up by a review of the specific equipment requirements for each building component, as opposed to the preliminary budget which set furnishings at 20% of construction costs. All in all, the detailed budget came in slightly higher than the preliminary budget. One should expect some difference between the preliminary estimate and the detailed budget.

During the design phase the architects or engineers would need to evaluate issues such as costs for removal of asbestos or the quality and capacity of existing electrical and plumbing systems. Also, most capital budgets include an escalation factor to capture the effect of cost increases.

Many larger organizations will have a capital planning group that supervises the development of project designs and budgets. This group is

Exhibit 6.3 Detailed Budget

Fees	
Environmental Impact Survey	$1,000
Architectural Fees	64,000
Document Reproduction	1,000
Permits	2,000
Subtotal fees	68,000
Construction Contracts	
Site preparation	35,000
Facility	605,000
Subtotal construction	640,000
Equipment and Furnishings	165,000
Contingency	87,300
Total Project Budget	**$960,300**

also likely to specify a format for budgeting, and to prepare budget materials for the review and approval process

Each capital project will be different, often unique in the history of the organization. Therefore, major projects must be reviewed individually, and the specific project's characteristics will determine the information required to conduct the review and make an approval decision.

6.3 EVALUATING CAPITAL PROJECTS

The most fundamental requirement for a capital project is that its purpose be clearly stated—that is, the proposal must clearly articulate the benefits that the organization will receive from the project. The definition of a capital project rests on the benefits received over a period greater than a year. A clearly defined purpose allows leadership and governing bodies to assess the value of the project relative to its costs and risks, and to assess the project's success after completion.

This requirement may sound overly simple, but many projects present a muddled set of objectives. The appearance, and often the reality, is that the project has not been thought out well, or its sponsors hesitated to present its real purpose. Perhaps a donor came forward to offer some money and the internal project sponsor tried to craft a project to fit the gift rather than to fit program needs. Perhaps the main benefit of the project is that it will bring attention to a manager who wants advancement outside the organization. The project's sponsor may try to get approval by justifying the project on as many levels as possible, losing sight of its main purpose along the way.

Without a clear explanation as to how this project serves the organization and its needs, it is impossible to assess the value received in relation to its costs. Most projects of any complexity will have several levels of benefit, but there should be a primary driver for the project. It may fit into one of several categories:

- Improves services to clients, customers, and other external groups
- Supports and fosters the development and effectiveness of the organization's staff or volunteers
- Improves the organization's financial position
- Improves the organization's operations and systems

If a project's main selling point comes from financial returns, the proposal will be evaluated as an investment opportunity, with an emphasis on showing substantial financial returns. If it will improve services, those reviewing the proposal need to articulate and demonstrate in detail how the project will achieve those improvements and should evaluate whether other investments would have a larger impact. If the project focus is not clear, it is too easy to cover failure by shifting the focus to another objective: The project may be losing money, but wasn't it about improving working conditions for the staff all along? Clarity of purpose promotes accountability.

Under some approval systems, all projects may be classified according to their primary purpose. In one state government system, projects are classified according to one of the following primary purposes:

- Health, safety and legal requirements
- Sustain current programs
- Growth and transformation

The categories chosen will depend on organizational objectives and issues. On the west coast, some organizations have a separate category for "Earthquake Retrofitting," for projects to improve buildings' capacity to withstand a major earthquake, or for earthquake repairs if the organization was hit by one of the major earthquakes in recent years.

The project proposal will include a description of the project, being clear about the major elements involved: proposed acquisition of land, construction or improvement of building or equipment, activities taking place in new facilities, new systems and their use. A proposal to the church to install central heating and cooling in its aging building should describe the type of system to be installed, its impact on the building's design and architecture, improvements in the efficiency of air conditioning, noise, disruption to church activities during installation, maintenance, and fuel requirements. It should have enough detail that nonexperts on the property or building committee can evaluate the proposal.

The project should include a budget and financial plan. This budget should describe all cash flows and their timing: required costs for acquisition of the capital item and an assessment of future returns from the project. It should also identify the source and timing of cash to support project acquisition. Part of the complexity of approving capital projects is that they will not all draw from the same source of funds, so the decision is not as "simple" as making tradeoff decisions on how to allocate resources from one pool to competing projects. Projects will compete on some dimensions, others stand on their own merits.

In addition to the financial dimensions of the project, those evaluating the project need to understand:

- *Key assumptions behind the proposal.* Does the proposal for a new HVAC system at the church assume no cost for asbestos abatement? Why does the project sponsor believe it is the right technology for this facility?
- *Primary elements of risk for the organization.* Could the system fail to function at all when installed?
- *Other ways the same results could be achieved.* Could the existing heating system be upgraded?
- *Other uses for the same resources (facilities, land, money, gifts, or borrowing capacity).* Would the church be better off spending money on programs or salaries than on the HVC system?
- *The fate of similar projects in comparable situations.* Have other churches or groups with similar buildings (age, size, use, construction) tried to install this kind of system, and what was their experience?
- *Dependence of the project on key personnel and the demands it will place on staff, board members, and volunteers.* Will the new heating system's computerized controls require higher technical skills to operate than those possessed by the current building steward?
- *Background of key external individuals or groups involved in the proposal.* What is the background and experience of the HVAC contractor who prepared the estimate? Can they be relied on to make a realistic estimate and deliver high quality work?

6.4 ORGANIZATIONAL CAPITAL SPENDING PLAN

The organization's capital spending budget for the year consists of the anticipated current year portion of projects approved in previous years and the current year portion of projects approved during the most recent budget development phase. Some projects will appear on the capital budget for several years running, and new ones will be introduced and removed each year as projects start and conclude.

In a large organization, the capital budget process will constitute a discrete stream of activity that parallels development of the operating budget. The organization may have separate internal and board committees that meet to consider capital spending plans and major capital projects over an institutionally established dollar threshold. In some cases, it does not subject capital projects to a firm deadline—projects come forward for approval as they are developed. However, the lack of a capital project approval schedule makes it more difficult to prepare the organizational capital spending plan for review and approval, and makes it difficult to make trade-off decisions when projects compete for the same financial resources.

In smaller organizations, capital projects and the capital budget may be submitted as part of the operating budget approval process, and may not be identified as a separate component of the budget. The Presbyterian Church, for example, may submit its capital projects as a line on its operating budget and may fund them through an extra appeal to parishioners that will be recorded as part of their pledges for the year. However, the session should examine the proposed projects and have the chance to assess the value of each.

Under a system with a schedule for developing the capital budget, the capital budgeting process will have a similar structure to the budget process described in Chapter 3.

- The process should flow out of early assessments of organizational strategy. In this phase, leadership will identify priorities for capital investment and set some guidelines for how much unrestricted revenue may be dedicated to this purpose.
- Central staff will establish a schedule for the year that will start with a call for proposals for capital projects and should specify a format for submissions. They will also establish the schedule for internal review meetings, derived from the board's schedule for reviewing the organization's capital budget.
- Operating departments and central offices such as information technology, telecommunications, and facilities that are responsible for organization-wide infrastructure will develop proposals.
- The organization's review group—a special capital projects review committee, the budget committee, the standing leadership group, or the organization's director—will review the proposals and approve some of them.
- This set of proposals is compiled and presented to the board for approval.
- Projects that are approved will be established with project accounts in the accounting system.

Different staff may support the capital budgeting process than those who support the operating budgeting process. Some organizations with large budget offices split responsibilities between analysts assigned to capital and operating budgets. Others rely on a separate facilities planning group to manage the capital budgeting process.

Some organizations have a formal method for scoring capital projects. Often these methodologies have a number of factors and assign points for each factor. The scores allow comparisons between projects or can be used to establish a threshold for approval. As an example of this sort of scoring system, suppose the University of Okoboji uses a simple scoring system to help in making the initial decision on project approvals. The university scores each project according to the following dimensions:

- Legal or safety mandate
- Degree of financial risk
- Advances one of the 10 key initiatives in Okoboji 21, a university-wide planning document
- Improves services to students
- Improves faculty effectiveness
- Achieves greater operational efficiencies
- Improves services to alumni and the community

Each project would be rated high, medium or low on each of these dimensions. Recognizing that some of these factors are more important than others, high, medium, and low are assigned different numeric weights depending upon the factor (Exhibit 6.4).

These weights give special emphasis to projects that respond to legal and safety requirements or that advance some of the major initiatives stated by the university in a key strategy document. Note that this system is designed to reward projects which represent a low financial risk or reduce the university's financial risks; a different set of factors

Exhibit 6.4 Scoring System Weights

	Low	*Medium*	*High*
Legal/Safety	0	5	10
Financial Risk	5	2.5	0
Okoboji 21	0	5	10
Serve Students	0	2.5	5
Faculty Effectiveness	0	2.5	5
Operating Efficiency	0	2.5	5
Alumni/Community	0	2.5	5

might emphasize projects that serve to strengthen finances or carry the potential for strong financial returns. The definition of the decision criteria and the weighting will have an effect on which projects do well under this scoring system.

After materials have been distributed and the sponsors have made presentations before the capital projects committee, each member of the committee is asked to score the projects under consideration. Then the results are compiled, average scores are calculated, and these results are discussed along with any other aspects of the project in the committee's deliberations. The university does not use these scores rigidly in choosing projects, but as one piece of data among many, akin to the way some colleges use SAT and ACT scores as one factor in making admissions decisions. One set of ranks for the hypothetical projects came out as follows:

Exhibit 6.5 Project Scores, High/Medium/Low

Project	*Legal/ Safety*	*Financial Risk*	*Okoboji 21*	*Student*	*Faculty*	*Efficiency*	*Alumni/ Community*
Biotechnology Center	L	H	H	M	H	L	H
Business School addition	L	M	M	H	H	M	M
Res Hall Renovations	M	M	H	H	L	H	L
New Main Telecom Switch	M	L	L	L	L	H	L
Elevator replacement, Admin Bldg	H	L	L	L	L	M	L
Irrigation system for grounds	L	L	L	L	L	H	L

This translates into the following scores:

Exhibit 6.6 Numeric Scores

Project	*Legal/ Safety*	*Fin. Risk*	*Okoboji 21*	*Student*	*Faculty*	*Efficiency*	*Alum/ Comm.*	*Total*
Biotechnology Center	0	0	10	2.5	5	0	5	22.5
Business School addition	0	2.5	5	5	5	2.5	2.5	22.5
Res Hall Renovations	5	2.5	10	5	0	5	0	27.5
New Main Telecom Switch	5	5	0	0	0	5	0	15
Elevator replacement, Admin Bldg	10	5	0	0	0	2.5	0	17.5
Irrigation system for grounds	0	5	0	0	0	5	0	10

If the university wanted to do so, it could establish a hard threshold which projects must reach to receive approval. That approach may be useful in a politically-charged environment where every decision the committee makes will be scrutinized. A firm scoring system protects the committee from charges of improper decisions. However, heavy reliance on a scoring system can remove some of the committee's freedom to exercise its judgment. In the example above, the irrigation system did not score strongly, but the committee may want to approve it for a number of reasons—perhaps the plant department has not gotten many capital appropriations to support its operations and the group feels they are due, or the problem of retaining enough maintenance workers for manual watering of the lawns has been a particular thorn in everyone's side.

The funding of capital projects complicates the process of evaluating and approving them. Capital projects are funded from various sources. Some projects will be funded from organizational funds earmarked for capital spending or carved out of the operating budget. The organization may have a great deal of latitude in determining how to spend these funds. In other cases, donors will provide part or all of the required funds. Donors are likely to limit their gift to a particular project, and if that project is not approved the funding may go away. Special sources of funding may be available, such as state building funds, and the organization can borrow money, sometimes through tax-exempt bond programs.

Even if special sources of funds are available for a project, all capital projects constitute a commitment by the organization and carry financial risk. At the very least, these projects will require management time; whatever time is devoted to the project is time that cannot be used for other assignments, and major projects usually require lots of time. Often the projects involve ongoing maintenance, and the organization may carry liability and responsibility if the project fails. Finally, major projects will most likely shape the organization's future directions and plans—if the Arts Council receives a major grant to renovate the gallery space, the organization will start to look for ways to reinvigorate that program and will abandon talk of scaling it back in light of deficits in the program.

Once approved, capital budgets differ from operating budgets in that they must cover multiple years, which requires capital accounts in the accounting system that retain their balances of funding and records of transactions across fiscal years. Typically, the entire project budget is approved at one time. The timing of funds flowing into the capital account may depend on the particular source of funds. A donor may give her entire gift at once, so it might be credited to the project account at one time, or she may choose to deliver the gift in installments, which would be recorded as received. Even if the entire gift is received at the beginning of the project, the organization may choose to credit the capital account in installments and hold the remainder in its short-term investment pool if acceptable to

Exhibit 6.7 University of Okoboji Capital Budget Proposal ($000s)

	Expenditures		Future Commitments				Source of Funds					
	To Date	Year 1	Year 2	Year 3	Year 4	Year 5	Gifts	Grants	Reserves	Debt	Unrestricted Revenue	To Be Determined
Ongoing projects												
Science building renovation, phase II	$1,500	$1,400	$500	$0				$1,500	$300	$1,600		$0
Admissions building	450	1,050	750	65	0		2,000		315			0
Network backbone wiring, phase III	500	300	250	100	0				500		650	0
New gym	1,200	780	25	0			2,000				5	0
Roof replacement program	170	85	85	85	0				425			0
Administration building	1,300	60	0				1,000				360	0
New projects												
Biotechnology Center		1,105	950	800	100	0	1,500			1,455		0
Business school addition		600	330	30	0	0	500				460	0
Residence hall renovations		650	450	500	350	350	0			2,300		0
Main telecom switch		100	0									100
Elevator replacement, Administration		75	0									75
Irrigation system		60	0									60
Minor renovations, various		600							300			300
Major equipment		125						95	30			0
Equipment purchased from operations		10									10	0
Total capital expenditures		$7,000										$535

The University of Okoboji's capital budget proposal shows that about half of the proposed $7 million budget will be consumed by projects already under way and the remainder will be for new projects. Some of the projects proposed for this year can be completed in a single year, such as the new telecommunications switch.

Sources of funding have been identified for all of the ongoing projects, and much of the funding has been identified for the new projects; $535,000 remains to be funded. The Capital Budget Committee in consultation with university management will determine how much of the remainder to fund from unrestricted revenues, how much should be funded from reserves, and whether any of this amount can and should be funded from gifts, grants, and borrowing.

the donor. Similar variants are found with grants and borrowing. The manager of this project will need to monitor receipts and expenditures in the account to make sure costs of the project stay within guidelines and funding comes as planned.

The result of the capital budgeting process should be a multi-year capital spending plan as in Exhibit 6.7. The total spending budgeted for future year 1 is integrated into the annual budget. These expenses would be included in the cash budget, as would be the anticipated receipts of funds for the year, which might lead or lag expenditures, depending on the balance of ongoing and new projects and the relative timing of expenditure and funding.

6.5 CONCLUSION

Though it usually involves fewer people than the operating budgeting process, capital budgeting consumes a great deal of time and energy in many organizations. Capital budgeting decisions are critical, because they determine how the organization will apply its long-range assets to programs and departments. For these reasons, organizations require well-defined project proposals and budgets for capital projects. In many cases, capital projects are subject to a formal approval process that runs parallel to the process for developing the operating budget. The result of this process is a multi-year capital budget, which feeds information to the operating and cash budgets.

CHAPTER SEVEN

Cash Budget

7.1 INTRODUCTION

In Chapter 5 we discussed the operating budget at length. It might be assumed that if the budget stays balanced, meaning that total revenues always stay ahead of expenses, the organization will do well. Unfortunately, this is not always the case, because operating revenue and expenses do not always translate directly into cash receipts and outlays. Most medium and large nonprofit organizations use an accrual method of accounting based on the following:

- Revenues are recognized when the organization receives an unqualified right to receive the funds. Thus, an organization that issues a bill for services rendered will recognize the amount billed as revenue and record it as an account receivable until cash payment is received.
- Expenses are recognized when the organization becomes obligated to make payment and they are associated with the period in which the organization will benefit from the resource acquired. Thus, if an organization recognizes the expense for an item purchased by purchase order at the time the item is received, the expense is recorded as an account payable until the organization issues a check. Also, if the organization prepays for a service, such as a

year's equipment rental, it would divide the expense by 12 and recognize a portion each month as it uses the item it has rented.

In organizations that use accrual accounting, it is important to budget and monitor cash as well as income and expense.

Here are some examples of the differences between cash and income:

- When capital equipment is purchased, only part of the cost will be considered an expense in the current year, in the form of depreciation. The rest will be applied in future years, reflecting the multiple years of use the organization will get from the equipment.
- When an organization issues a bill for services, such as a college tuition bill, it records the amount of the bill as income immediately, even though it may take months to collect the cash payment. Until it receives the cash, it records the income as an account receivable on its balance sheet. Recognizing that it will not collect all of its tuition bills, colleges also book an offsetting expense item to fund a bad debt reserve. However, if it has done a good job of calculating bad debt, it treats the difference between the gross billings and the reserve as an asset as good as cash, which in theory could be transferred to another party for collection. In the for-profit sector, receivables can form an important part of a company's value in the market if they can realistically be collected.
- Financing and spending on capital projects are not treated as income. As the funds are expended for purchases or construction, the value of the newly acquired assets is added directly to the assets the organization records on its balance sheet.
- Many organizations do not recognize receipts of restricted funds or grants as income until they spend the money. Restricted funds are often disbursed to an organization well in advance of their use. One reason for not recording them as income at the time they are received is to make sure that the organization and its managers do not behave as if this were income available for any purpose.

The differences in accounting for income and cash require that organizations take special measures to budget cash and monitor and project its levels continuously.

7.2 STATEMENT OF CASH FLOWS

The basic accounting statement used to record cash activity is the organization's statement of cash flows, which forms one of the three basic financial statements, along with the balance sheet and the income statement or statement of changes in net assets. The statement of annual cash flows is constructed by starting with the change in net assets for the year. This figure is then adjusted in three ways:

1. *Noncash operating activity is backed out.* This amount includes reserve expenses, depreciation, noncash contributions and payments in kind, and changes in receivables.
2. *Cash flows from investing activities are documented.* These adjustments include costs for purchases and proceeds from sales of any asset, such as investments, property, or equipment.
3. *Cash flows from financing activities are recorded.* These items include restricted funds for investment, proceeds from loans and bonds, and payments of principal on debt.

This statement yields a record of the change in the organization's cash position, which shows the organization's ending cash balance when applied to the beginning balance of cash and cash equivalents (very liquid short-term investments). See Exhibit 7.1 for the university's statement of cash flows.

In a small organization, developing the statement of cash flows will be a fairly simple task that reconciles activity shown in the income statement with the balance in the organization's checking account, a task not much different from what any household goes through to determine how much money is really in the checking account when the checks are factored in that have not cleared yet.

7.3 BUDGETING CASH FLOW

Cash budgeting involves converting the income statement budget to a projected statement of cash flows. Once the budget model has generated the expected net income or net change in assets, finance staff can work out estimates for each of the main reconciling items the organization finds on its statement of cash flows. As in operating budget items, each reconciling item may require a different approach for estimation.

For some items, the best guide will be previous history. In many cases, the estimating technique will involve historical relationships between the reconciling item and the operating statement. For example, the organization may analyze its gifts income and determine that 10% usually comes in noncash forms. Therefore, it can link this reconciling item in the projected statement of cash flows to the estimate of gift income in the operating statement.

Exhibit 7.1 University of Okoboji Statement of Cash Flows

Cash balance at beginning of year	$51,025,003
Cash flows from operating activities	
Net increase/(decrease) in assets	(7,330,000)
Adjustments to reconcile increase in net assets to net cash provided from operating activities	
Depreciation	700,000
Net gain on sale of investments	(250,000)
Excess receipts of restricted gifts and grants	4,025,117
Changes in accounts receivable	(353,000)
Prepaid expenses and other assets	157,300
Changes in accounts payable and other liabilities	(79,000)
Loans disbursed	(1,230,675)
Principal collected on loans	980,755
Total adjustments	4,200,417
Net cash provided by (used in) operating activities	(3,129,583)
Cash flows from investing activities	
Purchase of investments	(4,381,413)
Proceeds from sale of investments	3,900,143
Acquisition of land, buildings, equipment, and books	(6,000,365)
Disposal of land, buildings, equipment, and books	154,935
Net cash provided by (used in) investing activities	(6,326,700)
Cash flows from financing activities	
Proceeds from issuance of notes and bonds payable	5,575,000
Principal payments on notes and bonds payable	(1,005,125)
Investment income from restricted private gifts and grants	2,025,766
Net cash provided by (used in) financing activities	6,595,641
Increase/(decrease) in cash and cash equivalents	(2,860,642)
Cash balance at end of the year	$48,164,361

Other items require analysis of the cash stream itself. If grant receipts are composed of many relatively small grants, finance staff may project receipts mathematically from past history. If some particularly large grants stand out, the staff will want to estimate the expected receipts on those grants individually. If the organization is trying to fund postretirement benefits or other future liabilities, it will need to review the schedules created to book those noncash expenses.

The organization will want to create a schedule of major capital projects that shows the timing and amounts of funding receipts and expenditures on project expenses and principal repayment. These items will depend heavily on specific large projects that should be factored in on a case-by-case basis rather than through a trend-based calculation.

The information on the projected cash flow statement can feed back into the operating budget if the organization wants to model interest income from cash balances more precisely. Many organizations will want to develop a cash budget, usually on a monthly basis, so that they can monitor cash fluctuations throughout the year. The monthly cash budget is usually expressed directly in terms of categories of receipts and outlays rather than in terms of a reconciliation from net income. The organization will need to identify the major sources and uses of cash, starting from the revenue and expense categories shown in the operating budget and making changes as needed. When these categories have been identified, the next step is to classify each as to whether it is evenly spread throughout the year, follows a seasonal pattern, or is incidental (hits the budget in a lumpy pattern on a few occasions throughout the year). In many cases, the cash budget can be derived from the operating budget, or with small modifications. Personnel costs are considered to be cash costs. If staffing is stable throughout the year and staff are paid on a monthly basis, the cash expense of payroll is projected by dividing the budget by 12. However, even if staffing is stable throughout the year, an organization with a biweekly payroll will need to adjust the cash outlays for payroll to reflect that some months have two paydays and others have three: Costs for a biweekly payroll are divided by 26 and distributed according to the organization's payroll schedule for the year.

The Victim Assistance program, whose monthly cash budget is shown in Exhibit 7.2, times expenditures when it can to coincide with receipts of its primary grant from the state attorney general's office. Some costs, such as the director's salary and the expenses of transportation for clients, are ongoing throughout the year. At midyear the program usually gets close to overdrawing its cash balances before it receives the second installment of its grant.

7.4 CONCLUSION

In constructing a cash budget, the organization should focus on the items with the largest cash impact. The primary goal is to determine whether the organization risks running out of cash at any point during the year. An organization with a healthy operating budget can run short of cash if expenses and revenues are timed poorly relative to each other—that is, expenses are concentrated earlier than revenue. Also, cash budgeting reminds the organization to consider the effects of capital activity on its budget. If it is funding capital costs out of operating revenue, these costs can consume a lot of cash quickly. If the organization has a tendency to overlook the operating impact of capital costs (such as neglecting to add future depreciation and interest payments into budgets following major capital investments), cash flow budgeting will bring these items to the fore and may help avoid a costly oversight in planning the operating budget.

Exhibit 7.2 Victim Assistance Association Monthly Cash Budget

	July	*Aug*	*Sept*	*Oct*	*Nov*	*Dec*	*Jan*	*Feb*	*Mar*	*Apr*	*May*	*June*	*Total*
Receipts													
State grant			$23,040						$23,040				$46,080
Plate collection								1,000					1,000
Total receipts	0	0	23,040	0	0	0	0	1,000	23,040	0	0	0	47,080
Salaries													
Director	2,666.67	2,666.67	2,666.67	2,666.67	2,666.67	2,666.67	2,666.67	2,666.67	2,666.67	2,666.67	2,666.67	2,666.67	32,000
Office assistant (part-time)			1,000	1,000	1,000	1,000	1,000	1,000	1,000	1,000	1,000	1,000	1,000
Health insurance	200	200	200	200	200	200	200	200	200	200	200	200	2,400
Telephones	40	40	40	40	40	40	40	40	40	40	40	40	480
Supplies	10	10	20.50	20.50	20.50	20.50	20.50	20.50	20.50	20.50	20.50	20.50	225
Equipment			30	30	30	30	30	30	30	30	30	30	300
Events				100			50	50			200		400
Travel (clients)	20.83	20.83	20.83	20.83	20.83	20.83	20.83	20.83	20.83	20.83	20.83	20.83	250
Travel (staff)	20.83	20.83	20.83	20.83	20.83	20.83	20.83	20.83	20.83	20.83	20.83	20.83	250
Memberships			100			150				50			300
Publications				75			25		75				175
Total expenses	2,958	2,958	4,099	4,174	3,999	4,149	4,074	4,049	4,074	4,049	4,199	3,999	46,780
Net receipts	(2,958)	(2,958)	18,941	(4,174)	(3,999)	(4,149)	(4,074)	(3,049)	18,966	(4,049)	(4,199)	(3,999)	300
Cash balance	$6,500	$3,542	$583	$19,525	$15,351	$11,352	$7,203	$3,129	$80	$19,047	$14,998	$10,799	$6,800

7.4 CONCLUSION

Larger organizations will use cash budgeting and monitoring to achieve more sophisticated cash management goals. As they assemble sufficient cash balances, they will want to consider different combinations of investment vehicles to maximize investment returns. They will want to analyze "float" effects—the difference in timing between issuing payment and that payment clearing the bank—during which time the funds can still be invested to produce returns that over time and a large number of transactions can add significant increments of interest income. Finally, cash planning at large organizations will analyze the organization's capacity to generate enough cash to fund major capital investments or to create endowments. All these aspects of cash management are part of the treasury function at a large organizations and require sophisticated professional advice to manage optimally.

P A R T   T H R E E

Managing an Organization's Finances

CHAPTER EIGHT

Long-Range Financial Plans

8.1 INTRODUCTION

The organization's financial plan forms the link between strategic planning and budgets, and budgets bring the plan to the level of operations. The financial plan gives a roadmap for the organization to follow in trying to achieve its objectives, whether they focus on institutional survival or call for major initiatives. After introducing the basic principals of long-range financial planning, we will illustrate them by creating a hypothetical planning process for our church example.

8.2 BASIC PRINCIPLES

Before creating budgets or making any plans for the year immediately forthcoming, an organization should go through a strategic planning process to establish its major goals and the directions it will pursue for several years. There are many books on strategic planning that the reader is advised to consult for a detailed description of this process (several are cited in the bibliography), and many consultants provide services to assist in strategic planning. Common elements of a strategic plan are to:

- Develop a statement of the organization's mission and its vision of itself. For nonprofits, it is particularly important to identify why the organization exists so that down the road it can make good decisions about which programs to build. In addition to or as part of the mission statement, the organization will state a number of component goals that relate to its key programs. It can be argued that the programs should flow from the goals, but in most cases the organization already exists, so part of the job of the strategic planning process is to determine how programs fit together coherently.
- Analyze the organization's external environment and its internal capabilities. A common technique is to assess the organization's strengths, weaknesses, opportunities, and threats. These provide the framework for picking feasible strategies.
- Identify the primary strategies or programs that the organization will use to achieve its mission and goals, and identify the initiatives it needs to take to put itself in a position to execute those strategies.
- Identify barriers to success and required resources, and design plans to overcome barriers and secure resources.
- Assign responsibility for executing strategies and establish timelines.

The strategic planning process may involve a large number of people in the organization. A core group may be assembled to lead the effort, with contributions coming forward from all parts of the organization, or with input being solicited through focus groups, surveys, and other methods. The plan itself must receive strong endorsement from the organization's leaders, who may form the core planning group.

The strategic planning process can end up with a document that describes grandiose, unachievable goals. It is the job of financial planning to determine the concrete requirements and limitations of the strategic plan, reconciling statements of intention with the mundane issues of running an organization—providing enough money to pay rent and keep the lights on, providing staff to open the doors each day and get paychecks out. Therefore, the organization will want to create a long-range financial model with which it can describe the results of a "business as usual" baseline and then see how strategic planning objectives fit with financial realities. The baseline case itself may reveal additional organizational strengths or weaknesses that will lead the planners to add new initiatives to the list generated in the planning process, particularly if the long-range baseline projects budget deficits.

The financial model may contain several components. All revenue and cost factors will be integrated to give a complete picture of organizational finances. A common and simple approach is to apply increase factors to the different categories of revenue and expense shown in the budget. This can be done on the very detailed level of every object code or account, but often it is easier to work with summary data for purposes of long-range planning. When conducting long-range planning, there usually is not time to carefully consider the likely activity in each object code, so general rates of increase are applied to all of the object codes in a category. Therefore, it is often just as effective to work with higher-level expense and revenue categories.

The financial model may also contain component models that analyze important features of the budget, such as a key revenue source and the activity that drives it. Most colleges build a model to predict tuition revenue under various enrollment and pricing assumptions. In the example that follows, the church will build a model for pledge income, driven by membership increases. Separate models may be required for endowment income (reflecting additions to endowment as well as investment returns), interest cost or income, costs associated with capital projects, and other key cost elements.

Once the baseline has been created, the initiatives laid out in the strategic plan can be integrated into the model. The results of that modeling may show that the organization can move forward with the initiatives it proposes with currently forecasted resources. In most cases, the organization will need to find new revenue for initiatives and growth, or make tradeoffs. The financial model lets planners test different revenue sources and the timing of expense growth and initiatives until they arrive at a combination that appears feasible.

A model represents only a projection, not a guarantee of future events. The model can be used to test several variations of factors to understand the impact of results better or worse than expected. Modeling's greatest value lies in proving that a course of action has a chance of succeeding. Without a model, the organization may embark on a course that will almost certainly throw it out of balance—for example, taking on huge debt for capital projects that would require quantum growth in membership revenue out of all proportion with the organization's ability to attract new members.

The final iteration of the long-range plan often provides the guideline rates of increase for the budget process. Budget guidelines derived from modeling give the organization's leader some sense of assurance that these rates will deliver a balanced budget. One of the most troubling aspects of budgeting for leaders is the concern that they will commit to increases the organization will not be able to sustain.

Full-blown strategic plans take a great deal of effort to prepare, so most organizations do not do one every year. However, in "off" years the organization's leaders should revisit the strategic plan before starting budget development. This review process allows the organization to assess progress and revalidate or amend its goals. Often some initiatives will lose urgency as conditions and opportunities change, and new projects will emerge.

Many organizations have not done a formal strategic plan. In those cases, the organization's leaders may still meet before starting budget development to discuss organizational goals, initiatives, and priorities. Whatever level of strategic planning the organization conducts (even none), it needs a long-range financial plan to develop baseline projections and budget guidelines.

It is difficult to generalize further about long-range financial plans. Each organization needs to chart its own course through the process of developing a strategic plan and designing a long-range financial plan that has the right structure and level of detail. Some form of long-range financial plan is needed to bridge the sometimes lofty statements of the strategic plan and the practical considerations reflected in the budget. Organizations that fail to integrate their strategic plans with the budget process are likely to find that the strategic plan is considered an empty document.

8.3 CASE STUDY

As an example of how a long-range financial plan is constructed and used to bridge strategy and budgets, consider the Presbyterian Church example. We assume that the church has assembled a group of parishioners and staff to serve on a planning committee to create a strategic plan.

The church's declared mission as an urban church is to translate the gospel into action in a modern urban setting. The planning group interpreted this mission statement into goals related to nurturing and spiritually supporting a congregation of urban worshippers, and to serving the neediest people in the downtown area, particularly the large homeless community. The planning group conducted a SWOT (strengths/weaknesses/opportunities/threats) analysis, with the results seen in Exhibit 8.1.

From this analysis, the group discussed the resources the church requires to achieve its goals of congregational care and service. The church needed to be a good home for its members, providing them with meaningful worship experiences and spiritual nurture as well as involving them in important service missions. Also, while the church's programs to assist the homeless were successful, there was so much more to do. The pastor was considered an excellent preacher and an inspiring leader of service programs but could not do everything.

Exhibit 8.1 SWOT Analysis

Strengths	Weaknesses
• Established leadership position in service to homeless • Downtown location • Small but dedicated congregation • Endowment • Strong pastoral leadership	• Operating income • Small congregation • Low pay rates • Condition of building
Opportunities	**Threats**
• Move from service to advocacy for homeless • Address root causes such as availability of mental health services • Develop theological basis for service to the homeless • Develop ways for suburban congregations to support this effort	• Job offers to pastor • Legal liability due to building condition

To take on initiatives in the missions to homeless, take care of members, and free the pastor to develop the theological dimensions of homelessness and other urban problems, the group recommended that the church add staff support: an associate pastor, to help with worship planning and ministry to church members and share other pastoral duties; and a coordinator for homeless programs, to help take that service to a new level of impact and to organize extensions of the program that might involve many volunteers from other congregations. Staff salaries also had to be upgraded to avoid losing staff.

The group realized two practical considerations interfered with the church's ability to pursue these goals:

- Even to keep up with its current level of activities, let alone go to a new level, the church needed to upgrade its building, which would be very expensive.
- The church's current operating revenues were insufficient to cover its operating expenses, forcing it to draw $27,000 over the last three years from its endowment principal. The church session had agreed that the draw from endowment must stop and the $27,000 had to be paid back from operating sources.

With this analysis completed, the church was ready to build its financial plan. The plan would determine what the church would have to do to achieve its objectives and it would feed back to the strategic planning process. If it proved impossible to create a realistic plan, the planning group would need to revise its strategic objectives.

The plan would need to assemble some historical data, build a baseline financial projection, and then evaluate the financial impact of five major initiatives identified in planning:

1. Stop draw on endowment.
2. Increase staff salaries.
3. Add associate pastor.
4. Add position to manage outreach to homeless.
5. Upgrade condition of building.

Before adding any of these initiatives, the church created a five-year baseline. The group discussed and settled on rates of increase for each expense and revenue category, based in part on three years worth of actual results and in part on the planning group's assessments of future trends. These rates resulted in a model (see Exhibit 8.2) that shows the draw on endowment would continue but would decrease.

The group worked with the model to discover that the church could end the draw on endowment if it cut spending on local missions to 22% of revenue, as seen in Exhibit 8.3. Also, the budget is very vulnerable to changes in the pledge income and endowment returns. If investment performance results in 5 percent rather than 7 percent growth in income available and pledges increase at a rate of 3 percent rather than 3.5 percent, the church shows a persistent deficit of $11,000, as seen in Exhibit 8.4.

The church then needs to figure out the total impact of its strategic goals, to determine how big the final gap will be. The following costs are estimated:

- Operating costs of $91,320 in the first year, or $484,830 over five years
- Capital costs of $120,000
- Pay back previous draws from endowment of $27,000 (the session agreed not to insist on the original draw plus interest)
- Projected cumulative deficits of $38,017

If the capital costs are funded by borrowing, principal and interest payments will need to be factored into the operating costs. The church gets a bank to quote terms on a 20-year note that would allow for payback at a rate of $12,000 a year. Now the church has to find revenue to

Exhibit 8.2 Two-Year History and Five-Year Financial Plan

	Year Before Last	*Last Year's Results*	*This Year's Budget*	*Out-Year 1 Projection*	*Out-Year 2 Projection*	*Out-Year 3 Projection*	*Out-Year 4 Projection*	*Out-Year 5 Projection*
Pledges	$168,000	$174,000	$172,000	$178,020	$184,251	$190,699	$197,374	$204,282
Plate	17,000	16,500	18,000	18,540	19,096	19,669	20,259	20,867
Special offerings	9,000	9,500	12,000	12,240	12,485	12,734	12,989	13,249
Endowment	29,000	40,580	53,558	37,450	40,072	42,877	45,878	49,089
Rentals	6,000	8,000	10,500	11,550	11,897	12,253	12,621	13,000
Interest	2,500	2,700	2,700	2,578	2,678	2,782	2,891	3,005
Total revenues	231,500	251,280	268,758	260,378	270,478	281,015	292,012	303,492
Expenses								
Operations								
Salaries	120,725	138,000	141,000	145,230	149,587	154,075	154,697	163,458
Benefits	28,000	27,000	27,000	27,810	28,644	29,504	30,389	31,300
Supplies	1,050	1,100	1,000	1,020	1,040	1,061	1,082	1,104
Phones	1,000	1,100	1,158	1,170	1,181	1,193	1,205	1,217
Equipment	1,500	1,700	2,500	2,500	2,500	2,575	2,575	2,575
Utilities	7,500	4,900	10,300	10,712	11,140	11,586	12,050	12,532
Contract services	6,725	5,980	8,000	8,320	8,653	8,999	9,359	9,733
Mission								
Presbytery	15,000	17,500	20,000	22,500	25,000	27,500	30,000	32,500
Local mission	36,000	39,500	40,800	34,535	34,498	34,570	34,756	35,061
Ghana hospital	2,000	2,000	2,000	2,000	2,000	2,000	2,000	2,000
Church development, Brazil	3,000	3,000	3,000	3,000	3,000	3,000	3,000	3,000
Special offerings	9,000	9,500	12,000	12,240	12,485	12,734	12,989	13,249
Total expenses	231,500	251,280	268,758	271,036	279,729	288,797	298,101	307,729
Net surplus/(deficit)	0	0	0	(10,658)	(9,251)	(7,782)	(6,089)	(4,237)
Endowment budget	29,000	32,000	35,000	37,450	40,072	42,877	45,878	49,089
Additional draw required	$0	$8,580	$18,558	$10,658	$9,251	$7,782	$6,089	$4,237

Exhibit 8.2 Continued

	Year Before Last	*Last Year's Results*	*This Year's Budget*	*Out-Year 1 Projection*	*Out-Year 2 Projection*	*Out-Year 3 Projection*	*Out-Year 4 Projection*	*Out-Year 5 Projection*
Revenue								
Pledges		3.6	–1.1	3.5	3.5	3.5	3.5	3.5
Plate		–2.9	9.1	3	3	3	3	3
Special Offerings		5.6	26.3	2	2	2	2	2
Endowment		10.3	9.4	7	7	7	7	7
Rentals		33.3	31.3	10	3	3	3	3
Interest		8	0	–4.5	3.9	3.9	3.9	3.9
Expenses								
Operations								
Salaries		14.3	2.2	3	3	3	3	3
Benefits		–3.6	0	3	3	3	3	3
Supplies		4.8	–9.1	2	2	2	2	2
Phones		10	5.3	1	1	1	1	1
Equipment		13.3	47.1	0	0	3	0	0
Utilities		–34.7	110.2	4	4	4	4	4
Contract services		–11.1	33.8	4	4	4	4	4
Mission								
Presbytery		16.7	14.3	12.5	11.1	10.0	9.1	8.3
Local mission		9.7	3.3	–15.4	–0.1	0.2	0.5	0.9
Ghana hospital		0	0	0	0	0	0	0
Church development, Brazil		0	0	0	0	0	0	0
Special offerings		5.6	26.3	2	2	2	2	2
Percent mission	25.2	25.6	25.6	25.0	25.0	25.0	25.0	25.0
Interest as percent revenue	1.1	1.1	1.0					
Interest calculated				2,578	2,678	2,782	2,891	3,005

Exhibit 8.3 Two-Year History and Five-Year Projection (22% Mission Alternative)

	Year Before Last	*Last Year's Results*	*This Year's Budget*	*Out-Year 1 Projection*	*Out-Year 2 Projection*	*Out-Year 3 Projection*	*Out-Year 4 Projection*	*Out-Year 5 Projection*
Revenue								
Pledges	$168,000	$174,000	$172,000	$178,020	$184,251	$190,699	$197,374	$204,282
Plate	17,000	16,500	18,000	18,540	19,096	19,669	20,259	20,867
Special offerings	9,000	9,500	12,000	12,240	12,485	12,734	12,989	13,249
Endowment	29,000	40,580	53,558	37,450	40,072	42,877	45,878	49,089
Rentals	6,000	8,000	10,500	11,550	11,897	12,253	12,621	13,000
Interest	2,500	2,700	2,700	2,578	2,678	2,782	2,891	3,005
Total revenues	231,500	251,280	268,758	260,378	270,478	281,015	292,012	303,492
Expenses								
Operations								
Salaries	120,725	138,000	141,000	145,230	149,587	154,075	154,697	163,458
Benefits	28,000	27,000	27,000	27,810	28,644	29,504	30,389	31,300
Supplies	1,050	1,100	1,000	1,020	1,040	1,061	1,082	1,104
Phones	1,000	1,100	1,158	1,170	1,181	1,193	1,205	1,217
Equipment	1,500	1,700	2,500	2,500	2,500	2,575	2,575	2,575
Utilities	7,500	4,900	10,300	10,712	11,140	11,586	12,050	12,532
Contract services	6,725	5,980	8,000	8,320	8,653	8,999	9,359	9,733
Mission								
Presbytery	15,000	17,500	20,000	22,500	25,000	27,500	30,000	32,500
Local mission	36,000	39,500	40,800	27,090	26,758	26,522	26,385	26,353
Ghana hospital	2,000	2,000	2,000	2,000	2,000	2,000	2,000	2,000
Church development, Brazil	3,000	3,000	3,000	3,000	3,000	3,000	3,000	3,000
Special offerings	9,000	9,500	12,000	12,240	12,485	12,734	12,989	13,249
Total expenses	231,500	251,280	268,758	263,592	271,989	280,749	289,731	299,021
Net surplus/(deficit)	0	0	0	(3,214)	(1,512)	267	2,282	4,470
Endowment budget	29,000	32,000	35,000	37,450	40,072	42,877	45,878	49,089
Additional draw required	$0	$8,580	$18,588	$3,214	$1,512	($267)	($2,282)	($4,470)
Percent mission	25.2	25.6	25.6	22.0	22.0	22.0	22.0	22.0

Exhibit 8.4 Two-Year History and Five-Year Projection (Lower Revenues)

	Year Before Last	*Last Year's Results*	*This Year's Budget*	*Out-Year 1 Projection*	*Out-Year 2 Projection*	*Out-Year 3 Projection*	*Out-Year 4 Projection*	*Out-Year 5 Projection*
Revenue								
Pledges	$168,000	$174,000	$172,000	$177,160	$182,475	$187,949	$193,588	$199,395
Plate	17,000	16,500	18,000	18,540	19,096	19,669	20,259	20,867
Special offerings	9,000	9,500	12,000	12,240	12,485	12,734	12,989	13,249
Endowment	29,000	40,580	53,558	36,750	38,588	40,517	42,543	44,670
Rentals	6,000	8,000	10,500	11,550	11,897	12,253	12,621	13,000
Interest	2,500	2,700	2,700	2,562	2,645	2,731	2,820	2,912
Total revenues	231,500	251,280	268,758	258,802	267,185	275,854	284,820	294,092
Expenses								
Operations								
Salaries	120,725	138,000	141,000	145,230	149,587	154,075	154,697	163,458
Benefits	28,000	27,000	27,000	27,810	28,644	29,504	30,389	31,300
Supplies	1,050	1,100	1,000	1,020	1,040	1,061	1,082	1,104
Phones	1,000	1,100	1,158	1,170	1,181	1,193	1,205	1,217
Equipment	1,500	1,700	2,500	2,500	2,500	2,575	2,575	2,575
Utilities	7,500	4,900	10,300	10,712	11,140	11,586	12,050	12,532
Contract services	6,725	5,980	8,000	8,320	8,653	8,999	9,359	9,733
Mission								
Presbytery	15,000	17,500	20,000	22,500	25,000	27,500	30,000	32,500
Local mission	36,000	39,500	40,800	34,141	33,675	33,280	32,958	32,711
Ghana hospital	2,000	2,000	2,000	2,000	2,000	2,000	2,000	2,000
Church development, Brazil	3,000	3,000	3,000	3,000	3,000	3,000	3,000	3,000
Special offerings	9,000	9,500	12,000	12,240	12,485	12,734	12,989	13,249
Total expenses	231,500	251,280	268,758	270,642	278,906	287,507	296,303	305,379
Net surplus/(deficit)	0	0	0	(11,840)	(11,721)	(11,653)	(11,484)	(11,286)
Endowment budget	29,000	32,000	35,000	36,750	38,588	40,517	42,543	44,670
Additional draw required	$0	$8,580	$18,558	$11,840	$11,721$11,653$11,484		$11,286	
Pledges		3.6%	–1.1%	3.0%	3.0%	3.0%	3.0%	3.0%
Endowment		10.3%	9.4%	5%	5%	5%	5%	5%

fund additional costs of $91,000 to $103,000 a year (and pay back previous draws on the endowment) and a total of $65,000 related to deficits and endowment borrowing, or adjust the scope or timing of its plans.

The church's main source of income is pledges. The most obvious way to increase revenue is to increase the number of members and their rate of giving. To assess the feasibility of making up the forecast budget gap from higher pledges, the church develops a separate model for pledge income that factors in the number of members and the percentage who will give at various levels. The church looks at the data and decides that people tend to fall into five groups:

1. Nongivers
2. Up to $200, averaging $110
3. $200–$700, averaging $437
4. $700–$1,200, averaging $993
5. over $1,200, averaging $4,750

For each group it calculates the rate of increase in numbers and includes a factor for adjustments in the average gift within each group. See Exhibit 8.5, which shows increase factors set at baseline values.

The church would need additional revenue over the five years of $549,986, or $609,986 if the church takes out a loan for capital improvements. It would take a sustained 19–20 percent annual increase in members to make this up from pledge revenue. The picture is better if it can be assumed that the average gift in all ranges will rise by a modest 2 percent—approximately a 17 percent sustained rate in membership growth is then required. Eliminating the homeless program coordinator reduces the income requirements to $390,000 to $450,000, which can be attained with a 13–14 percent growth in membership.

The church will work with these tools to try different combinations of membership and income goals, change assumptions on all cost and revenue factors, and change the timing of initiatives to arrive at a workable plan. It ends up realizing that increased membership is key to any strategy, and gives priority to hiring an associate pastor and adjusting the senior pastor's salary, treating these as investments to building the membership base.

Even with this fairly short set of goals, the church needs a long-range financial model to test many combinations of a few variables. Larger organizations will need more complicated models, with more component models such as the one the church developed for pledge income. It should be clear that these models can become very complicated. Therefore, a critical task of the person building the model is to choose areas on which to focus.

Exhibit 8.5 Pledge Model

		Current	Current	Out-Year 1 Projection		Out-Year 2 Projection		Out-Year 3 Projection		Out-Year 4 Projection		Out-Year 5 Projection	
	Average Gift	*Number*	*Budget*	*Number*	*Income*	*Number*	*Income*	*Number*	*Income*	*Number*	*Income*	*Number*	*Income*
Nongivers	$0	22	$0	23	$0	24	$0	24	$0	25	$0	26	$0
$0–200	$110	45	$4,950	47	$5,123	48	$5,303	50	$5,488	52	$5,680	53	$5,879
$200–$700	$437	105	$45,885	109	$47,491	112	$49,153	116	$50,874	120	$52,654	125	$54,497
$700–$1,200	$993	12	$11,915	12	$12,332	13	$12,763	13	$13,210	14	$13,673	14	$14,151
$1,200+	$4,750	23	$109,250	24	113,074	25	$117,031	26	$121,127	26	$125,367	27	$129,755
Total		207	$172,000	214	$178,020	222	$184,250	230	$190,699	238	$197,374	246	$204,282
			Nongivers	3.5%		3.5%		3.5%		3.5%		3.5%	
			$0–200	3.5%	0.0%	3.5%	0.0%	3.5%	0.0%	3.5%	0.0%	3.5%	0.0%
			$200–$700	3.5%	0.0%	3.5%	0.0%	3.5%	0.0%	3.5%	0.0%	3.5%	0.0%
			$700–$1,200	3.5%	0.0%	3.5%	0.0%	3.5%	0.0%	3.5%	0.0%	3.5%	0.0%
			$1,200+	3.5%	0.0%	3.5%	0.0%	3.5%	0.0%	3.5%	0.0%	3.5%	0.0%

Computer software such as spreadsheets or PC-based database management systems assist in constructing models, and allow the user to build very large, complicated models. However, the additional detail technically possible with current software will not necessarily make the model a more effective decision support tool. The real challenge in building a useful model is to arrive at the best organization of information, identifying and building in the critical variables that give a reasonable model of economic conditions and changes. Models are simplified versions of the real world—simplified in order to allow the user to focus on and test key variables.

8.4 CONCLUSION

Long-range financial planning can be a powerful tool to an organization for converting its strategic objectives into concrete action plans. A long-range plan is probably a requirement for giving the budget process relevance to the organization's strategy. Long-range planning or projections are also useful in organizations that do not engage in formal strategic planning. The long-range model allows the organization to see the implications of following its current or proposed track into the future. The response to those projections is best when informed by the organization's strategy, but a tactical response is possible as well, in which the organization identifies the most feasible options within the current organizational context and chooses a course of action that seems least disruptive or most likely to succeed.

CHAPTER NINE

Monitoring Budget Results

9.1 INTRODUCTION

In chapter 3, we identified the second phase of the budget cycle as being the process of monitoring, tracking, and adjusting the budget. This portion of the cycle may take up the largest part of managers' time in many organizations, much of it consumed by making sure that transactions have been correctly posted to accounts. However, the key institutional issue during this phase of the budget cycle is to make sure the organization is on track financially, identify any need for midstream corrections, and choose a course of action. In this chapter we go into more depth on the techniques for monitoring budgets.

9.2 DEVELOPING THE INSTITUTIONAL ASSESSMENT

Monitoring the budget during the year must occur on both an institutional level and at the level of departments, programs or units. On an institutional level, staff must develop a full picture of the organization's financial status, which includes all funds and covers capital spending and cash flow as well as operating results. Current year financial analysis needs to assess the organization's performance so far relative to expectations, predict results for the year, and identify any longer-term issues.

After assembling the year-to-date financial results, the first question will be whether the organization has brought in as much revenue and spent as much as it expected, or whether it is running ahead or behind. The budget should offer the best reflection of the organization's expectations for the year. However, most organizations do not divide their budgets into part-year segments. Those that do can compare results to the part-year budget and assess their financial position.

Organizations that work from annual budgets use several methods to assess status midyear, and some of these methods are advised for organizations with part-year budgets as a reality check. The organization can estimate the portion of the budget it expects to have spent at this point in the year. This estimate will be built up by analyzing the different cost and revenue elements. A parallel approach is to project expenses forward to the end of the year rather than rolling the budget backward. Similar analytical effort yields an answer to the question, Where will we end up if we continue on the course indicated by the results so far?

Previous history can provide a basis for assessing the current period. See Exhibit 9.1. Previous years can be analyzed to determine what portion

Exhibit 9.1 Victim Assistance Association Comparison of Actuals to Same Period in the Previous Year

	Annual Budget	*Actuals Through Nov*	*Same Period Previous Year*	*Variance*
Revenues				
State grant	$46,080	$23,040	$22,580	$460
Plate collection	1,000	0	0	0
Contributions (rent)	12,000	5,000	5,000	0
Total revenues	59,080	28,040	27,580	460
Salaries				
Director	32,000	13,333	12,933	(400)
Office assistant (part-time)	10,000	3,333	4,167	833
Health insurance	2,400	1,000	1,000	0
Telephones	480	200	200	0
Rent	12,000	5,000	5,000	0
Supplies	225	190	105	(85)
Equipment	300	170	95	(75)
Events	400	350	200	(150)
Travel (clients)	250	85	105	20
Travel (staff)	250	105	110	5
Memberships	300	200	150	(50)
Publications	175	130	175	45
Total expense	58,780	24,097	24,240	143
Net surplus/(deficit)	$300	$3,943	$3,340	$603

of the budget was consumed at different points in the year and what revenues were received. Also, comparing current year-to-date figures with the actual results for the same period in previous years can indicate where performance is headed. Simple comparison of the amounts on a year-to-year basis or a comparison of the percentage of the budget consumed may be relevant.

The comparison in Exhibit 9.1 shows that the program is generally running ahead of last year, primarily due to a temporary vacancy in the part-time assistant position. This comparison is useful in understanding some specifics of the budget—for example, the lack of plate collection revenue might cause concern if the reviewer did not know that this sort of revenue was based on one collection a year that takes place in the last half of the year. The comparison with the previous year underscores this timing effect. Alternatively, a comparison of the percentage of each element consumed emphasizes the magnitude to which the program is going over in some expense categories. See Exhibit 9.2.

Exhibit 9.2 Victim Assistance Association Comparison of Percent Expended to Same Period in the Previous Year

	Previous Year			*Current Year*		
	Annual Budget	*Actuals Through Nov.*	*Percent Expended*	*Annual Budget*	*Actuals Through Nov.*	*Percent Expended*
Revenues						
State grant	$45,160	$22,580	50.0	$46,080	$23,040	50.0
Plate collection	1,000	0	0.0	1,000	0	0.0
Contributions (rent)	12,000	5,000	41.7	12,000	5,000	41.7
Total revenues	58,160	27,580	47.4	59,080	28,040	47.5
Salaries						
Director	31,040	12,933	41.7	32,000	13,333	41.7
Office assistant (part-time)	10,000	4,167	41.7	10,000	3,333	33.3
Health insurance	2,400	1,000	41.7	2,400	1,000	41.7
Telephones	480	200	41.7	480	200	41.7
Rent	12,000	5,000	41.7	12,000	5,000	41.7
Supplies	225	105	46.7	225	190	84.4
Equipment	300	95	31.7	300	170	56.7
Events	400	200	50.0	400	350	87.5
Travel (clients)	250	105	42.0	250	85	34.0
Travel (staff)	250	110	44.0	250	105	42.0
Memberships	300	150	50.0	300	200	66.7
Publications	175	175	100.0	175	130	74.3
Total expense	57,820	24,240	41.9	58,780	24,097	41.0
Net surplus/(deficit)	$340	$3,340		$300	$3,943	

Institutional monitoring may also focus on major trends and categories. Projected surpluses or deficits in these areas may have a determinant effect on other financial activity if the organization adjusts spending to reflect these trends. For example, a church may focus its analysis on pledge revenues. If pledge revenues are falling behind plan, the congregation and staff will start looking for ways to cut back expenditures. If this key revenue source looks better than expected, the church will start considering what to do if it actually has excess funds available at the end of the year.

In the example of church pledge results through July in Exhibit 9.3, or seven months into the year, the church experienced a setback in February and March from which it started to recover. However, the recovery has been unreliable, just barely beating the budget in May and now dipping back into a current month surplus for July. The church may need to be sensitive to the possibility that a stronger decline will start, or that the good months will continue to be too weak to offset the deficit.

Once the source of a problem has been identified, it should be verified and explained by identifying the root causes of the variance in specific transaction streams or in operational detail. An accounting error or an unusual pattern of transactions may have distorted results, or the worse-than-expected results might have to be viewed in conjunction with better results in another category (such as is the case when costs of goods sold increase along with sales revenue). If the results are true, the cause needs to be understood in order to develop responses. For example, if staff salary costs have exceeded expectations, was this due to lower vacancies, the addition of positions, unusually high salary increases, overtime expenses, temporary staff, or other causes? Once the source of the problem has been identified, the organization can take steps to make sure the problem does not get worse (e.g., freeze use of overtime) and can start to evaluate whether it can respond by taking action in the area that generated the problem (e.g., reduce the use of temporaries and/or hold positions vacant longer), or whether it will have to compensate through improved financial performance in other areas.

Even in the case of results better than expectations, the variance from expectations needs to be verified and explained so that the organization can decide how to make use of the unexpected resources. The better-than-expected results could have been caused by transitory effects such as an accounting anomaly, which will be offset to come back into line with the budget in a future period. The organization needs to make sure the resources really are going to be there before committing itself to new spending, or assuming the windfall will cover problems in other areas.

Exhibit 9.3 Presbyterian Church Pledge Revenue Comparison of Performance Against Budget

	Jan	*Feb*	*Mar*	*Apr*	*May*	*June*	*July*	*Aug*	*Sept*	*Oct*	*Nov*	*Dec*	*Total YTD (Jan-July)*
Budget	$19,000	$14,000	$20,000	$22,000	$14,000	$5,000	$5,000	$5,000	$10,000	$12,000	$20,000	$35,000	$99,000
Actual	21,094	12,003	13,413	23,121	14,002	6,135	4,808						94,576
Difference	2,094	(1,997)	(6,587)	1,121	2	1,135	(192)						(4,424)
Cumulative difference		$97	($6,490)	($5,369)	($5,367)	($4,232)	($4,424)						

9.3 MONITORING CAPITAL AND CASH

On a periodic basis throughout the year, someone in the organization should monitor the progress of capital projects and spending and the level of cash balances. In capital projects, the organization needs to know whether projects will be completed on time, and whether the project budget is holding up. If a project incurs cost overruns, the organization will need to start looking for ways to fund the gap, either from new sources of funds or by cutting other costs. Also, late delivery of a project may have serious effects on operations—if a new facility is late in opening, the organization may have to extend rent payments for temporary space.

It is critical that the organization maintain adequate cash balances to meet its current obligations, both in operating costs such as payroll and for capital projects. In addition to compiling information on current cash balances, someone needs to evaluate what new receipts of cash are expected and determine whether the balance and new receipts will be sufficient to cover anticipated cash obligations. If a cash shortfall is predicted, the organization will have to look for ways to reduce cash outflows, such as delaying expenditures or capital purchases, or letting staff go (decisions to cut staff to reduce cash obligations must factor in cash severance costs that will offset the cash savings).

9.4 ASSESSING DEPARTMENTS, PROGRAMS, OR UNITS

While central staff will analyze the current results on an institutional basis, departments, programs, and units need to monitor their own budget status, in more detail and usually more often. Most immediately and parochially, the budget manager needs to make sure the department is staying within its budget for the year to protect the department and herself from criticism, and to guide decisions about purchases or staffing.

In some cases, the institutional analysis is built up from unit-level analysis. Units should conduct the same sorts of analysis that consider the amount of the budget that was expected to be consumed within the period and compare results with the same period in previous years. Managers who have been in place a long time may have a strong intuitive sense of the annual pattern of expenditures in their area and may be able to perform this analysis simply by looking at the financial statements that come out of the accounting system.

Units often will go into more detail on spending and receipts by type. In smaller units with less budget flexibility, the level of review will be more detailed to ensure that enough money is available. Also, unit budget managers' detailed understanding of their budgets is one of the best sources for the organization as a whole to assess the root causes of variances. The relevance of the concept of budget transparency becomes apparent when an organization starts trying to "drill down" to find an explanation for variances and develop a solid midyear assessment of results. Often there is no substitute for turning to the managers who are closest to the transactions and therefore have a grasp on the most specific details of the financial results.

Monitoring of unit finances may be mirrored by central staff who also monitor expenses on a unit level. In some cases, the manager gets information from the unit's staff, and central administrators turn to central staff for an independent assessment of the same budget. The presence of parallel monitoring efforts may indicate distrust between central administrators and departments. In other cases, units do not have the responsibility or capacity for this analysis.

9.5 STATUS MEETINGS

Just as the budget development process may be built around a timeline whose major milestones include meetings between central staff or leadership and internal managers and meetings in which the budget is presented to external groups, the process of monitoring the budget may be structured around a calendar of meetings. These meetings may be conducted separately and parallel to the budget development cycle, or they may be combined with those meetings. Current year status and plans for next year can be two items on the agenda for a meeting with the board or internally with budget managers.

Some organizations will schedule formal meetings of central administrators and budget managers to review their financial position for the year. Such meetings can serve as milestones that spur everyone to undertake the analytical effort. They also allow central administration to learn what is going on in departments, alert them to impending problems, and permit them to initiate corrective actions. Departmental managers may see these meetings as intrusive, taking them away from the business of running their department. Those running the budget process need to take steps to make sure these meetings are constructive and create an environment in which managers feel they can openly discuss financial issues, rather than simply try to get through the meeting without being chewed out.

In addition to these internal meetings to review budget status, the organization's board is likely to ask for updates throughout the year on budget status for some of the same purposes: to learn what is going on and let them know when corrective action needs to be taken. Internal meetings can help prepare central administrators to brief the board.

9.6 CONCLUSION

Monitoring the current year budget constitutes a significant analytical effort on the part of central staff, leadership, and budget managers. If an organization uncovers worrisome trends in its current year budget, verification and evaluation of those trends becomes critical, as does the search for feasible responses. If results are better than expected, the sooner the organization knows that, the sooner it can start deciding how best to use its enhanced resources in service of its strategy and mission. In larger organizations, this situation requires separate and coordinated effort by both central staff and departmental or program budget managers.

CHAPTER TEN

Managing the Process

10.1 INTRODUCTION

In the previous chapters, we discussed the steps in developing, monitoring, and evaluating budgets. In each of these discussions, we have talked about different roles of leaders, central finance staff, departmental managers, boards, and others. It should be obvious at this point that every organization has a different configuration of positions and distribution of responsibilities among participants in the process. In spite of the diversity of configurations encountered among organizations, there is a set of functions that must be performed in every budget process. These functions get rolled up into five typical roles that can be staffed in various ways.

10.2 BASIC FUNCTIONS

There is a set of basic functions that should be performed to manage the budget process in an organization. In some cases the organization will be so small or the parts of the process so truncated that the functions being performed are hardly noticed. The functions are described here, not the job descriptions of people in the process—these functions can be divided between positions in many different ways. In Section 10.3, we describe typical roles or positions that are defined to make sure the key functions in the budget process are performed.

(a) Timeline and Scheduling

Someone needs to establish the timeline for budget development and schedule meetings required for review, discussion, and approval. This function may be split: The person scheduling board meetings establishes schedule parameters for budget development by default. Someone needs to work back from the dates scheduled for board review and approval and establish reasonable time lags for preparation and distribution of basic materials, preparation of proposals, review, modification, compilation, and presentation.

Furthermore, someone needs to make sure review meetings happen in a timely fashion, and that all parties receive materials they need with advance review time, or to make sure that materials are clear enough that previous review is not necessary. One of the most disruptive elements to a budget process can be when parties are not informed about meetings, meetings are scheduled with calendar conflicts, and the parties involved are not adequately prepared. These are the basics of administrative work, but their importance cannot be overstated.

Participants in the process are rarely satisfied with the timelines provided. A common complaint is lack of adequate time to prepare proposals once the budget materials are received. A common budget process crisis occurs when the budget materials are late, and managers have only a week to return the budget sheets with their proposals once the materials arrive. Those preparing the materials should try to provide adequate time for managers to develop proposals, but they are often subject to their own constraints—they may be squeezed from both ends, waiting for information from the officers on the results of a planning retreat, and having strict instructions that the Finance Committee is to be given an advance copy at a certain date, during which time they need to compile and check proposals. The more communication the better between all parties so that everyone understands the constraints of others' work situations.

(b) Prepare Data

We have discussed places in each stage of the budget process that require the assembly and analysis of data. Developing a budget requires data on the current budget, current and recent activity, and any key factors that are considered in making long-range projections, developing guidelines, supporting proposals, and testing alternatives. Monitoring results requires both detail on current activity and historical data for comparative purposes, and year-end analysis also requires detail and comparative results. It is not possible to create an exhaustive list of the data required by any one organization, let alone a list that applies to all organizations.

Some of the keys tasks related to preparing and handling data are as follows:

- *Assemble data.* (1) Budget bases. Assembling the base data may simply require knowledge of the definition of the budgets by accounts or departments, but may also require cleanup to back out one-time changes or mistakes. Assembling the budget base for the personnel budget can be particularly time-consuming if it is built up from personnel rosters—keeping up-to-date on these records is harder than it might sound. Fundamentally, someone needs to define the starting point for budgeting. (2) Historical budgets and results: Each organization will look at different comparisons, but someone needs to be responsible for assembling the authoritative data. (3) Current period and year-to-date results and comparative results for similar periods in previous years: Putting together data for partial year periods can be more difficult than pulling together the year-end results or full-year budgets, which are more often documented in well-circulated sources.
- *Calculate guidelines or pools.* In a system where managers are given pools of funds to budget, someone needs to be responsible for calculating those pools. Most organizations calculate this figure centrally and give it to department managers rather than simply giving them rates and instructions for applying them. This tends to cut down disagreements about the correct size of the pool and the proposal's compliance as it comes in.
- *Calculate variances.* Each organization will decide which variances are important: budget to actual, actual to previous year actual, actual to current year budget, and so forth. In some cases, the organization will ask departments to take responsibility for calculating and analyzing these variances, but doing the calculations centrally increases the likelihood that central and departmental staff will be explaining the same figures.
- *Review submissions.* As proposals come back, someone needs to make sure that the math is correct and that the proposals meet the rules for the process.

As in each function in this section, these tasks related to preparing data can be performed by different people in the organization, from its leader (often the case in small organizations) to staff working for individual budget managers.

(c) Analysis and Modeling

Most organizations do some sort of projections and modeling. We have already discussed techniques for projections and modeling, in particular in Chapters 5 and 8. In small organizations the function may be limited to putting together the next year's budget in a test form to see if it is likely to balance. The extent of this function will be larger in larger organizations, which are more likely to do more formal modeling and analysis, reflecting the greater complexity of their operations, a possibly longer-term focus in financial planning, and greater resources available for managing finances.

Thus, in a large organization that is engaged in formal budget modeling, someone should develop and maintain an institutional financial model. This model factors in all key aspects of revenues and expenses and projects financial results for several years. It is used to test initial assumptions and to establish budget guidelines that are likely to work. Once budget proposals come in, the model is used for testing a preliminary budget proposal and for testing the longer-term effects of these proposals as a group.

Models may be developed on multiple levels. An institutional budget model may be built on a summary level, but it may contain feeder models to project specific cost or revenue elements or to model departmental budgets. A model that is designed to integrate departmental financial planning with institutional budgeting will need to have a more sophisticated design to allow it to roll up departmental and object code detail into more summary levels. As an example, some of the detailed revenue and expense models that may be in use at a college or university are:

- Enrollment (feeds several of the other models)
- Tuition
- Financial aid
- Housing
- Food services
- Faculty
- Benefits
- Depreciation schedules
- Cash balances

(d) Systems and Tools

Someone will need to develop and maintain whatever systems and tools are used for developing, testing, or reporting the budget. This task may be as simple as designing a budget submission sheet that managers use in hard copy only. Many organizations have some sort of electronic tool such as spreadsheets that are prepared for departments, distributed to them, modified, and returned to a central office for compilation. Others use modules in their financial system that must be maintained and updated, including managing user access and providing training.

(e) Make Decisions

Obviously, throughout the budget process participants need to make a whole series of decisions ending up with the approved budget. Ultimately the board is responsible for approving a budget, although the effective decision can lie with staff. Before the final budget reaches the board, there are many decisions that must be made by some combination of the board, officers, managers, and staff of the organization. The decisions include:

- Distribution of authority and responsibility for developing and managing budgets
- Goals and guidelines for the upcoming budget
- Exceptions to guidelines, reallocations, or special appropriations
- Major capital expenditures
- What information to present to the board and other groups

Each organization will distribute the responsibility for these decisions as it sees fit. Generally more far-reaching decisions should be reserved for the board, officers, or leadership of the organization. Most importantly, the organization needs to define and articulate who is responsible for which decisions, and establish processes to make sure that those responsible for particular decisions can and do make them.

(f) Document Decisions and Prepare Reports

Documenting decisions is another aspect of basic good administrative behavior. It mst be clear who is responsible and accountable for documenting decisions. It is easy to neglect clearly documenting agreements made in the budget process. Confusion about what was decided causes unnecessary tension. A particularly common phenomenon is that deals are made to reach a balanced budget and then they do not come up again until the following year's budget preparation cycle when managers are trying to sort out the starting assumptions for the budget. A year later, it may be difficult to remember or agree on the details of the deal.

For instance, perhaps a manager agrees to hold a position vacant for five years to pay for a deficit in one year. If that agreement is not documented, the manager might argue every year that the position should be included in the budget base for the next year. Furthermore, the manager may argue that even though the position is to be held vacant, the agreement was that the position would be included in the salary base for purposes of calculating the salary increase pool. Many people in the organization will spin their wheels trying to resolve this question if the decision has not been clearly documented.

Related to documenting decisions, from the final budgets for departments to the details that make them work, is the job of preparing reports, particularly for review by the board and external governing bodies. It is very important that these reports be correct (i.e., the numbers add across rows and down columns) and accurate insofar as they reflect the budget agreed to by all parties.

(g) Update the Accounting System

Once the budget has been approved, someone will need to update the accounting system. In the Victim's Assistance program, this means starting a new ledger book with the new budgeted amounts in the first column. At the Arts Council, it means updating the organization's Quickbooks files to start a new year. In large organizations, more effort and coordination are required. In the most advanced systems, the files that feed the approved reports contain the necessary detail to supply budgets electronically to the accounting system. It would then be the responsibility of a central staffer to initiate or perform the transfer. In other systems, budgets are input into a budget module that feeds the accounting system. Representatives of the departments may be required to do the input, or it can be a role for clerks in a central office. In this case, someone must have responsibility for coordinating and supervising the effort.

(h) Monitor Results

Various people inside and outside the organization have a role in monitoring spending and transactions during the year. In a small organization, this is often one of the many roles of the organization's director. In larger organizations, the role is split, with some staff watching certain revenue items, managers and their staff keeping an eye on departmental budgets and transactions, and central staff monitoring the overall effect.

(i) Control Spending

Budgets by themselves do not control spending, although they can be a tool that assists staff in this function. Centralized forms of control involve central staff reviewing transactions for budget availability or appropriateness and challenging them, or system-generated holds that kick out transactions that would push the object code, expense class, or account over budget. These transactions are then reviewed by central staff.

In a less centralized environment, managers are responsible for controlling spending. They may use the budget as a guide to alert them of expenses that will push their accounts over their overall funding level.

10.3 ROLES

Throughout this book, we have referred to various groups of participants in the budget process: boards, leaders, budget committees, central finance staff, department managers, and others. While every organization will have a different configuration of positions and participants in the process, there is a set of roles designated in most organizations. Responsibility for the functions described in Section 10.2 is distributed among participants playing one or more of the following roles.

(a) Approving Body

As we have mentioned frequently, there is usually a governing body that approves the organization's budget. Often this is a board and its Finance Committee. For organizations heavily supported by grants, the funding agencies effectively approve the organization's budget. State agencies typically have their budgets approved by a state body.

(b) Decision-Making Groups

Many larger organizations have a formal budget committee that reviews departmental budgets, sets guidelines, and decides on the final budget proposal. The committee may be advisory to the organization's leader or an inner circle of leaders, or it may hold power in its own right and make recommendations based on votes of its members. There may be a separate group responsible for reviewing and approving capital projects, which is particularly the case if the organization feels different representation is necessary to legitimize capital spending decisions.

(c) Central Staff or Office

In larger organizations, central staff members are responsible for many of the process functions described above, including management of the timeline and schedule, preparation of key data and reports, modeling, and coordination of budget entry. The central staff may be in a budget office or planning office primarily responsible for budgets, or staff in an accounting office who perform budget duties along with other responsibilities. The decision to establish dedicated budget staff is largely a function of the complexity of the process and its perceived importance in decision making. If the budget is not seen as the nexus of organizational decision making, there is no reason to dedicate staff to this role. In a smaller organization, the central staff may include the organization's chief financial officer or the director herself.

(d) Budget Managers

Leaders of units or programs are typically responsible for preparing budget proposals for their areas, or at least providing input to central staff where the process is heavily centralized. Budget managers are then responsible for monitoring financial activity on that budget and are accountable for outcomes. They will have a weaker sense of accountability if they feel the budgets were imposed from elsewhere rather than truly reflecting their plans and needs.

(e) Departmental Staff

Budget managers may assign staff in their department to many of the detailed tasks related to monitoring and managing budgets: checking transactions, tracking and projecting results, and preparing periodic reports. The responsibilities may include assignments during preparation of budgets, such as filling out budget worksheets or entering data into the accounting system. In some cases, the departmental staff will duplicate efforts of central staff, who also develop projections and reports. This situation may be due to mistrust between central staff and budget managers, or a lack of communication.

10.4 GAMESMANSHIP IN THE BUDGET PROCESS

Several authors have described various forms of gamesmanship in the budget process, or "budget ploys" as Robert Anthony and David Young call them (see Bibliography). It is important for both sides in the process to recognize in good faith the motivations of the other. Good departmental managers will focus on doing the best possible job in their program or aspect of the organization. Central staff are trying, often desperately, to make all the pieces fit together to produce a balanced picture. Dysfunctional budget processes are characterized by distrust on both sides of the table in budget negotiations and a lack of shared views of the organization's goals and outlook.

Much of this book focuses on design of the budget process, because the author believes that thorough examination of the fundamental aspects of the process design leadership can align managers more closely and effectively with organizational goals, reducing the ground for mutual distrust.

(a) Games Played by Budget Managers

In their book *Management Control in Nonprofit Organizations*, Anthony and Young list over 20 ploys used by managers in the budget process, which they advise financial administrators to anticipate and be prepared to counter. These ploys fall into four categories:

1. *Deception in the proposal.* There is a variety of ways in which budget managers can submit deceptive proposals. A small increment may be proposed first that becomes a sunk cost, which can form the basis for larger requests in the future. They may try to obscure the nature of a proposal by burying something within a proposal or naming it deceptively. Managers may use statistics deceptively, or inflate requests beyond what is needed. Most of these ploys can be combated by thorough scrutiny of the numbers, requesting that proposals be broken down into detail adequate for those reviewing them.

2. *Jumping decision channels.* Budget managers may try to go above the head of the person with initial review, muster public support, or play one decision maker against another. These methods are best combated by clear delineation of the process, with sanctions demonstrated for those who subvert decision paths. However, once a budget manager jumps the decision channels, it can be difficult for the reviewers to go against the proposal. Sanctions may have to come downstream.

3. *Bluster.* This covers a variety of strategies intended to convince the reviewer that he has no choice but to approve the proposal. The specific behaviors may be to imply high-level support for the proposal, arguing that the proposal must be accepted to stay current or to maintain appropriate levels of service. Another strategy is to claim special expertise or a difficult-to-describe technical reason why approval is obligatory. In general, these strategies are

best resisted by an insistence that claims for a proposal be backed up by proof and a refusal to be embarrassed by the need for more information or a clearer explanation.

4. *Halfhearted compliance.* These passive-aggressive strategies appear to comply with the budget process, but do so in a way that appears to cause more problems that can only be solved by a higher level of funding. Again, the best response is to insist on further analysis to determine whether all options have really been considered or whether the reasons for rejecting more acceptable alternatives are valid.

When confronted by these strategies, it is important to keep in mind the following:

- Many of the actions described as budget ploys are so only if they are done in a spirit of subverting the process. It is not necessarily bad to gauge support for a proposal from the public or organizational leaders. Outside experts can provide a useful perspective on a proposal, as long as they are not given too much credit.
- Apparent ploys may be due to a lack of expertise. A proposal may contain deceptive or badly organized statistics because the unit lacks staff with the time or expertise to prepare effective materials.
- What is causing someone to try to "game" the system? He may be discouraged after years of failure in his requests or by the unresponsiveness from leadership. The behavior of leadership and central staff may be responsible for breeding managers who do not trust the budget process.
- What are the incentives in the process? The system may reward managers for building programs rather than complying with the spirit of the budget process. The organization may have fostered a "nice guys finish last" culture in which results are emphasized at the absolute expense of behaviors.

(b) Games Played by Central Budget Staff and Leadership

Central staff and leadership engage in the following budget ploys that budget managers widely recognize:

- *Withholding information.* Central staff issue guidelines but give no information on why the guidelines were set at that level. There may also be references to instructions and desires from leadership that are never spelled out or put in the context of their full justification.

- *Making things out to be worse than they are.* Even when central staff do share the information on their assumptions and projections, they may make things out to be worse than they are. To the central staff this is a cautious approach, assuming the worst case so that there are no unpleasant surprises at year-end. That way they can be congratulated by the board for snatching surpluses from the jaws of a deficit once again. To budget managers, this situation causes undue hardship at the expense of trying to implement programs.
- *Insisting that hard-pressed departments achieve higher productivity.* This can take the form of mandating across-the-board cuts or holding budgets flat, justified by the undocumented assertion that the department can and should work harder and smarter and get more from its resources. Sometimes this is a fair response to overall decreases in funds available to the organization, but not always.
- *Refusing to listen.* Budget managers can develop solid data to support their proposals and contentions, but central staff and leaders refuse to listen if the data do not support their goals. The plant manager explains that oil prices have gone up 15 percent and so heating costs will definitely go up, but the central staff refuse to make any adjustments to the plant budget, either instructing the manager to fund the fuel increases with cuts in other areas or challenging whether the manager is making overpessimistic assumptions about fuel consumption and the expected severity of the winter. Another form of this ploy is to request departmental input and then consistently ignore it, based on the assertion that the department's work is always wrong or biased and the central staff's version is correct.
- *Creating unnecessary work.* After submitting budget materials, central staff and leadership seem to be constantly asking for more data, a different presentation of the data, or consultation with additional parties. These requests seem to do little to clarify the proposal, but seem better designed to convince the manager to give up the request or to put off a decision.
- *Undercutting budget managers.* This can take the form of setting one manager against another, or failing to warn managers when they submit proposals that they know will provoke a severe reaction upstream in the review process. By making it clear that managers are competing for the same funds, an environment can be created in which managers criticize each other's proposals to better position their own. Central staff may also set managers up by asking them to submit information without all of the context, on

the assumption that without that context the departmental staff is bound to be perceived as out of line with institutional policies, goals, or guidelines; the department is forced into a guessing game for the "right" answer.

Many of these ploys by central staff result from the pressures they face in trying to respond to demanding leaders and difficult financial times. They may not have the time to communicate everything they should to managers, who perceive worse motivation than is in fact the case.

The obvious conclusion is that all parties in the budget process need to communicate as openly as possible, truly listen to each other, and try to accommodate each other's legitimate concerns.

10.5 CONCLUSION

The first task in managing the budget process is to make sure that the functions described in this chapter are performed and to assign people to fill the key roles in the process. We have attempted to describe these functions and tasks in generic terms, acknowledging the diversity of forms they take in individual organizations. In addition those responsible for managing the process need to understand and anticipate the behavior of everyone in this process.

CHAPTER ELEVEN

Financial Analysis

11.1 INTRODUCTION

Financial analysis forms one of the key disciplines of budgeting and financial planning. Every stage in the budget process requires significant analytical efforts to make sense of numbers and guide decisions. Without financial analysis, budgeting becomes little more than an empty, bureaucratic process. In the budget development process, analysis identifies the true dynamics of the organization's finances to provide realistic projections, which in turn should produce more realistic guidelines or allocations. Once the budget is in place, analysis allows the organization to evaluate performance to date, make intelligent assumptions about the immediate future, and identify the adjustments that are needed. Finally, the assessment of year-end results is pure analysis, which allows the organization to take stock of its performance as a whole and the performance of its units or programs, and to guide development in the next round of budget development.

The first step to good financial analysis is to understand that it is much more than cranking out variance results between actuals and budgets, between projections and budgets, or between one year and previous years. This mistake is made all too often—for example, when a finance staff views its job as issuing financial statements, with the "analytical" element being a column that shows the difference between the budget and actuals. Financial analysis must go further and sort out the reasons for variances.

The task of financial analysis is not to produce certain documents but to develop a story line—that is, describe the organization's financial results, why they occurred (or will occur in the case of projections), and what the organization should or could do. Often, the best financial analysis, while rooted in numbers, can take the form of a narrative explanation that can be conveyed easily in words and is comprehensible to everyone associated with the organization, regardless of their level of financial expertise.

11.2 COMPARISONS, RECONCILIATIONS, AND DETAIL

To get to the storyline, the financial analyst must engage in a disciplined process of assembling and going through data. All analysis needs mileposts which provide fixed reference points for all numbers and statements. These mileposts will generally include a set of authoritative annual financial results from previous periods and the approved budget. In larger organizations, each set of financial statements will be divided into a set of statements for the component units of the organization.

For example, a university will have a set of historical operating results for the entire organization, verified by its formal audit. For internal purposes, it may use a different format, but the statements in this format must be reconciled to the audited financials, with a formal schedule that shows the specific differences between the audited statements and internal documents. Exhibit 11.1 shows three years of the audited statements for the University of Okoboji plus the budget stated in the same format.

The figures shown here constitute the most fundamental touchstones for financial analysis at the university. Every time an analyst looks at a part of the university's finances, whether the slice being examined is a unit, an expense type or a period of time, he or she must be able to show how figures ultimately trace back to these statements, and to the bottom line results in particular.

The audited financial statements follow Financial Accounting Standards of Financial Account Standards Board Statement Number 117, and recognize contributions in the period in which they are received. For internal purposes, the University of Okoboji prefers to show restricted revenues during the period in which they are expended, so that the receipt of these funds will not disguise weakness in general operating finances. Therefore, the audited statements must be reconciled to the reports used by management. Once the reconciliation has been spelled out, the management reports can be treated with the same authority as the audited financials. Exhibit 11.2 shows what this reconciliation might look like.

In addition, the university will have financial statements for each of its major units. The financial statements for all of these units, taken to-

Exhibit 11.1 University of Okoboji Multi-Year Results and Budget ($000s)

	1994-95 Actual	*1995-96 Actual*	*1996-97 Actual*	*1997-98 Budget*
Tuition and fees	$42,000	$44,000	$49,000	$52,000
Federal appropriations	8,200	7,000	6,550	7,280
State appropriations	525	970	4,535	5,455
Local appropriations	120	140	600	750
Grants and contracts	3,330	4,300	4,500	5,500
Private gifts	29,500	38,500	26,100	33,750
Endowment income used	7,500	7,800	8,040	8,050
Sales and services	250	650	400	500
Other sources	6,500	6,850	7,900	7,350
Auxiliary sales	35,000	33,000	29,000	34,000
Total revenue	**132,925**	**143,210**	**136,625**	**154,635**
Educational & General Expenses				
Instruction	46,650	49,075	53,050	59,300
Research	5,500	5,650	6,100	6,700
Public Services	2,230	2,450	2,600	2,500
Academic support	2,870	3,090	3,040	3,740
Student services	2,600	2,875	3,050	4,000
Institutional support	3,400	4,200	5,140	5,750
Op and maintenance of plant	10,700	10,400	12,000	13,000
Scholarships	6,500	7,500	10,070	13,700
Mandatory transfer	650	200	800	1,560
Total E&G	**81,010**	**85,440**	**95,850**	**110,250**
Auxiliaries	28,000	31,200	30,100	30,920
Interest paid	225	240	220	210
Depreciation	640	675	680	700
Other costs	7,500	7,900	7,100	7,000
Total expenses	**117,375**	**125,455**	**133,950**	**149,080**
Net income	**$15,550**	**$17,755**	**$2,675**	**$5,555**

gether, will equal the institution-wide statements or will be formally reconciled to that statement. The same organizational divisions and detail should exist for the budget as well. The component figures for the University are shown in Exhibit 11.3. These are the figures for one year—the University would have a similar table for each year and could create multi–year series for each component. Once one expands financial figures into two layers of detail (time and division overlaid on a basic summary by expense and revenue type), the data takes on three dimensions and can only be viewed in partial view in the two dimensional context of a printed sheet or a single computer screen.

During the course of the year, financial statements will be issued for part-year results or projections. These statements should reconcile to

Exhibit 11.2 University of Okoboji Reconciliation of Audited Financial Statements and Internal Statements ($000s)

	1994-95 Actual	*1995-96 Actual*	*1996-97 Actual*	*1997-98 Budget*
Net operating results from audited financials	$15,500	$17,755	$2,675	$5,555
Less excess receipts over expenditures, Federal sources	(1,200)	(1,000)	(1,050)	(980)
Less excess receipts over expenditures, local appropriations	(75)	(70)	(135)	(155)
Less excess receipts over expenditures, private gifts	(5,000)	(10,500)	(6,600)	(11,750)
Net income on internal management statements	$9,275	$6,185	($5,110)	($7,330)

historical statements following the same structure. Each round of statements should use consistent definitions, or again, the differences should be reconciled. The accounts that constitute a unit in financial terms should be consistent across statements, and the statements should use a consistent treatment of transactions or types of revenues and expenses.

In addition, any new financial statements should be reconciled to previous statements that have covered the same topic. Some of these cases may be obvious. For example, if the budget included enrollment projections, later projections must be compared to the earlier projections. In other cases, the relationship may not be as obvious—one report may focus on enrollment for one school, whereas an earlier report offered a projection on enrollment for the whole institution. That institution-wide projection implicitly included assumptions on enrollments for each school. As school-level projections are done later, implicit assumptions from earlier work need to be spelled out and the differences reconciled.

A core concept for financial analysis is "drill down" and "roll up." Figures are assumed to be composed of a number of elements. Taken together (or rolled up), these elements compose the total. The elements can be different organizations or more detailed types of revenues and expenses. To understand phenomena at one level of detail, analysts can drill down into the figure's component elements to identify more specific information on what drives the change. The data must be constructed consistently across levels of detail. If a university's institution-wide data break salaries into faculty, staff, and temporaries, detailed data for individual units should not have just a single salary category that includes all

Exhibit 11.3 University of Okoboji Current Year Budget Breakout by Division ($000s)

	Arts & Sciences	*Business*	*Pharmacy*	*Social Work*	*Total Academic*	*Student Services*	*Adminis-tration*	*Develop-ment*	*Institutional*	*Total*
Tuition and fees	$26,000	$15,600	$5,200	$5,200	$52,000					$52,000
Governmental appropriations					0				3,850	3,850
Grants and contracts					0					0
Private gifts	1,500			1,500	3,000				12,000	15,000
Endowment income used					0				8,050	8,050
Sales and services		375			375	125				500
Other sources					0	350				350
Auxiliaries					0	25,500	8,500			34,000
Restricted revenue	8,400	700	1,400	3,500	14,000					14,000
Plant revenue					0				7,000	7,000
Total revenue	**35,900**	**16,675**	**6,600**	**10,200**	**69,375**	**25,975**	**8,500**	**0**	**30,900**	**134,750**
UR[1] Faculty salaries	19,560	6,520	3,260	3,260	32,600					32,600
UR[1] Staff salaries	2,627	2,627	730	438	6,420	292	6,129	730	1,021	14,592
UR[1] benefits	5,547	2,287	997	924	9,755	73	1,532	182	255	11,798
Total UR[1] compensation	27,733	11,433	4,987	4,622	48,776	365	7,661	912	1,277	58,990
UR[1] financial aid	3,400	80	240	280	4,000					4,000
Other UR[1] operating costs	2,626	2,100	1,313	525	6,565	135	7,716	1,050	10,793	26,260
Total UR[1] E&G[2]	33,759	13,614	6,540	5,427	59,341	500	15,377	1,962	12,070	89,250
Auxiliaries					0	23,190	7,730			30,920
Total rest expense	8,400	700	1,400	3,500	14,000					14,000
Total plant expense					0				7,910	7,910
Total expenses	**42,159**	**14,314**	**7,940**	**8,927**	**73,341**	**23,690**	**23,107**	**1,962**	**19,980**	**142,080**
Net surplus/(deficit)	($6,259)	$2,361	($1,340)	$1,273	($3,966)	$2,285	($14,607)	($1,962)	$10,920	($7,330)

[1]Unrestricted
[2]Educational and General

three. If anything, the organizational detail should offer the option of more detail for expense types.

The analysis may require the inclusion of nonfinancial data, such as numbers of client visits or enrollments. Nonfinancial data are subject to the same requirements for consistency and for being anchored to accepted reference points. A church's count of members should use consistent criteria for defining who is included on the membership roll. Are inactive members taken out of the count at consistent intervals? Are children included as well as adults?

It is very tempting to neglect these comparisons and reconciliations. Often a set of statements will look fine and the analyst may feel she can explain each element. Reconciling the statement to earlier work may unearth problems or raise questions that would not come up otherwise. Perhaps the questions would all end up having simple answers, but thorough reconciliation will open many cans of worms. Human nature probably naturally resists disrupting this sense of order once it is achieved. However, the chance that something important was overlooked requires that analysts redouble their energy and integrate one round of work with previous efforts.

11.3 JUDGMENT AND INTERPRETATION

Developing the financial story line involves judgment. Simply calculating variances is not sufficient, and following the chain of variance and detail mindlessly can lead to endless work—there is always one more variance to calculate, one more level of detail to pursue. Success in analysis depends on focusing on what is essential. Analysts should examine the largest variances. They must also understand the critical elements of an organization's finances, the places where even small variances can have profound effects.

Once the data have been assembled and the main variances have been calculated, the analyst faces a maze of choices about what to investigate, what to explain, and what to highlight:

- Some variances are large, but are actually offset by something else, such as the increased cost of goods sold that may go with higher sales.
- A variance may appear to be small, but underlying it are large offsetting variances that need to be explained.
- In some cases, an expense type is less predictable and may be expected to show large variances, such as major gifts.

In a complicated organization, the analyst needs to select from many small and large variances to construct a story line. Some instincts about the organization are required to lead her to the essentials. Analysts hone and build these instincts through experience within the organization, experience and knowledge of the particular sector (churches, arts organizations, etc.), and outside experience that gives new perspectives on what might be happening.

After finding the main sources of variances from expectations, the analyst must explain why the variance occurred (which may lead to reinterpretations of the significance of variances). If a church is headed toward a deficit because of lower pledges, it needs to know why pledges went down. The trend in pledges or members may come down to nonfinancial things such as degree of satisfaction with worship services, which can only be recognized if the analyst knows the organization well.

If the analyst does not understand the organization well enough to explain all significant results, he must be willing to go to those in the organization with enough operating knowledge to provide this interpretation. Sometimes the operating managers will identify anomalies in the data that require a reassessment of the calculations. For example, a certain category of construction projects may indicate an improvement in the time required for completion. In discussing this result with operating managers—why did this figure improve so much?—it may turn out that the operating department started including some shorter projects in that category, resulting in a change in the mathematical results. In large organizations, central analytical staff rarely will have sufficient knowledge to interpret results without significant input from operating staff.

Again, the analyst must resist the temptation to cut corners. Sometimes she may find it easier not to ask others for help in interpreting information and to go with her own judgment or guess. Working with others takes time, may be frustrating as they ask questions that have already been answered or have trouble understanding the information, may undermine efforts to hold information from others in the organization (for good or bad reasons), and may hurt the analyst's pride to admit that she does not know something. For the sake of the quality of the analysis and to save time later on (when the points missed by the analyst finally emerge), the analyst must talk to the line staff.

11.4 CONCLUSION

The best financial analysis will do more than lay problems at the feet of the organization. It will point toward possible solutions. It may identify options and test their possible impact. It should provide decision makers with the information they need, including what questions to ask and decisions to make, and with data to support the decision. The main point of developing a financial story line is to promote effective decision making. Financial analysis can encourage decision makers to take action by giving them something to go on and can help avoid decisions that absolutely conflict with knowable, objective conditions. Good analysis still leaves decision makers with some uncertainty, but too much uncertainty can lead to paralysis or foolhardiness.

CHAPTER TWELVE

Controlling Costs

12.1 INTRODUCTION

Control is a process through which the management of an organization makes reasonable assurance that resources are used effectively and efficiently to further the organization's mission and plans, financial reporting is reliable, and organizational policies and relevant laws and regulations are followed. Established control procedures provide a means to demonstrate to donors, boards and other external groups that the organization is run properly. The challenge of management control is easiest to see in a large organization—if an organization receives hundred of payments a day or a week at multiple locations, how can the director of that organization make sure all are being properly deposited in the organization's accounts? If an organization employs hundreds of people, how can the director be sure that all of those people are doing what the organization hired them to do?

Internal control is a broad concept that encompasses all of an organization's system, processes, operations, functions and activities. The budget is one important part of the control system. The control system includes many other types of activities, procedures, and policies: e.g., review and reconciliation of financial transactions, physical control of assets, segregation of job duties, and differing levels of authority.

One of the budget's control roles is to influence how the organization spends money. The organization needs to make sure that people do not spend more than it can afford, nor spend funds on inappropriate things. The budget can provide people with guidelines on how much they can spend and on what. With a coherent budgeting system, an organization knows how much money it can spend and when to hold back. It can exercise systematic control over the distribution of resources between parts of the organization or types of expenses. While these broad statements are true, how budgeting controls costs varies significantly under different management models.

12.2 TRADITIONAL MODELS OF BUDGET CONTROL

In the most traditional model, budgets are prescriptive, telling people in the organization at the beginning of the year how much they can spend that year on what types of expenses. When this approach works well, it simplifies financial management. The manager receives a budget at the beginning of the year. As long as he does not go over that amount, he is doing fine. As an organization, the sum of all departmental budgets fits within the organization's income. As long as all managers follow their clear instructions for spending, the organization will do fine as a whole. If a department does go over budget, someone has to take money from another budget to make up the difference and keep the total within its limits. By committing themselves to the spending plan in the budget and to strict policies on budget overruns, the organization's leaders can assure the board that the organization will remain financially stable in the year to come.

An organization that establishes a strict expense budget may do so at a very detailed level, such as the individual object code and account. For example, a unit's budget might have sections for personnel costs and operating expenses, with the operating expense budget divided into the following object codes: telephone charges, photocopies, office supplies, and subscriptions.

Object Code	*Description*	*Budget*
2011	Telephones	$300
2025	Photocopies	$150
2100	Office supplies	$100
2124	Subscriptions	$ 75
	Total	$625

This budget may be based on historical spending patterns, historical budget levels (which may vary greatly from actual spending patterns), or the unit's request. The organization's financial leadership assumes that if the unit has budgeted $75 for subscriptions, that is what it needs for subscriptions. Therefore, the unit is allowed to exceed $75 for this expense type only after submitting a special request to change the budget, preferably by transferring budget dollars from one of the other lines shown here. Under extraordinary conditions, the central finance staff will consider requests to adjust these budgets with funds from outside this manager's budget.

Object Code	*Description*	*Original Budget*	*Adjustment*	*Revised Budget*
2011	Telephones	$300		$300
2025	Photocopies	$150	($15)	$135
2100	Office supplies	$100		$100
2124	Subscriptions	$ 75	$15	$ 90
	Total	$625	$ 0	$625

(a) Problems with Traditional Budget Controls

This approach to budgeting locks the organization into a specific pattern of spending and should encourage thoughtful planning during the development cycle. It also protects the organization from managers who might show no restraint in spending, authorizing purchases far beyond the budget's ability to support them.

This approach will strike some readers as cumbersome and overly restrictive. How can budgets possibly be established with so much precision? Won't managers always need to spend a little less in one category and a little more in another than they predicted? Why put everyone through the paperwork of budget adjustments? Won't the adjustment transactions create the need for reconciling these transactions and rounds of corrections? Won't the managers be tempted to misclassify expenses to put them in lines that have funds available, compromising the accuracy of financial statements?

In the previous example, say that the department found that its photocopier budget was far less than required. If the central finance staff makes budget transfers painful (perhaps by treating the requester as if he were demonstrating gross incompetence in having to make a request, since the budget should have been prepared correctly in the first place), the department may decide to charge $50 in photocopying expenses to object code 2100. If this action were repeated across a large organization, photocopying expenses could be understated by 25 percent, which would cause a problem if the organization wanted to investigate a photocopier management program in which it contracted with a single vendor to provide leased photocopier machines and maintenance. The organization's financial analysis would understate photocopier expenses, perhaps making the vendor proposals look less attractive.

Most organizations find that setting budget limits on the basis of object codes requires too much effort and invites as many problems as it solves. However, there are situations in which this level of budget control is appropriate or inevitable. For example, external funders may agree to a detailed budget and expect spending to follow the agreed distribution of funding. Perhaps finding agencies would be well advised to adopt more flexible spending policies, but strict budgeting allows them to compensate for the difficulty they face in overseeing the groups spending their money. An agency may distribute money to a large number of groups, geographically dispersed, which do not operate under the same roof or under the same management. Still, the agency is held accountable to other groups that provide the funds or oversee their use—boards, donors, legislatures, and so forth—that want assurances the funds are not being misused. Given this difficult oversight assignment, it is not irrational for funding agencies to insist on detail-level budget controls that will mean the same things across organizations. An organization heavily funded by grants may find it easier to adopt this approach for all of its spending.

(b) Higher Level Traditional Controls

Organizations may establish budget controls at a higher level within the chart of accounts, such as by categories that include a number of expense items. Managers can spend over or under on any one item, as long as spending in the expense category as a whole stays within the total budget. In our previous example, the unit could spend up to $625 on operating expenses, but would be free to follow any spending pattern within that category.

Object Code	*Description*	*Budget*	*Actual Spending*	*Variance*
2011	Telephones	$300	$297	$ 3
2025	Photocopies	$150	$105	$45
2100	Office supplies	$100	$125	($25)
2124	Subscriptions	$ 75	$ 98	($23)
	Total	$625	$625	$ 0

This form of budget control is more common and frees organizations from some of the problems of detailed budget controls—it cuts down on budget transfers and reduces the temptation to misclassify expenses. Higher-level controls focus on:

- *Limiting long-term liabilities*. Salary expenses typically involve long-term commitments of the organization's resources, unless it has a practice of maintaining short-term contracts with people. In most cases, an organization that hires someone will feel a commitment to try to keep that person on the payroll. The employment relationship may have legal obligations as well. Therefore, many organizations separate personnel and nonpersonnel budgets, and do not allow managers to transfer budget between them or allow excess personnel spending to be offset by savings in nonpersonnel costs (an implicit budget change!).

- *Shaping patterns of spending*. Although the organization may not want to try to control its managers' spending patterns in detail, it may want to shape broader patterns of spending. Another effect of restricting movement of funds between personnel and other costs is to make sure managers do not succumb to a temptation to add people and find themselves short of necessary operating costs. An organization may also want to plan and control capital expenditures or expenditures on a particular item, such as computer hardware and software. The purpose may be to force these decisions on certain expenditures through a review process, or to control an area in which there is seemingly insatiable demand on the part of managers.

12.3 ALTERNATIVE APPROACHES TO CONTROL

Traditional approaches to cost control through budgets have a number of limitations. These include the tendency to increase administrative burdens through budget adjustment processing and the negotiations that occur as managers look for exceptions to the strict rules. At the bottom, the problems with traditional approaches boil down to the inherent difficulties of enforcing budget discipline on unit managers through central control. As long as unit managers do not feel vested in careful budget management, but instead see the budget process as a set of rules standing between them and effective management of their units, central financial leadership will attain influence and control over their actions only through painful cycles of bureaucratic wrangling.

Traditional budgetary approaches are analogous to quality control in the manufacturing sector. In manufacturing, quality used to be assured by having quality assurance specialists inspect all of the parts at the end of the manufacturing process or at various stages in the process. Once these inspectors identified defects, the parts were sent for rework or were discarded. As long as the inspectors and rework sections did their job, no unacceptable parts went out the factory doors. However, it was found that this process did little to reduce the number of defects during the manufacturing process, and that rework cost a lot. This led to the quality movement, which among other things argued that quality should be built into the process from the very beginning, with workers controlling for quality themselves through process changes, team problem solving, and worker empowerment, not relying on a specialist at the end of the line to find defects. It was much more effective to build quality into the process rather than inspect it in, and for everyone at the plant to feel responsible for quality rather than looking to a small group of inspectors to determine whether parts met standards.

Budgeting practices in the nonprofit sector have taken an analogous turn toward trying to build budget control and fiscal responsibility into the whole financial management process. The organization will spend its resources much more effectively if it can find a way to engage all of its managers and staff in thinking about financial decisions in ways that benefit the organization as a whole as well as the unit, and that are consistent with the organization's goals.

(a) Staff and Management Accountability

The first requirement for an organization that wants to move from a traditional control model is that budget responsibility must be part of the human resources cycle. If a job will have control over budgets, the job description needs to include the budgetary responsibilities, and hiring decisions need to factor in ability to handle budgets. Financial goals for managers need to be clearly stated, they should be discussed and agreed to, and managers should have access to training and advice to help meet those goals. Finally, managers need to understand that their performance will be evaluated in part on budget performance. The organization must show a willingness to reflect strong or poor budget performance in decisions on pay, promotion, and retention. There must be both rewards and consequences associated with budget management.

This level of accountability for budgets stands in contrast to what occurs most typically under traditional control methods. In those systems, managers frequently believe that responsibility for coming in on budget lies with whomever checks their spending against budget funds available. If they happen to go over budget, they will argue that it was the responsibility of the Budget Office or the Comptroller to tell them and cut them off, or to help them find an alternate source. Every time central financial staff take an active role in solving a specific budget dilemma, it gives the impression that they have taken responsibility for that budget. Also, to the extent that trade-offs between object codes or expense categories are difficult, budget managers will not look for responsible trade-offs within their budget. They will have no incentive to optimize their spending, only to follow the budget.

In an environment in which managers understand that budget management forms a key part of their success, and in which financial goals and trends have been discussed openly, analysis during the year is one of the primary means of exercising control. As the year progresses, the organization should have a coordinated program of analyzing budget variances. Large variances need to be investigated and explained, particularly in cases that put expenses on a trend line to exceed budget. Large increases may indicate poor management, or areas for taking specific actions: finding cheaper sources, enforcing reductions in consumption, changing processes, applying technology, consolidating activity.

Midyear variance analysis at the University of Okoboji might show the following results for three of its schools. We will assume that spending and revenues follow an even pattern of distribution through the year, so these units will spend 50% of their budget and receive 50 percent of their revenues by midyear.

	Annual Budget	*6-Month Budget*	*Year to Date*	*Variance*
Arts and Sciences	($6,259)	($3,130)	($3,600)	($470)
Business	$2,361	$1,181	$1,400	$220
Pharmacy	($1,340)	($670)	($650)	$20

These results seem to indicate that the biggest issues lie in Arts and Sciences, with its $470,000 deficit. However, this level of detail does not offer much information about what is really going on. Moving to the next level of variance, we find the following variances by major category:

	Arts and Sciences	*Business*	*Pharmacy*
Revenues	($950)	$233	$400
Faculty salaries	(30)	(60)	5
Other compensation	287	37	(7)
Other expenses	223	10	(379)
Total variance	($470)	$220	$20

At this level, a different story emerges. Arts and Sciences is having trouble, with a real revenue problem, but the school apparently has tried to cut back expenses in other categories. The financial management task from here forward is to look for other ways to reduce current year expenses, and to take actions to avoid a similar revenue shortfall in the future or to make further changes to the expense base.

The second-level variance reveals new issues for investigation, particularly in Pharmacy. While overall the school has stayed within its budget, it had stronger than expected revenues, which would lead managers to expect stronger-than-budget financial performance. Instead, nonsalary expenses have eaten up most of the revenue surplus. At this point, analysis would focus on determining the reasons for the higher-than-expected nonsalary expenses in Pharmacy. They could be related to the increased revenue, such as financial aid or advertising expenses), they could reflect unusual expenses (such as start-up costs for a major new lab), or they could have resulted from sloppy expense control.

(b) Budget Incentives

Moving one step beyond establishing goals and integrating them into human resource practices, an organization can adopt budget rules that encourage managers to find ways to cut costs or generate new revenue. If managers can retain part or all of any savings achieved in one year for use in their unit in future years, they will have incentives to save money in every way possible. A rule that allows units to retain surpluses must be paired with a rule that makes units responsible for making up deficits in future years by cutting costs or increasing revenue to achieve a surplus. The rule on carrying deficits forward provides an incentive to units to generate surpluses and save the funds for the "rainy day" of a deficit year. This type of rule forms a dramatic contrast with most traditional systems, in which funds left over at the end of the year are rolled back into central accounts to either offset deficits in other areas or support the organization's general fund balance.

Such a budget rule, while temporarily holding down spending, appears not to help the organization overall. What good is it to the University of Okoboji if the Business School runs a surplus, which it retains, while Pharmacy runs a deficit? In the short run, the excess cash sits in university accounts, allowing it to cover expenses not supported by revenue in other schools. However, as soon as the Business School decides to start spending that money, the deficit in other areas will come back to haunt the institution as a whole. If the pattern of surpluses in Business and deficits in Pharmacy goes on year after year, it simply perpetuates an imbalance—Pharmacy goes deeper in the hole each year, while Business continues to build up its war chest. Pharmacy will start acting like an impoverished institution, paring salaries to the bone, letting facilities deteriorate, and cutting back services.

In contrast, Business will behave like the wealthy operation it is, paying premium salaries, improving its buildings, setting up strong services operations, and installing state-of-the-art technology. Business's success will build on itself, while Pharmacy will enter a "death spiral" of disinvestment. Before long, the university will close the Pharmacy program.

Some at the university will ask whether efforts should be made to use resources to maintain more consistent quality and service levels, and to maintain a full range of programs. Also, as the Business School builds its surpluses, it will tend to become sloppy in its spending decisions—its success may result simply from strong demand for an MBA, not from any particularly good or bad management decisions. Given these concerns, the rules can be modified and still retain incentives:

- *Partial carry forward.* Units carry forward part of their surplus; the rest is retained by central administration to help other areas. Central administration jointly shoulders responsibility for part of a unit deficit. While the incentive effect is somewhat muted, if the portion retained by the unit is large enough it will still be better for it to hold off on spending than to spend to the last dollar available in order to earn future flexibility.

- *Central contingency.* A large central contingency can be funded from surpluses to allow central administration to bail out struggling areas.

- *Periodic review of allocations.* Fundamental budget allocation patterns between units should be reviewed to balance structural deficits and surpluses between units. This is a politically difficult process, discussed in more depth in Chapter 16.

- *Restrictions on spending surpluses.* The organization may establish rules on how surplus funds can be used to limit the organization's future exposure from temporary windfalls in one area. For example, the organization can prohibit units from spending surplus funds on salaries, which avoids building a set of ongoing obligations on temporary funds. The organization could require that surplus funds be used for capital expenditures, which assures that one-time funds go to one-time expenses and has the advantage of retaining some of the gains achieved on the organization's balance sheet. Spending surplus funds on capital items constitutes a shift on the balance sheet from one asset (cash) to another form of asset (long-term financial instruments, plant, equipment, etc.), rather than immediately depleting the asset by spending it on operating expenses. In the best case financially, the cash will be directed to endowments, where the principal value will be retained. In other cases, the capital item will be depleted through depreciation, but this takes place more slowly, depending on the item. In the meantime, the organization's asset base stays almost as high, boosting its position in financial markets.

- *Central review of expenditures of surpluses.* A more free-form method of exerting central influence over surplus funds is simply to require central review when a unit wants to spend those funds to make sure the decision is financially prudent. This method allows the organization to take any number of factors into consideration. Of course, the lack of clear, simple rules creates uncertainty for unit managers and opens up a potentially protracted political process of negotiations as these requests come forward.
- *Reward below-budget spending in future decisions.* Without allowing units to retain their surpluses, an organization can give them an incentive to save by making it clear that below-budget spending will improve their chances for approval for future requests and will work in their favor in future allocation decisions. A declaration of this policy will have very little effect—this policy may come to life through leadership's actions only, and there is still likely to be debate as to whether it has been enforced. What strikes one person as generous treatment under the budget process will strike another as entirely unresponsive to pressing needs.

Any number of these rules can be adopted, or variations on them. The common purpose is to mobilize the creative energy of all managers, directing them toward cost control and stronger revenues. These rules are combined with rules that focus on personnel decisions rather than transaction decisions to create a system in which cost control is carried on throughout the organization.

12.4 CONCLUSION

Budgeting is an essential part of the financial management control system. Traditionally, this meant that the budget laid out detailed spending limits for managers and staff. Such restrictive systems can have the negative effect of creating extra administrative effort to make even small adjustments and tradeoffs, and may leave managers feeling that the system, not they, exercise control. In response, organizations are moving to new understandings of budgetary control that rely on increased accountability and better alignment of rules and incentives to enlist staff and managers in actively contributing to effective control of financial activity.

CHAPTER THIRTEEN

Deficits and Surpluses

13.1 INTRODUCTION

Much effort and debate in the budget process goes into deciding whether an organization, department, or program is running a surplus or deficit. An organization must know if it lacks the proper resources to cover its expenses or deliver its programs or if additional resources are available. Once a deficit or suplus is identified, the organization must respond.

13.2 DEFINING DEFICITS AND SURPLUSES

On the face of it, the definitions of *deficit* and *surplus* are clear—respectively, spend more money than you bring in; bring in more money than you spend. However, organizations make several distinctions in defining these terms, and then in determining the relevance of the different kinds of surpluses and deficits in the organization's financial management.

Financial managers must distinguish between absolute deficits and surpluses and deficits and surpluses against plan. An absolute surplus or deficit is the simple mathematical definition—when all of the revenues are added and expenses are subtracted, is the result a positive or negative number. It can be calculated for the organization as a whole and for its component units. In many cases, managers will focus more on surpluses and deficits from plan. In this case, the surplus or deficit is measured against the expected results, presumably documented in the budget. An organization may expect to achieve a positive net income of $10,000 in one year. If its net income is $100, it has still achieved an absolute surplus, but has fallen short of plan by $9,900. This gap may be critical to the organization if it had planned on using those funds for future initiatives. The financially strongest organizations are those which have been able to fund future spending from current operations, in the form of cash balances to protect against temporary shortfalls, endowments to provide ongoing, assured support for programs, or capital investments. On a departmental or program basis, achieving the organization's overall plan will depend on some areas producing net surpluses to balance areas that run deficits. On the detail level, deficits against plan can be critical to the organization's overall balance.

Organizations also need to determine which fund groups will be evaluated in defining surpluses and deficits. Many organizations limit their analysis of the overall deficit and surplus to unrestricted funds, leaving aside restricted funds or institutionally designated funds. The restricted and designated funds are analyzed and controlled on a case-by-case basis, since spending in each account is limited to the funds available in that account. It is assumed that only in unrestricted accounts can a deficit in one account be offset by a surplus in another. Some organizations include restricted funds in the analysis of unit balances because units may have the ability to shift expenses to restricted accounts. For example, a university school may have a number of scholarship accounts and a budget of unrestricted funds for scholarships. If it has underspent the income available in a restricted account, it may be able to apply those funds to a student receiving unrestricted scholarship funds. In the case of designated funds, the organization's flexibility is even greater.

Institutionally designated funds have been set aside by the organization for specific purposes, often in very specialized accounts. An example at a university would be research funds set up for professors from a percentage of the indirect cost recoveries associated with grants they received. In the case of extreme financial demands at the institution, current year income to these accounts could be redirected to unrestricted purposes to make up deficits in other sorts of unrestricted revenue.

By analyzing unrestricted and restricted balances together, managers can find sources of relief from the drain on unrestricted funds. Viewing unrestricted funds alone, the University of Okoboji Business School appears to be headed toward a deficit. Stronger revenue is more than offset by deficits in several categories. See Exhibit 13.1.

Adding restricted funds changes the picture. The Business School is running an $80,000 surplus in its restricted funds, giving it overall a deficit projection of only $20,000. Moreover, the source of the restricted funds surplus is in financial aid, an area where unrestricted funds show a deficit. The management of the Business School needs to review its financial aid

Exhibit 13.1 University of Okoboji Business School Projected Results, Unrestricted Funds ($000)

	Unrestricted Budget	*Projected*	*Variance*
Tuition and fees	$15,600	$16,000	$400
Sales and services	375	380	5
Total revenue	15,975	16,380	405
Faculty salaries	6,520	6,805	(285)
Staff salaries	2,627	2,623	4
Benefits	2,287	2,345	(58)
Total compensation	11,433	11,773	(340)
Financial aid	80	150	(70)
Other operating costs	2,100	2,195	(95)
Total expenses	13,613	14,118	(505)
Net surplus/(deficit)	**$2,362**	**$2,262**	**($100)**

decisions for the year and determine whether any of the unrestricted financial aid awards could be replaced with restricted funds. This is likely to be the case. By utilizing all of the restricted funds available, the Business School can significantly mitigate its unrestricted deficit. See Exhibit 13.2.

On an organization-wide basis, leadership must take into consideration different rules on accounting for restricted revenue. In the past, many organizations set restricted revenue equal to expenses, in recognition of the assumption that funds not spent in this period would only be recognized as revenue if an appropriate use were found for them in the future. The funds would be of no practical use to the organization until an expense that matched the fund's purpose came forward. However, Financial Accounting Standards Board (FASB) 117 has required nonprofits to record more restricted funds as revenue at the time of receipt rather than at the time of expenditure, reflecting the flexibility organizations have in matching expenses with the fund's purpose.

13.3 RESPONSES TO SURPLUSES OR DEFICITS

There are four general responses that an organization can make to current year surpluses or deficits.

1. *Make cuts or increase revenues within the current year*. As a deficit (from plan) starts to emerge, the organization can move to cut expenses or look for ways to boost revenue within the current year.

Exhibit 13.2 University of Okoboji Business School Projected Results, All Funds ($000)

	Unrestricted			*Restricted*			*Combined*
	Budget	*Projected*	*Variance*	*Budget*	*Projected*	*Variance*	*Variance*
Tuition and fees	$15,600	$16,000	$400				$400
Sales and services	375	380	5				5
Restricted revenue				700	705	5	5
Total revenue	15,975	16,380	405	700	705	5	410
Faculty salaries	6,520	6,805	(285)	450	450	0	(285)
Staff salaries	2,627	2,623	4				4
Benefits	2,287	2,345	(58)	150	150	0	(58)
Total compensation	11,433	11,773	(340)	600	600	0	(340)
Financial aid	80	150	(70)	100	25	75	5
Other operating costs	2,100	2,195	(95)				(95)
Total expenses	13,613	14,118	(505)	700	625	75	(430)
Net surplus/ (deficit)	$2,362	$2,262	($100)	$0	$80	$80	($20)

This action could take the form of freezing hiring for vacant positions or initiating a special fund-raising appeal to members.

2. *Return surplus funds to cover balances in other areas.* Surplus funds can be returned to the central administration at the end of the year to make up deficits elsewhere. The result might be a year-end purchasing rush as units scramble to spend right up to their budget, whether they are budgeted at a surplus, a deficit, or to break even.

3. *Cover deficits through transfers between funds.* Deficits in one area may be covered by transferring funds from another account that is running a surplus. A department could be forced to perform a transfer from designated funds to make up a current period deficit in its unrestricted budget. In many larger organizations, budget analysts and accountants in the Comptroller's Office work with departments to identify possible sources to cover deficits.

4. *Roll over deficits and surpluses into fund balances to be addressed in future periods.* Surpluses and deficits can be carried forward. Surpluses from one period might be considered to offset deficit spending in future periods, and a deficit might be carried forward with the unit then assigned to "pay it back" by running a comparable surplus in future periods. On an organization-wide basis, the final results generate a positive or negative fund balance. The organization may experience both surplus and deficit years, but an

overall positive fund balance for the organization indicates that its assets exceed its liabilities. The fund balance is analogous to retained earnings on for-profit balance sheets. A positive fund balance is one requirement for an organization to be able to represent itself as being in good financial health. An organization may decide it can accept a deficit in one year because it has enjoyed strong financial results in previous years, giving it the flexibility to take initiatives that may require spending more than it takes in.

13.4 DEFICIT BUDGETS

The phrase *deficit budgeting* may strike the reader as an oxymoron. After all, isn't the purpose of budgeting to ensure that an organization does not run a deficit? The counterargument is that avoiding deficits is a function of financial planning and management that must be viewed over a long-range perspective. The budget is the tool for implementing the long-range financial plan. In an ideal world, every organization will run a surplus every year (let us go further and ask for a *large* surplus every year for good measure). Unfortunately, that is not always possible. Any number of factors may require an organization to dip into resources it has accumulated in the past or to extend beyond its resources to make a place for itself in the future. The critical requirement is that spending and revenue generation take place within the context of a plan for the organization that has a view toward its long-term survival and long-term fulfillment of its programs and mission. While not a crisis, consistent generation of large surpluses without a plan for how they will be used constitutes a management failure. In the most extreme cases, excess surpluses would call into doubt the organization's status as a nonprofit entity. Short of that legal dilemma, managers of a nonprofit organization that runs consistent surpluses face the ethical question of whether they are serving as good stewards of these resources and advancing the organization's eleemosynary purposes.

(a) Reasons for Approving a Deficit Budget

Given the realities of running an organization, its leadership may decide to approve a deficit budget. The legitimate reasons for approving a deficit budget will primarily fall into one of two rationales:

1. The organization needs to embark on major initiatives to put it in a better position for the future. This may include hiring staff for new programs that will build revenue over time. An example would be the initiation of a new three-year degree program. First, the school must hire new staff to design the program. Then, they

are ready to receive the first class. However, the full revenues assumed in the program are not achieved for two more years until they have three full classes in attendance and paying tuition simultaneously. A new nonprofit may need to borrow money to cover initial operating deficits, just like a start-up company in the for-profit sector.

2. Negative financial results require a multiyear response to turn around. On an organization-wide level, this is the most common reason for approving a deficit budget. Many nonprofits have experienced major shifts in their funding in recent years, which has driven them into deficits. In order to climb out of those deficits, many of these organizations have built back their revenue stream, an exercise often requiring multiple years. Building revenue often requires upfront expenditures—an organization may need to embark on an advertising campaign to market its services more aggressively. Restructuring costs can also require time—when cost reduction is a function of adopting new technologies and processes, the technology must be installed and paid for and the processes redesigned before cost savings can be realized. Given the profound restructuring of the nonprofit economy in recent years, organizations may need to run deficits for several years before they can see the effects of their actions on producing surpluses.

(b) Paying for the Deficit

If an organization decides it must run a deficit, it must also have a plan for how it will pay for the spending in excess of revenues. The primary sources are:

- *Cash balances.* If the organization has run surpluses in previous years, it presumably will have cash balances that can make up the difference in current year income. Spending against cash balances must take place in the context of careful cash budgeting, making sure that normal swings in cash balances will not coincide with the deficit draw on cash to exceed cash available. For example, if a church has approved a deficit budget, it needs to be sure that excess expenses will not hit disproportionately during the summer months when pledge receipts are low.
- *Borrowing.* Borrowing can be internal or external and includes special appropriations from funders. External sources include standard bank loans or debt issuance from larger organizations.

Organizations with large asset bases and well-defined sources of future revenue have the option of using those assets as collateral. Borrowing provides new cash to the organization but creates a long-term financial obligation for debt service and interest payments that become an almost permanent part of the expense base, creating a higher hurdle for financial success in the future. Some organizations may be able to receive funding from foundations or donors to get them through, which they must pay back. An organization may be able to make a loan to itself by temporarily drawing funds from endowment, with the requirement that they will be replenished at an internal interest rate that reflects the amount of investment proceeds that would have been returned to principal under the organization's endowment spending policies.

- *Liquidating assets such as investments or real estate.* Unlike borrowing against long-term assets, this response constitutes a permanent conversion of long-term assets into operating funds, with no explicit provision for paying them back. Obviously, the organization cannot liquidate truly restricted funds, except to return them to the donor. However, the organization can liquidate endowment that has been funded from unrestricted resources, or sell off physical property or real estate, and it can reclassify restricted funds as unrestricted funds. While legal, liquidating such assets runs the risk of damaging the organization's long-term financial stability.

In looking at any of the sources of funds to cover deficit budgets, it is clear that the organization must do so only if it has a clear understanding of how the money will be spent and how it will help the organization achieve long-term financial health. Such moves are ill-advised simply to buy the organization time to figure out a financial strategy. If the organization really has no idea how to get out of its financial difficulties, it needs to first concentrate on budget cuts and enhancing revenues. Budget cuts are discussed in Chapter 14.

(c) Dangers of Deficit Budgeting

The dangers of deficit budgeting should be clear, but we will point out the most obvious ones:

- Expected improvements do not occur. Any deficit budget is a gamble. The organization embarks on excess spending based on the prediction that improvements will come, either as a result of this spending or as other factors take effect. In some cases, it may be difficult for the organization to realistically assess the plan's chances for success—wishful thinking may take hold as an option emerges that saves everyone from difficult decisions such as staff reductions. One area of particular caution is in the argument that new technology will result in cost savings that pay for the technology itself and change the organization's expense structure. While there have been examples of this occurring, they usually take place when there is a radical transformation of the entire business through technology, not through marginal administrative changes.

- Debt burden becomes too heavy. While borrowing may allow the organization to take on new initiatives that are critical for its success, borrowing leaves a long-term legacy of financial obligations. If the debt service and interest costs are large enough, they alter the expense structure in such a manner that the original survival plan has to be completely rethought in light of this new expense stream. Debt service and interest payment simply must be incorporated into financial analysis of any strategy or proposal that involves borrowing.

- Endowment is never replenished. When borrowing against unrestricted endowments, the organization has no externally driven requirement to replenish the endowment, only its own knowledge that preserving the level of endowments provides financial assurance for the organization's future. When an organization has drawn funds from endowment, paying them back is a matter of documenting the amount borrowed and the terms and timing of repayment, and maintaining the managerial discipline to stick to this schedule. An organization may be tempted to relax its discipline and let the schedule slip as demands arise for uses of net income other than making good on this internal commitment to rebuild its long-term financial base.

- The organization loses credibility with the board, funders, donors, and the government. Any decision to adopt a deficit budget is likely to be viewed with disfavor by external parties. The stronger and more persuasive the long-term plan, the more these groups will accept the decision. However, the organization will run the risk that the decision to adopt a deficit budget marks it in the eyes of external parties as an organization with weak management and unhealthy finances, which may color future decisions on funding and regulation.

13.5 CONCLUSION

Much of the effort that goes into reviewing and analyzing budgets revolves around the question of whether the budget is on balance, whether a significant surplus or deficit is projected. While the terms *surplus* and *deficit* may seem simple, they are subject to interpretation. Once the surplus or deficit has been defined and identified, an organization may have a number of legitimate options for response. An organization may even choose to budget at a deficit for a limited time, although this strategy carries risks. In the next chapter we discuss budget cutting, not-for-profit organizations' most common response to deficits or the fear of deficits.

CHAPTER FOURTEEN

Budget Cuts

14.1 INTRODUCTION

Budget cutting has become one of the most common and unpleasant jobs of managers in the nonprofit sector. It might seem like an aspect of normal cycles of deficit and surplus, of organizational growth and demise, but in recent years budget cutting seems to have taken on a life of its own. "Doing more with less" is seen as a virtue worth pursuing for its own sake. That assertion is debatable, but waves of budget cutting will likely continue to hit different parts of the nonprofit sector for the foreseeable future.

The toughest issue for not-for-profit organizations is how to reduce the budget without harming the mission. Put differently, budget cutting in this environment usually requires scaling back well-justified activities. Most organizations do not find that they have lots of unjustified spending they can eliminate. This may be due to the inherent prudence and responsibility of the organization and its people, or to skills members of the organization cultivate for developing mission-based explanations for what they do. The lack of easy "targets" requires that the organization's leadership approach budget cutting with care, so as not to harm its capacity to continue to deliver on its mission.

In this chapter we will focus first on some of the technical considerations in budget cutting, and then return to the more difficult decision-making questions.

14.2 REASONS FOR BUDGET CUTS

As a first step in developing a strategy for cutting budgets, the organization needs to understand the reasons driving the cuts. Some of the most common are:

- *Cutbacks by funders and governments.* Government funders will reduce funding as government revenues decline or policies change. A governmental budget deficit is likely to result in reduced funding for nonprofit organizations. At times, funding cuts will be driven more by changes in policy, such as the cutbacks in appropriations to the National Endowment for the Arts that were driven by congressional skepticism about the government's role in funding arts. Foundations and other funders may also cut back funding in the light of poor stock market performance or changes in their program focus.
- *Lower demand for services and the emergence of new providers.* Like any organization offering services in a market environment, a nonprofit organization may experience fluctuations or steady reductions in demand, or find new providers emerging who take market share. In the education marketplace, the demand for admission to degree programs may decline as the number of high school students declines or the economy improves. Nonprofit schools catering to adult students have found new for-profit competitors entering the market, threatening to take students away from the traditional nonprofit provider.
- *Spending not controlled in the face of slower revenue growth.* In a period of slowing revenue, expense growth must be contained to maintain financial equilibrium. This cause for cutbacks reflects the organization's failure to respond to changes in revenue and exercise adequate financial discipline, as opposed to the purely external factors cited above.
- *Price competition.* A nonprofit may find that its prices for services have gotten out of line with the market. A good example is found in health care, where some nonprofit providers have been pushed by lower-cost providers to reduce their prices, forcing them to undergo serious programs of cost reduction.
- *Unusual cost events.* In some cases, singular events may occur that drive up costs independent of the organization's ability to raise more revenue. An example of such a watershed event was the oil crisis of the 1970s, which resulted in large increases in energy costs for institutions and arguably drove up inflation for other costs as

well. Such events can force organizations to realign costs and revenues across the board.

14.3 DETERMINING THE SIZE OF CUTS

Once an organization has determined that cost reductions are required, it needs to determine the extent of the cuts. The size of the cuts may be mandated, in the case of government agencies, or may be determined through some sort of financial modeling. Financial modeling may take a relatively informal form, such as the organization's leaders reviewing projections or actual programs that show a deficit and deciding what portion of the gap they will make up from revenue increases and cost reductions. In most cases, more formal financial modeling is advised to take into account timing effects and the combination effect of different factors. The types of financial models described in Chapter 8 can be invaluable in testing the effect of budget cuts on regaining financial equilibrium.

For example, if positions are held vacant, the effect will build over time as the vacancies actually occur. An organization with 10% turnover will not experience cost savings of 10 percent in the first year of a freeze—it is more likely to see savings of around 5% if vacancies are evenly distributed throughout the year. In its second year of the freeze (discussed as an example only, since hiring freezes can seldom be maintained that long), the organization would have a reduction of about 15 percent in salary costs from the baseline year.

In assessing the financial effect of this hiring freeze, modeling would be used to factor in the offsetting effect of salary increases for the positions that remain filled. Combining a wage freeze with a hiring freeze might hobble the organization as it asks employees to do more while their wages shrink in real terms. In that case, the organization would want to give a minimal 3% raise. The net one-year savings from the hiring freeze would then be about 2.15 percent. Salary costs are just one aspect of the overall organizational financial equation that would need to be analyzed, and additional interaction and offsetting effects would be encountered.

Combined Effect of 3% Increase and Salary Freeze	
Base wages	$100,000
3% increase	$3,000
New wage base	$103,000
5% savings from freeze	$5,150
Projected annual salary cost	$97,850
Net savings	2.15%

In the example in Chapter 13 (Exhibit 13.1) the University of Okoboji's Business School experienced its single largest negative variance in faculty salaries, while staff salaries were essentially in balance. To illustrate the timing effects of a hiring freeze, we will switch these results and locate the variance within the staff salaries line. See Exhibit 14.1.

If the Business School has 10% staff turnover, not filling vacancies might make up the gap in that line—after all, 10% of $2,627,000 is about $263,000, just about the size of the variance! The problem with that conclusion comes clear when you lay out the results for staff salaries on a month-by-month basis. Exhibit 14.2 shows the data and projections that were assumed for the projection of $2.9 million. If vacancies had been offset by hires throughout the year, the Business School would have hit its budget. However, hires have exceeded new vacances, resulting in increasing costs. In the example shown below, each month the cost of new hires exceeds the savings from new vacancies by about $3,750. This excess cost continues for each subsequent month. Each month, the monthly cost of salaries exceeds the budget by an additional multiple of this gap. By the end of the year, the monthly gap has grown to $43,000, and the cumulative impact reaches the projected variance of approximately $285,000.

If the Business School initiates a hiring freeze in January, it will be relieved of the additional cost of new hires. Assuming the rate of vacancies continues at the same pace, as positions come vacant in the second half of the year, the monthly gap falls. However, since the rate of vacancies was less than the rate of new hires, it reduces the gap at a slower rate than it was built up. Also, it does not reverse the excess spending

Exhibit 14.1 University of Okoboji Business School Projected Results, Unrestricted Funds ($000s)

	Unrestricted Budget	*Projected*	*Variance*
Tuition and fees	$15,600	$16,000	$400
Sales and services	375	380	5
Restricted revenue			
Total revenue	15,975	16,380	405
Faculty salaries	6,520	6,516	4
Staff salaries	2,627	2,912	(285)
Benefits	2,287	2,345	(58)
Total compensation	11,433	11,773	(340)
Financial aid	80	150	(70)
Other operating costs	2,100	2,195	(95)
Total expenses	13,613	14,118	(505)
Net surplus/(deficit)	$2,362	$2,262	($100)

Exhibit 14.2 University of Okoboji Business School Staff Salaries Results and Projection

	Actual						Projected						Total
	July	*Aug*	*Sept*	*Oct*	*Nov*	*Dec*	*Jan*	*Feb*	*Mar*	*Apr*	*May*	*June*	
Previous month salaries	$218,917	$222,672	$226,397	$230,090	$233,753	$237,385	$240,987	$244,558	$248,100	$251,613	$255,096	$258,550	
Salary savings from new vacancies	(1,824)	(1,856)	(1,887)	(1,917)	(1,948)	(1,978)	(2,008)	(2,038)	(2,068)	(2,097)	(2,126)	(2,155)	
Salaries for staff new this month	5,580	5,580	5,580	5,580	5,580	5,580	5,580	5,580	5,580	5,580	5,580	5,580	
Total salaries	222,672	226,397	230,090	233,753	237,385	240,987	244,558	248,100	251,613	255,096	258,550	261,976	
Monthly gap, hires over vacancies (gap from previous month continues to next)	3,756	7,480	11,173	14,836	18,468	22,070	25,642	29,184	32,696	36,179	39,634	43,059	284,177
Projection based on starting salary level	$2,627,000												
Projection based on changes through 6 mos												$2,911,177	

that occurred—that can only be offset by running monthly costs that actually dip below the monthly budget. The result is that the negative variance is reduced significantly, from $285,000 to $169,000, but not eliminated. (See Exhibit 14.3.)

While this example was constructed to show the effects that timing and interaction of factors have on reducing the impact of cost cutting strategies, the Business School may decide that this would be a successful strategy. The Business School and the university may decide that reducing the deficit in staff salaries to $169,000 will suffice—along with it will come some savings in benefits costs, and the lower deficit in this compensation category does appear to bring the school's overall budget projection back into balance, thanks to the good news in tuition receipts. On the other hand, the university may want, as a matter of policy, not to go over budget in staff salaries and not to use excess tuition receipts to subsidize additional staff costs.

14.4 TYPES OF BUDGET CUTTING APPROACHES

Once a goal has been set, responses will tend to fall into three categories:

1. Across the board
2. Targeted
3. Process or technology driven

(a) Across-the-Board Cuts

Across-the-board cuts are in some ways the easiest to administer. The primary analytical effort rests in determining the amount to cut. For a government agency or institution, the percent may have been legislatively mandated. In other cases, the organization needs to determine the percentage for itself. Finance staff will need to conduct analysis and modeling to determine the optimal reduction, and leadership will need to exercise its judgment in determining the degree of reduction that is feasible. When an organization makes across-the-board cuts, the percentage is usually set and then managers are asked to develop proposals for achieving the cuts in their areas. This gives them the flexibility to take the cuts where they will do the least damage to their operations. If their budgets contain any slack, managers will identify these areas and cut them first.

The organization may decide to consider multiple levels of reduction proposals, asking for budget reduction proposals at the levels of 10 percent, 20 percent, and 30 percent. This process allows leadership to evaluate the degree of cut that can be sustained in light of the disruption to

Exhibit 14.3 University of Okoboji Business School Staff Salaries Results and Projection (with Hiring Freeze)

	Actual						*Projected*						*Total*
	July	*Aug*	*Sept*	*Oct*	*Nov*	*Dec*	*Jan*	*Feb*	*Mar*	*Apr*	*May*	*June*	
Previous month salaries	$218,917	$222,672	$226,397	$230,090	$233,753	$237,385	$240,987	$238,978	$236,987	$235,012	$233,054	$231,111	
Salary savings from new vacancies	(1,824)	(1,856)	(1,887)	(1,917)	(1,948)	(1,978)	(2,008)	(1,991)	(1,975)	(1,958)	(1,942)	(1,926)	
Salaries for staff new this month	5,580	5,580	5,580	5,580	5,580	5,580							
Total salaries	222,672	226,397	230,090	233,753	237,385	240,987	238,978	236,987	235,012	233,054	231,111	229,185	
Monthly gap, hires over vacancies (gap from previous month continues to next)	3,756	7,480	11,173	14,836	18,468	22,070	20,062	18,070	16,095	14,137	12,195	10,269	168,611
Projection based on starting salary level	$2,627,000												
Projection based on changes through 6 mos												2,795,611	

programs and services. If leaders cannot accept higher levels of cuts, they may renew their efforts to increase revenues to respond to the financial problem.

Across-the-board cuts have "surface" fairness, but they are indiscriminate. They do not account for differences in units' ability to absorb cuts, in their starting level of budget flexibility. Therefore, the organization may choose to pursue targeted cuts in which it identifies the best opportunities to reduce budgets.

(b) Targeted Cuts

Targeted cuts can be identified and chosen by leadership itself, or through a participative process. Leadership may make the cuts by deciding at a senior level where cuts can occur to achieve the required reduction. Each officer might offer to cut certain things in his area. A more participative process involves more managers in identifying opportunities to reduce budgets.

Targeted cuts will start with a search for excess funding that may have been used in the past but is not entirely necessary to maintain programs and services at a minimally acceptable level. Units will also look for places in which they can hold positions vacant without undue disruption to services. Targeted cuts may extend to higher-impact decisions such as ending certain services, closing programs, or cutting back on support services. Such strong cost-cutting moves will tend to bring larger reductions in costs but will come at a higher cost in organizational morale and external relations. Therefore, it is crucial that these decisions be consistent with the organization's core strategies and with the interests of the key clients, customers, or constituencies.

A participative approach to targeted cuts may require more cooperation and voluntary sacrifice than managers can muster. In that case, leadership may choose a select group of staff or may hire consultants to try to find these opportunities for cost reduction.

Although somewhat more extreme than most of the examples cited so far, an organization that needs to significantly reduce costs may decide that it needs to do more than that, that in fact it needs to undergo a major restructuring. This would involve reevaluating the services it offers, reassessing how many departments and managers it should have, taking a fresh look at how many and what kinds of staff it has, and developing fundamentally new models for such things as the use of technology in its operations and service delivery. An organization may decide it must restructure if it determines that its financial problems are due to major changes in its service delivery arena. Perhaps the populations it serves has changed, or new options for serving those needs have emerged. Once an organization decides it needs to restructure, it has definitively moved from the realm of budgeting to that of strategic planning.

(c) Process or Technology-Driven Cuts

One way to target cuts is to link them to process or technology changes. In this approach, the organization's staff and/or consultants analyze processes to identify ways to change procedures or apply technology that will reduce the work required. Once processes are changed and technology is installed, positions and other costs can be eliminated.

This strategy usually will not produce net savings in the short run—the changes usually require time to implement—suggesting that an organization may adopt deficit budgets as it goes down this path. Also, this strategy may involve a shift from operating costs to capital as new technology is acquired. Capital costs will not immediately hit the operating statement as a drain on net income, since for accounting purposes they are treated as a transfer of assets from one asset category to another, but they may strain the organization's cash balances. Also, the long-term costs of the capital investment, in terms of depreciation, replacement, and ongoing support, must be evaluated against the realistic savings projected in other cost categories. However, process or technology changes have the potential to produce substantive changes in the way an organization does business which can result in structural, sustainable reductions in cost. By contrast, organizations that implement across-the-board cuts often find that the costs return quickly after the sense of crisis and the period of intervention start to lift.

(d) Cost Cutting and Budget Cutting

Cutting budgets and cutting costs are not the same thing. Cutting the budget gives the organization a plan for lower spending, but achieving this plan requires discipline in specific decisions on hiring and buying made throughout the year. An organization with a strong culture of taking budgets seriously and managing to budget will find that reducing budgets results in lower spending by managers. However, it may be necessary to adopt additional policies and procedures in order to enforce lower spending in keeping with the reduced budget. These may include a freeze on filling vacancies and the establishment of a review process for exceptions. In any situation in which managers are required to achieve budgeted cost reductions, budget performance must be incorporated in a rigorous performance evaluation system that reinforces the need to achieve specified financial goals.

14.5 MAKING DECISIONS ON BUDGET CUTTING

Organizations have several kinds of options for cutting budgets, but they still must decide how much to try to cut, over what time frame, and choose an approach. First, the organization's leaders need to have a clear understanding of the nature of their deficit.

- *Is it a cash deficit, an operating deficit, or both?* The organization's full operating statement may show a deficit, but most operating statements will include non–cash items such as depreciation. A non–cash deficit is a serious matter, because the organization is not generating the resources to replenish itself, but the negative effects may play out over a longer time frame, giving it more time to develop a response.
- *How strong are cash balances?* Deficits pose a much more immediate threat to an organization with low cash balances, leaving it with much less room for error in assessing the situation and developing the response.

Once the organization understands these basic facts about its deficit, its leaders need to consider the following factors in making the decisions about how to cut budgets and costs. First, they must consider:

- *Existing budget rules.* Certain budgeting systems include explicit or implicit rules about how to handle budget deficits. If the organization has adopted a Responsibility Center model (see Chapter 16), in most cases the managers of units which have run deficits will have the responsibility for reversing those deficits within their own unit's finances. An organization may have an understanding that once certain budget resources have been allocated to units for the year, they will not be taken back mid-year—therefore midyear adjustments must come from resources over which the central administration retains control. A deficit can get bad enough that an organization must suspend its rules due to the extreme exigency of the situation. In that case, it is critical that leadership acknowledge that it is suspending or changing the rules and be prepared to explain what about the situation is so severe as to justify this strong response.

Within the context of these budget rules (or a period of exigency that requires a suspension or change in rules), leadership needs to consider the following issues:

- *Time available for achieving a change in results.* Does the organization need to avoid a deficit in the current period, try to come up with a balanced budget for next year, or develop a multi–year recovery strategy? Financial considerations such as the size of cash balances can drive this decision, but organizational policies or politics can play an equally important role. The board may not accept deficits, or leaders may find that tolerating deficits sends the wrong message to the organization.

- *Risk tolerance.* Some strategies for cutting budgets and costs carry more risk. Investing money in technology in order to bring about major changes in the cost structure runs the risk that the cost savings returns will not equal the investment. A major organizational restructuring to reduce positions runs the risk of disrupting programs. Holding reductions to a minimum while trying to boost revenues runs the risk that the revenues will not materialize. The organization's tolerance for riskier responses is a function of the organization's culture, its resources, and the potential for positive changes in the future.

- *Dependence on and impact on external groups.* The organization also needs to assess the ways in which reductions could influence their relations with external groups, such as clients, donors or volunteers. Will cuts in certain services disadvantage the organization relative to other groups that could serve the same client base, thereby reducing its ability to win funding for its programs? Would cuts in certain services or programs inconvenience or put off significant numbers of volunteers who would then start giving their time to other organizations? Are other entities poised to pick up clients, donors or volunteers if the organization falters?

- *Quality of information.* Does the organization understand the sources of its deficits, and does it understand costs well enough to identify areas which might be better places to cut or which it can restructure through process and technology changes? The information can include how well it has articulated goals and strategies, and whether those strategies have been linked to operating activities in a way that allows the organization to make differential judgments about how activities and cost areas contribute to achieving those goals.

- *Quality of managers.* Do the managers understand their operations and costs well enough to help assess costs, do they have the good judgment to make recommendations that have the optimal impact on costs without undercutting programs and the organization, and do they have the skill to implement major changes? If leaders do not trust their managers, or do not trust them consistently, it will be hard to adopt a program that pushes much of the decision-making about budget cuts back onto the managers. Some recovery strategies, such as implementing major process change in a way that reduces staff levels, require significant management skill to pull off.

- *Trust levels within the organization.* Are the members of the organization well-aligned around a common vision of the organization and its situation? Do they work well together and support each other? Has leadership succeeded in establishing communications within the organization? Trust may need to extend to board members, donors and volunteers as well. The trust levels in the organization may determine its ability to accept differential cuts, or for some units to sacrifice resources on behalf of the whole. Establishing trust is a matter of behavior as well as communications—leaders need to behave in ways that inspire trust. For example, if leaders ask for some units to bear the brunt of budget cuts, they must make sure they chose those cuts based on legitimate operating considerations, and did not inflict cuts on managers or units which had fallen out of favor for one reason or the other.
- *Political clout of leadership within the organization.* Does leadership have the ability to align people behind a course of action and to convince them to accept some moves which may be unpopular or distasteful? When an organization needs to cut budgets, it often does not have the time to wait for consensus to develop behind a response. The organization's leaders may need to use political influence within the organization to get people to go along with something. If leaders do not have the political skills or weight, they may need to avoid strategies which require higher levels of participation and collaboration from people throughout the organization.

Based on their answers to these questions, leadership should develop its approach to cutting budgets. In an organization with low trust levels and relatively poor information, the best approach may be across-the-board cuts. Although it has the potential for more sustained impact, relying on process or technology changes is somewhat riskier, so it may be a better choice for an organization which has a longer timeline for its recovery, resources for investment, and management talent for implementation.

14.6 COMMUNICATING BUDGET CUTS

In addition to deciding how much to cut and what approach to take, the organization's leaders need to determine how to communicate their actions to the rest of the organization. Once people start to hear about budget cuts, they start to worry about their own jobs, programs and clients and about their friends in the organization. Morale may decrease and distractions increase. For these reasons leadership may want to keep its budget-cutting activity quiet. This may be a good idea, especially if their actions can be discrete and have minimal impact on members of the organization, such as negotiating better rates when contracts come up for renewal or changing expenditure patterns out of central funds.

However, in most cases leadership cannot insulate members of the organization from budget and cost cutting. Therefore, they must say something about the reasons for taking action and about what will happen. Each organization will need to make its own judgment about the amount of information shared and the tone of it. It may not be appropriate or useful for leadership to share everything it knows about its cost trends, although some information about its specific expectations can be useful. The organization also needs to decide whether to describe its situation in terms of a crisis, or to soft-peddle it. Some writers on organizational change have argued that an organization will change only if the people in it share a sense of crisis and can mobilize themselves to respond to it, as a nation does in time of war. However, in some situations the sense of crisis can get exaggerated beyond the true scope of the situation, and distract people unduly from the organization's normal business. One way of looking at the decision about tone of the communications is to ask whether this a situation in which the organization needs everyone to drop what they are doing, roll up their shirt sleeves, and help dig out of this mess, or is this a case in which people should know that the organization is facing some difficulties, but leadership is working on it and is confident that they can respond with minimal disruption, so people should just keep doing what they are doing and be prepared to help out when they are asked.

In communicating about budget cuts, leadership needs to keep in mind a few points:

- Assume that everyone is looking for one piece of information within everything said—will I lose my job? This means that everything said by or on behalf of the organization and leadership will be scrutinized very closely, hunting for implicit clues that suggest the extent of layoffs or that jobs will be guaranteed or protected. This means that if a dollar savings target is announced, some people will divide that by what they believe is the average salary to come up with the number of positions they think will be eliminated, even if there is no intention to cut positions. On the other hand, an announcement that the organization expects to achieve cost reductions through attrition may be taken as a guarantee of no layoffs.

- Keep the messages clear. People can exercise selective hearing during this process. If leadership tries to make an overly nuanced pronouncement on the budget cutting process, the nuance may be missed and people may hear a more discouraging or encouraging message than was intended. If leadership has decided to try to place everyone who wants one in a new job, but wants to retain the right to offer a lower salary for the new position, they need to be careful not to say something that is interpreted as a guarantee that no one will lose their job and everything that goes with it—responsibilities, pay, etc. On the other hand, in this case one would want to be careful not to suggest that the organization is going to cut pay rates if that is not the case.

- Be careful what you promise. People will remember the statements leaders make. The organization should be sure it won't have to lay off people before anyone makes a statement that rules out layoffs or some other painful move. Once the statement has been made, it either limits the actions the organization can take or forces leaders to forget about the earlier statement (usually people in the organization don't allow these statements to be forgotten) or to recant it, exacerbating the negative effects on morale and trust.

- You won't make everyone happy and can't control everyone's interpretation of events. Periods of budget cutting are difficult times, and after making a good effort to communicate effectively, management has to accept that some people in the organization will be angry and will not accept the organization's "party line." Leaders will move forward in spite of these sorts of difficulties, although they will do what they can to reduce them. Communicating during a period of organizational stress is not easy.

Many organizations find it useful to adopt a formal communications plan early on in such a painful process. This plan would specify the audiences for communications, the information they should receive, and the timing and vehicles for communicating to them. Certain messages need to come directly from the organization's leader, others can come from more immediate supervisors. Often an organization needs both face-to-face communication of information and formal documents that record and disseminate key elements of the analysis, process and response. The organization should assess the need for messages to outside groups, including in some cases the local media. An organization which has a significant profile within its community may find that the media start to pick up news of its internal actions, and may need to take action to educate the media about what it is doing.

14.7 CONCLUSION

Due to a variety of factors ranging from changes in government policy and funding to demographic and cultural shifts, budget cutting has become a major and seemingly permanent fixture in the management of not-for-profit organizations. Once an organization decides it needs to cut its costs, leadership first has to determine the size of the cuts it needs, and then choose approaches for achieving those reductions. The best approach for a particular organization depends on its leadership's interpretation of a set of issues related to the organization's finances, management, culture, and environment. Ultimately, the best approach is that one that an organization's leaders think they can make work. In addition to identifying the size and timing of cuts and the most likely workable approach, leaders must take care to communicate with the members of the organization about the need, the process, and the impacts of budget and cost cutting.

CHAPTER FIFTEEN

Planning and Managing Human Resources

15.1 INTRODUCTION

As we pointed out in Chapter 5, salaries and benefits constitute a majority of the costs in most organizations. While decisions about an organization's human resources costs may be expressed in terms of finances, in important ways the decisions about the human resource budget really concern the fundamentals of running the organization:

1. On a high level, human resources budgeting takes place within the context of an implicit or explicit human resources plan which identifies how the organization will get its work done.
2. On a more detailed level, the human resources budget comes from an accretion of decisions about specific salaries for specific individuals. Setting individual pay rates is one of the most important ways in which a manager can influence individuals' performance.

In these apparently financial considerations—how much to spend on staff and how much to pay individuals—operating decisions loom large.

15.2 HUMAN RESOURCES PLANNING

Human resources planning is a formal process of projecting the need for different types of labor based on projected activity and program levels and patterns of attrition. Not many nonprofit organizations do formal human resources planning, but some do it informally or under a different name, and many others would be well advised to address their human resources needs more systematically.

A formal human resources plan lays out how many people will be on the payroll in future periods, what they will do, how much they will get paid, and how many hires or promotions will be required. The human resources planning task is clear when a program or organization is starting up. The plan will show how many people will be needed to start the program and the timing of additions to the staff. Very often the organization or program will be required to present at least the initial staffing levels to whomever it asks for funds. An organization may start with a director who designs the programs and facilities and hires staff as needed or as funding becomes available. Even if program growth depends on service demand or funding, the board should have an idea of how big it thinks the organization will get and how quickly.

One of the first human resources questions a new organization will face is the degree to which it will use paid staff members as opposed to relying on volunteer effort. Many small organizations start with primarily volunteer staffing and then move to paid staffing over time. Eventually most organizations find volunteers cannot make a long-term time commitment to the organization. Sooner or later, demands from jobs or family encroach on the time a volunteer can give. Volunteers come and go as their interest in the organization changes, new priorities emerge, or they move away. They may show a preference for some activities and less interest in other, maybe more mundane activities (such as reconciling bank accounts, staying late to clean up after an event, or filing tax returns). Eventually the organization's activity levels may outstrip what it can handle with volunteers.

In deciding to add paid staff, the organization's board needs to decide what level of staffing it can support with reliable revenues and what activities it most needs paid staff to perform. This analysis leads to a decision on the number and level of staff: Is an executive director needed to take over management of the organization, a bookkeeper to pay bills, or a secretary to answer phones and handle correspondence? Are full-time or part-time services required from these people? It costs less to hire someone part-time, but part-time employees are less likely to take on new responsibilities; the organization will tend to occupy a more secondary place in the priorities of a part-time employee.

The organization also needs to assess whether it has staffing needs that can be accommodated with temporary employees or independent contractors rather than permanent employees. The Arts Council hires artists working as independent contractors to deliver educational programs.[1] Its commitment to pay them extends only for the length of the program and will not exceed the grant funds that support this program.

In addition to deciding how many people to add, human resources planning requires decisions about compensation strategy. The organization needs to decide whether it will use pay as a way of attracting and retaining staff, or rely on other factors such as institutional loyalty or dedication to a cause.

Any organization, even a long-established one with stable programs, should think about its future staffing needs. If recruitment for staff takes a long time, as it does for university faculty, the organization needs to anticipate when it will need to replace staff who leave for other jobs or retirement. Staffing in some organizations will fluctuate directly with demand for services, so human resources planning is an integral part of revenue/expense planning.

Human resources planning can also be directed at changing the nature of the workforce to achieve objectives other than simple growth. An organization that wants to improve the diversity of its workforce needs to evaluate its current staff demographics, set goals, determine appropriate hiring strategies, and develop realistic timetables based on funding, rates of hiring, labor markets, and so forth. Organizations may also use human resources planning to alter the skill or experience mix of its workforce to change its position in the markets it serves. A university that wants to be perceived as a higher-quality institution on a national level may decide that it needs to add some high-profile senior faculty. It will need to plan which areas will get the "star" faculty, how the school will fund the hires, and the timing.

15.3 COMPENSATION STRATEGY

Once staffing levels have been determined, the organization must set rates of pay. Pay rates may be based on labor markets, equity within the organization, ability to pay, or some combination of these factors. Salary increases will be based on the same factors, plus job performance.

[1]Independent contractor is an employment status defined by the Internal Revenue Service, which has issued a series of questions that determine whether a person should be treated as an employee for tax and benefits purposes. Independent contractors are not just part-time or temporary workers—they generally provide a service to the organization whch they also offer to other clients, do not operate under the direct supervision of the organization's staff, set their own hours, and use their own equipment. Independent contractors are responsible for paying their own taxes to the IRS, whereas the organization is responsible for withholding all taxes from its employees. When in doubt, an organization is safer to treat the people it pays as employees.

(a) Labor Markets

A nonprofit organization offers its staff rewards other than compensation, such as the feeling that they have made a positive contribution to society. However, organizations can only depend on those sources of motivation up to a point and have to base their pay rates on labor markets. Different labor markets will be relevant for different positions. An organization may recruit from a national pool to find a director or a highly specialized professional. Other positions will draw from regional labor markets, and most support positions will be filled from a local labor market.

Organizations can assess market rates by reviewing salary survey data that they collect by calling other organizations or that they purchase from firms that issue salary surveys. More informal methods include asking board members what their companies pay for comparable positions.

Assessing market salaries is complicated by several factors. An organization needs to select the right comparisons. Not only will salaries vary according to the overall cost of living in an area and the area's wage scales, but some organizations will pursue policies of paying the top dollar or holding wages down. An organization that simply has a better capability of paying high wages may not be a great basis for comparison. Also, an organization needs to look at starting salaries, median or average salaries, and maximum salaries for a job, if this information is available. Some organizations may pay higher starting salaries but raise salaries more slowly. The organization needs to decide what strategy and position to take.

An organization that collects data from several sources—some published surveys, some direct calls—could end up with the following data for its assessment of rates for physical therapists. In addition to surveys published by the local hospital association and a survey conducted by a national compensation consulting firm, the organization calls several hospitals in the region with comparable operations that are not included in the surveys.

Source	*Range Minimum*	*Range Maximum*	*Average Starting Salary*	*Median Salary*
Local hospital association	$26,000	$52,000	$27,000	$35,000
Consultants' annual survey, regional results	$30,000	$54,000	$34,000	$46,000
Hospital 1	$29,000	$45,000	n.a.	$36,000
Hospital 2	$35,000	$57,000	n.a.	n.a.
Hospital 3	$32,000	$57,000	$33,000	$48,000
Organization's own rate	$30,500	$44,500	$30,500	$42,000

These results raise a number of questions. While the organization exceeds the minimum salaries in the surveys, it lags two of the hospitals it chose for direct comparisons, and its average starting salary is also low relative to the consultants' survey. Of course, this comparison is more difficult because two of the hospitals were not willing to share these data. One potential issue with the surveys will be the rate or pattern of nonresponse to certain questions. The results for starting salaries may be based on a smaller response base than the less sensitive information on classification range minimums and maximums.

These data also encourage questions as to whether the organization should focus on its starting salaries or the rate it pays people already on staff, which may require changing the pay ranges. One guide will be what management perceives is the greater problem—hiring or retaining people. In an active labor market, the answer may be both.

These data might be easier to interpret if they showed the organization seriously out of line with some part of the market. As it is, the organization generally appears to be in range with the market, and therefore must make more subtle judgments about the strength of its position.

(b) Equity Within the Organization

If the organization already has some staff and is adding positions, it needs to consider whether the pay rate for a new position will seem fair to current staff. Even if labor markets suggest paying a premium for a new position, current staff may feel that the importance of their job or their seniority merits a similar premium. The organization will need to consider adjusting all salaries or settling for a lesser candidate in order to maintain morale. While it is important to maintain confidentiality about salaries, creating salary inequities and then relying on keeping the staff from knowing each other's salaries is dangerous because this information tends to get out.

Equity is assessed by analyzing pay rates within the organization, job requirements, and seniority of incumbents. Large organizations will have compensation systems in place that quantitatively rate jobs. Small organizations will rely more on their managers' judgment to establish equitable relationships, or may be able to get assistance from external consultants.

(c) Ability to Pay

The organization's financial strength will put some limits on what it can pay people. Organizations with more money tend to pay more. In large organizations, it is common for some units to pay more than others because they generate more income, even though the organization may resist or deny it. At universities, schools of medicine, law, and business tend to pay all of their staff more because they have (or have had in the past) strong sources of revenue from clinical billings, tuition, and rich alumni.

Ability to pay is determined through analysis of the organization's financial condition. Organizational financial models can be very helpful in allowing management to test alternative levels of pay and assess its long-term ability to sustain these levels.

Organizations should exercise caution in committing to starting rates of pay and in making pay increases. Once a salary level is set, it is difficult and seldom reasonable to cut it. In periods of financial crisis, the organization may ask employees to accept a wage cut, but this is an extraordinary measure. Generally, employees should not bear the brunt of the organization's financial problems. Asking employees to skip a paycheck also pushes the financial problem into employees' personal lives, guarantees that people will start looking for new jobs, and creates a financial obligation that will have to be made up in the future. Board members need to remember that they may be personally liable for the organization's financial obligations.

Many organizations respond to economic downturns by holding positions vacant. This provides some budget relief, but the work performed by the position usually does not go away. It gets shifted to remaining employees, to volunteers, or into a backlog, creating a pent-up demand to fill the position and building the risk that a critical task will not get performed. Pushing work to remaining employees can have the same detrimental effect on retention and morale as a wage cut. Employees may see it as tantamount to a paycut if they feel they are performing two jobs for the price of one.

Organizations will reduce or forego salary increases in times of financial hardship. The impact on staff morale and retention depends on the organization's success in communicating its reasons for holding salaries back, the sense that the organization is doing everything it can to respond to the crisis (and did not bring it on through mismanagement), and the general economic climate. When the general economic climate is bad, staff may feel satisfied to have job security if they see their friends and neighbors suffering layoffs.

Compensation consists of fringe benefits as well as salaries, and organizations need to determine where benefits fit into their compensation strategy. Fringe benefits include health insurance coverage, retirement plans, life insurance, tuition benefits, and other services that an organization buys for its employees. In many cases, employees will have expectations about the kinds and levels of benefits coverage they should receive based on what they can get elsewhere.

15.4 INDIVIDUAL SALARIES

Given the proportion of organizational budgets that go to compensation costs, organizations will often budget these costs separately and in greater detail. The personnel budget is typically based on the salary for each approved position. In addition, costs for temporaries or contract employees are budgeted, and benefit costs are projected separately based on assumptions about participation rates, utilization, and external pricing.

The base personnel budget will include positions that are filled and vacant but approved positions. The filled positions usually show the actual salary of the incumbent, where vacant positions may show the salary for the last incumbent, the minimum starting wage for the position, or some other figure. The actual salary is not likely to be determined until the position is filled (with the exception of government agencies and other organizations with rigid salary structures that specify a single pay rate for all positions in a classification or grade).

Position Number	*Title*	*Name*	*Salary*
001	Director	Mary Brant	$56,250
052	Associate director	Russell Lee	38,000
032	Administrative assistant	Vacant	19,500
115	Database administrator	Andre Derain	19,200
047	Instructor	Clara Lemlich	28,000
098	Instructor (part-time)	Fred Ho	10,000
Total salaries			$170,950

As we have stated elsewhere, budgets are not the same as costs. Vacant positions do not cost the organization. They may lead to spending on temporaries, or payments to other staff for overtime or extra service. However, it is likely that the department will not spend every dollar of salaries for the positions shown above. Thus, there may be some flexibility to spend in other ways. Organizations that have extremely tight budgets may count on the savings from vacancies and may add a line to reflect that:

Position Number	*Title*	*Name*	*Salary*
001	Director	Mary Brant	$56,250
052	Associate director	Russell Lee	38,000
032	Administrative assistant	Vacant	19,500
115	Database administrator	Andre Derain	19,200
047	Instructor	Clara Lemlich	28,000
098	Instructor (part-time)	Fred Ho	10,000
Total salaries			170,950
Budgeted salary savings (10%)			(17,095)
Total salary budget			$153,855

Whether the organization insists on budgeting anticipated savings from salaries, managers will be aware that some flexibility is likely to come from this source.

When organizations are able to give pay increases, they will often express the increase in terms of a rate of increase on current salaries (as opposed to simply announcing a dollar amount available for increases). The increase may be applied across the board to all positions or all currently filled positions. Other methods leave the decision on allocating increases to managers, or ask them to make proposals that are reviewed centrally. A typical method of applying the increase is to calculate an increase pool for a department and ask managers to decide how to allocate it to employees. In the example above, the increase pool is based on 3 percent of the salary for all filled positions:

Position Number	*Title*	*Name*	*Salary*	*Increase Dollars*
001	Director	Mary Brant	$56,250	$1,688
052	Associate director	Russell Lee	38,000	1,140
032	Administrative assistant	Vacant	19,500	
115	Database administrator	Andre Derain	19,200	576
047	Instructor	Clara Lemlich	28,000	840
098	Instructor (part-time)	Fred Ho	10,000	300
Total			$170,950	$4,544

The manager is asked to make a proposal to allocate the $4,544 pool between the current staff. Organizations asking that the increase proposals reflect performance may request documentation of performance evaluations to accompany increase proposals. The manager makes the following wage proposal:

Position Number	*Title*	*Name*	*Salary*	*Increase Dollars*	*Proposed Salary*
001	Director	Mary Brant	$56,250	$1,250	$57,500
052	Associate director	Russell Lee	38,000	1,294	39,294
032	Administrative assistant	Vacant	19,500		19,500
115	Database administrator	Andre Derain	19,200	0	19,200
047	Instructor	Clara Lemlich	28,000	2,000	30,000
098	Instructor (part-time)	Fred Ho	10,000	0	10,000
Total			170,950	4,544	175,494
Total pool					175,494
Check					$0

The budget manager decided that two employees, the associate director and the full-time instructor, should receive increases higher than the guideline (3.4% and 7.1%, respectively) in recognition of their performance or to bring them in line with the market. Performance problems with the database administrator led to a decision to make no increase, and the manager decided it was not necessary to adjust the salary of the part-time instructor.

Central staff should review proposals to make sure they comply with guidelines. Typically they are reviewed at several levels before the final salaries are approved (often one of the last events in the budget cycle). The approved proposals are compiled to create the final personnel budgets, employees receive notification of their new salaries, and the new salaries must be entered into the payroll system so that employee paychecks will be calculated at the correct rate on the effective date.

15.5 MEASURING AND REWARDING PERFORMANCE

In the examples in the previous section, the manager decided to give some of the staff higher increases than others based on performance. These differential increases should recognize the behaviors, actions and outcomes that best serve the organization. An obvious question is how did the manager reach these decisions—how did she decide which behaviors, actions and outcomes deserved reward, and how did she measure what had occurred? If the basis for this decision is not clear, then the manager's decisions will be questioned and are more likely to produce resentment and bad morale and diminish performance overall rather than encourage improvement.

For these reasons, if an organization is going to realize the motivational potential of compensation decisions, it must have a coherent performance measurement and reward process in place.

Performance evaluation systems can take many forms. Basic elements of a good system are as follows:

- Clear decisions should be made on what will be evaluated. Organizations can evaluate performance on the basis of achieving specific goals or objectives, outcome or output measures, qualitative assessments, skills as demonstrated in the workplace or tests, and combinations of these factors.
- Evaluation criteria should reward performance that is congruent with organizational goals.
- Performance should be measured in ways that are verifiable, not totally dependent on the evaluator's subjective judgment.
- The basis for the evaluation system must be communicated to those being evaluated.
- Those making evaluations should have some oversight or training to make sure they are performing evaluations consistently with the organization's program.
- Performance assessments should be communicated to employees, giving them an opportunity to discuss the evaluation.
- Programs should be in place to correct performance problems and provide employees with training and other resources to improve performance.
- Performance evaluations should be documented in a consistent manner that can be accessed at a later date if disputes arise.

The system also needs to specify how performance will be rewarded:

- The extent to which pay decisions will be based on performance. Some systems combine an across-the-board increase given to all or most staff with an additional performance–based increment given to the best performers. Others base the entire increase on performance.
- The linkage between pay levels and increases and the results of performance evaluation. Some organizations may specify rates of increase for specific scores on an evaluation system; others will leave the decisions on pay for individuals to the manager's judgement.
- How performance–based pay will be structured. The most common choice is between delivering performance-based pay as a bonus or as an increase to the employee's salary base. Typically a

bonus is delivered as a one-time lump sum payment that does get carried forward in the person's salary in future years. Bonuses can seem like a bigger reward, coming in one large payment, and they can give employers flexibility—if an employee's performance drops, the employer is not locked into paying them at higher rates. Employees may prefer increases to their salary base because it contributes to a sustained increase in their means, which they can count on in planning their household finances.

Rewards can take forms other than pay increases. In designing a performance evaluation system, organizations need to consider including other factors as part of the reward structure:

- Increased responsibilities or promotions
- Improved resources for the manager's department
- Bonuses
- Nonfinancial recognition programs, such as awards or special events

15.6 CONCLUSION

All through this book we have argued that budgeting is a tool for general management of the organization, not just financial management. Nowhere is this clearer than in human resources. As an organization thinks in the long–term about its human resources costs, it must evaluate how it expects to get its work done, who it needs to have available to do that work, and thoroughly assess the role of the human factor in its operations. When the organization moves from setting total compensation budget pools to allocating salary dollars to individuals, it becomes apparent how well or poorly those salary dollars reinforce individual performance. The return on salary dollars comes from the organization's success in investing those dollars in specific people.

PART FOUR

Trends in Budgeting

CHAPTER SIXTEEN

Reallocation Systems (Zero-Based Budgeting and Activity-Based Budgeting)

16.1 INTRODUCTION

Several difficult questions lurk behind any discussion of budget methodology:

- How does an organization know it has a reasonable allocation of resources between units and programs?
- How does it establish the correct amounts?
- When should it take steps to readjust budgets?

To some extent, reallocation can be addressed in any budget review process—as leaders review budget proposals in comparison to actual financial results, staffing levels, and activity levels, they may decide that some units can afford to take a cut to provide more funds for a unit that clearly struggles to find enough resources. This situation is particularly likely to occur in a small organization in which budget decision making is concentrated in the hands of one person or a small number of people. For example, the executive director of the Arts Council each year may make some shifts in resources between programs. If people associated with one of those programs—say the editor of the council newspaper—disagree with the executive director, they can speak with her. Responsibility for the budget and the overall financial health of the organization rests squarely with this executive director. On a small scale, this is a highly centralized budget process.

Such ad hoc reallocation decisions are much more difficult in larger organizations for technical and political reasons. Every person in the organization will have a different assessment of the criticality of a particular activity, and many will have evidence to support their position. It is very difficult for central leadership to make a technical judgment on the comparative worth of one activity over another. Also, the possible trade-offs become very complicated—the solution set rarely boils down to binary choices such as either funding an activity in Arts and Sciences or an alternative in Student Services, but involves almost infinite combinations. The activities in Arts and Sciences and Student Services could be funded by trading them off against activities in other units or within their own units.

Given the technical difficulty of reallocation decisions, those who lose in this process will protest strongly. They will feel that their valid program concerns fell victim to an arbitrary decision on the part of leadership. Each reallocation decision will leave another manager feeling misused and disenfranchised, looking for ways to beat the budget process the next time.

In spite of these difficulties, organizations sometimes find they must reassess the fundamental allocation of resources within the organization. Two related techniques have emerged that provide a systematic means to achieve this goal. Zero-based budgeting and activity-based budgeting are both designed in the belief that to achieve major restructuring of budgets, an organization needs a system that it can explain to everyone in the organization and that subjects everyone to the same rules.

16.2 ZERO-BASED BUDGETING

Zero-based budgeting (ZBB) has both a general meaning and an application to a very specific system of budgeting. In general terms, zero-based budgeting is quite simple: It occurs whenever an organization builds up a budget from scratch, identifying each activity or position that must be funded. In its more specific definition, zero-based budgeting refers to a system for budgeting large organizations developed in the 1970s.

The phrase *zero-based budgeting* emerged in the 1970s, referring to a budgeting approach developed in private industry (and quickly applied to government and nonprofits) that required each part of the organization to identify its major activities, determine their criticality to the organization's mission, and describe the activity at several possible levels of funding and the implications of not funding the activity. In ZBB, a unit makes its budget request by preparing "decision packages" for each activity it undertakes. Funding decisions are made on an activity-by-activity basis.

An Admissions Office at a university might have five activities for which it would request funding:

Activity 1. Promote program.

Activity 2. Recruit and interview.

Activity 3. Process applications.

Activity 4. Make decisions and communicate with applicants.

Activity 5. Administer office and conduct research.

Each of these activities might correspond with different groups of staff in the office, or with major parts of their jobs. Activity 1 is the primary responsibility of a publications specialist, supported by clerical staff and external mailing services. Activity 2 corresponds with the activities of the office's admissions counselors, and so forth.

A sample decision package form for a university is shown in Exhibit 16.1. The decision package for each activity is developed at several funding levels, often three. The activity and department are named, and a budget for that activity at that level is filled out. The activity in general is described and the department identifies the results for each cost element. For example, under "consulting and services" the department might indicate it needs funding for program advertising to ensure the necessary level of applications. Volume indicators and outcome measurements are identified for the activity as a whole so that the funding decision will be linked to specific measurable outcomes. The volume of activity and expected outcome measurement results presumably will vary at different funding levels. The department also describes alternatives to the proposed activity, arguments for retaining it, and the consequences of dropping it.

The department is asked to rank order each level of all of its decision packages, indicating the single activity and funding level it considers most important. If a department's request consists of five activities, its ranking of activities might be as follows (with Level 3 corresponding with the highest level of funding for an activity, Level 1 with the lowest):

	Level 1	*Level 2*	*Level 3*
Activity 1	13	1	8
Activity 2	10	4	7
Activity 3	11	3	6
Activity 4	12	2	9
Activity 5	15	5	14

Exhibit 16.1 Decision Package Form

<table>
<tr><td colspan="2">Decision Package</td><td colspan="2">Level of ______</td><td>Rank: ______</td></tr>
<tr><td>Activity:</td><td colspan="4">Department:
Ranking of other levels:</td></tr>
<tr><td>Desired results:</td><td>Resources Required/Earned</td><td>Current Year Budget</td><td>Budget Year This Level</td><td>Budget Year Increase/Decrease</td></tr>
<tr><td></td><td>Revenue</td><td>$</td><td></td><td></td></tr>
<tr><td></td><td>Number of faculty</td><td></td><td></td><td></td></tr>
<tr><td></td><td>Faculty salaries</td><td>$</td><td></td><td></td></tr>
<tr><td></td><td>Number of staff</td><td></td><td></td><td></td></tr>
<tr><td></td><td>Staff salaries</td><td>$</td><td></td><td></td></tr>
<tr><td></td><td>Benefits</td><td>$</td><td></td><td></td></tr>
<tr><td></td><td>Consulting and services</td><td>$</td><td></td><td></td></tr>
<tr><td></td><td>Supplies and equipment</td><td>$</td><td></td><td></td></tr>
<tr><td></td><td>Computer hardware and software</td><td>$</td><td></td><td></td></tr>
<tr><td></td><td>Other expenses</td><td>$</td><td></td><td></td></tr>
<tr><td></td><td>Total</td><td>$</td><td>$</td><td></td></tr>
<tr><td colspan="5">Description of activity:</td></tr>
<tr><td colspan="5">Volume of activity:</td></tr>
<tr><td colspan="5">Outcome measurement:</td></tr>
<tr><td colspan="5">Alternatives to achieve same or partial results:</td></tr>
<tr><td colspan="5">Advantages of retaining activity:</td></tr>
<tr><td colspan="5">Consequences if activity is eliminated:</td></tr>
<tr><td>Prepared by:</td><td>Date:</td><td colspan="2">Approved:</td><td>Date:</td></tr>
</table>

In this case, the manager has given the highest priority to retaining current funding levels (Level 2) for all activities, and then has given various priorities to increases.

The decision packages with their rankings would be forwarded to the next level of review, where they would be compared with packages from other departments and ranked against each other. This process is repeated until it reaches an organization-wide level, in which all funding requests are assessed against each other. The organization now has a budget in which the funding for each activity has been set in light of its criticality to the organization and its need for funding. Alternatives have been considered, and outcome measurements are in place to determine whether the activity delivers its promised return on investment. Managers may not like the funding decisions, but they can see more of the rationale behind the decisions and where their request fell in relation to all other requests.

While theoretically sound, zero-based budgeting proved unwieldy to administer. Some organizations tried it for a few years and then returned to a more incremental approach. Many organizations who engaged in ZBB report that it was a useful exercise, helping them understand their budgets and activities better, and helping them realign funding levels.

Zero-based budgeting can be done in a less involved way that saves the administrative costs but may lose some of the sense of objectivity that it strives to project. In times of organizational change, tight finances, or mission redefinition, the organization's leaders will need to review budget allocations. One approach is to assign central staff and/or consultants to review budgets and activity levels and return with proposals on optimal budget and staffing levels. An organization may want to do a budget scrub, to identify budget lines that have consistently been underspent or positions that have been held vacant to offset expenses in other areas. One department may consistently come in under budget while another always runs a deficit—this could be due to good management in one area and bad management in the other, but it could be that one manager has budget flexibility the other lacks. The organization may want to increase the structurally underfunded budgets by transferring funds from better-funded budgets or central funds so that all managers face the same challenges in meeting their budgets. Using a more participative style, leadership could ask departments to prepare a full analysis and justification of their budgets that in a less formal manner hits the issues ZBB addresses and allows everyone to get a better understanding of what is funded and whether some reallocations may be in order.

16.3 ACTIVITY-BASED BUDGETING

In recent years, industry has started to move to activity-based budgeting, which grows out of activity-based costing (ABC) and bears similarities to zero-based budgeting. Many companies and some nonprofit organizations have engaged in activity-based costing exercises to understand the relationship between activities, costs, and outputs. In the for-profit sector, ABC has been used to gain a better understanding of the full costs and therefore profitability of products. Activity-based costing determines the full cost of each individual activity by surveying staff on how they allocate their effort between activities, which is particularly enlightening in the case of support staff, who may split their time between processing purchase requests, distributing mail, handling time sheets, and many other activities. Once the full cost of each activity has been calculated, drivers can be established that link support activities to the primary activities of the organization—in a manufacturing environment, they would be the direct costs of production; in the non-profit sector the primary activities would be the direct costs of program delivery. The full cost of each product or program can then be calculated and related to an outcome measure—units sold, units produced, clients served, and so forth.

Organizations use the cost data derived from ABC to assess the full efficiency of different parts of the organization, to identify places to cut, and to establish a cost baseline that may be influenced through process or technology changes that reduce effort requirements for an activity. Activity-based costing can also be used as the foundation of an activity-based budgeting (ABB) system. Under ABB, budgets for support costs within program departments and within central departments are based on standards of consumption of support services. Standards can be a function of activity driver relationships or overall cost structure:

- Activity-based costing analysis may determine that it takes one FTE (full-time equivalent) of effort to handle 500 purchasing transactions a year. Therefore, units that have 500 purchasing transactions would receive approval for one purchasing support person. Those with fewer transactions would have to combine the purchasing support role with other activities, or receive support for purchasing from another department.
- The analysis of staff effort may indicate that total administrative support salaries—purchasing, budgeting and accounting, human resources, and so on—within a department are on average 30% of the salaries for direct program delivery personnel. Departments might thus receive approval for support costs only up to 30% of direct salary costs.

Activity-based costing generally starts with a survey of staff effort. In some systems, all staff members respond to the surveys, others rely on a sample, and some draw their data from supervisor assessments. Each approach has its advantages. Also, the data may be collected through a paper survey, e-mail responses, or in interviews. These approaches yield a set of data with each employee's time allocated on a percentage basis to a predefined set of activities (see Exhibit 16.2). These percentage allocations can then be extended to project costs for each activity, either by linking the responses to the employees' actual salaries or by applying average salaries.

Exhibit 16.2 Determining Percentage Allocations

	Employee 1	*Employee 2*	*Employee 3*	*Employee 4*
Activity	*Secretary*	*Database Administrator*	*Counselor*	*Director*
Service delivery				
Promote services			10%	15%
Counsel clients			50	20
Conduct training			35	10
Purchasing				
Select items		5		5
Process purchases	10			
Finance				
Prepare grant request			5	15
Prepare budget	10			10
Reconcile monthly transactions	10			
Analyze results and do projections	5			10
Human resources				
Hire staff				5
Process payroll	5			
Conduct evaluations/performance management				10
Systems				
Design and purchase systems		10		
Generate reports		20		
Perform routine maintenance		5		
Support users		40		
Create applications		20		
Office support				
Answer phones	20			
Filing	15			
Schedule meetings and conferences	25			
Total	100%	100%	100%	100%

The data give the organization an idea of where it expends effort. The data in Exhibit 16.2 can be converted into FTEs for each activity or group, or can be expressed as a percentage of all effort in the department:

Area	*FTE*	*Percent*
Service delivery	1.4	35%
Purchasing	.2	5
Finance	.65	16
Human Resources	.2	5
Systems	.95	24
Office Support	.6	15
Total	4.00	100%

If these data are to be used for budgeting, the FTE figures must be converted to dollars to reflect the fact that 10% of the secretary's time costs less than 10% of the director's time. Summarizing the activity percentages in the first table above and multiplying them by each staff member's salary, the cost of each employee's effort is allocated in Exhibit 16.3.

On a percentage basis, the department allocates its budget as follows by area of activity:

Area	*Dollars*	*Percent of Budget*
Service delivery	$54,450	40%
Purchasing	6,100	4.5
Finance	23,050	16.9
Human resources	7,850	5.8
Systems	31,350	23.1
Office support	13,200	9.7
Total	$136,000	100%

The percentages indicated by these results might be compared to organization-wide data for setting the budget. Perhaps across the organization systems support constitutes on average 10 percent of departmental budgets. One conclusion for this department would be that the department should not have its own systems support person, but should share that position with another department. Of course, the department might take another approach and argue that the time spent developing applications or some other part of the database administrator's time is really direct service delivery, and might argue for reclassifying some of the hours and increasing the position's focus on those activities. Even if this argu-

Exhibit 16.3 Determining Dollar Value of Allocations

	Employee 1	*Employee 2*	*Employee 3*	*Employee 4*	
	Secretary	*Database Administrator*	*Counselor*	*Director*	*Total*
Salary	$22,000	$33,000	$36,000	$45,000	$136,000
Service			34,200	20,250	54,450
Purchasing	2,200	1,650		2,250	6,100
Finance	5,500		1,800	15,750	23,050
Human resources	1,100			6,750	7,850
Systems		31,350			31,350
Office support	$13,200				$13,200

ment for looking at the database administrator from a different angle carries the day, the ABC analysis may have served to keep the position focused on delivering service to clients rather than spending too much of the budget on maintaining the department.

16.4 CONCLUSION

Reallocating funds between units in a way that comes across as fair and is readily accepted by budget managers is probably one of the most difficult things to try to do in the budget process. As an organization changes, it is likely to reach a point where it cannot avoid the difficult issue of reallocation. Some organizations will feel that their environment is changing so rapidly that the allocation of resources within the organization should be subject to constant review. In such cases, an organization may want to adopt a formal system to conduct this review and make the inevitably politically charged decisions. Experience with these systems has found them to be somewhat cumbersome to administer, although an activity-based system that is integrated with an organization-wide use of activity-based costing holds some promise.

CHAPTER SEVENTEEN

Responsibility Center Management and Budgeting

17.1 INTRODUCTION

One of the most significant trends in budgeting for nonprofit organizations has been the move toward responsibility center budgeting (RCB). Under an RCB system, an organization divides itself into responsibility centers, each of which has a budget and a single manager assigned to managing that budget. The manager is accountable for meeting the financial target reflected in the responsibility center's budget. The manager is granted a great deal of freedom to make decisions on the use of resources within the responsibility center, as long as the goal is met.

This system has gained popularity as nonprofit organizations have struggled to find ways to align expenses and revenues in light of continued cost pressure and disruptions in traditional funding sources. Responsibility center management harnesses managers' knowledge and creativity to engage them in helping the organization find solutions to its financial problems.

17.2 DESIGNATING RESPONSIBILITY CENTERS

Responsibility center budgeting starts by defining responsibility centers. Responsibility centers include all of the activities and units that make up discrete programmatic areas and are controlled by one manager (possibly indirectly through other managers that report to him or her). It is important that the responsibility center include activities that the manager actually can control.

The best way to understand some of the issues in defining responsibility centers is through an example. A university might have the following activities or units:

- College of Arts and Sciences
- Undergraduate honors program
- Student computer labs
- Human resources
- Bookstore
- Controller
- Art museum
- Associate provost for research
- Vice president of administration
- President

In designating the responsibility center run by the dean of Arts and Sciences, the university includes the honors program and student computer labs with the Arts and Sciences responsibility center because these programs are integral aspects of the undergraduate program. The dean of Arts and Sciences may need to make trade-off decisions between Arts and Sciences, honors, and the computer labs when it comes to computer purchases.

While the bookstore, controller, and human resources all report to the vice president for administration, the university decides to establish the bookstore as a separate responsibility center. It often does better than its target, and the university wants to be able to share those gains across the campus. If the bookstore is grouped with the controller and human resources, those units will absorb gains from the bookstore's auxiliary operations.

The university faces some issues in assigning the art museum. Technically, only vice presidents report directly to the president, so the art museum, which has a small budget, is nominally assigned to the provost's office, and within the provost's office it has ended up in the portfolio of the associate provost for research. However, the director of the art museum has traditionally operated very independently. If the art museum is included in the responsibility center assigned to the associate provost, the associate provost will have difficulty exercising control over budgets in that area and will be resisted if she attempts to move funds from the art museum elsewhere in her responsibility center. The university wants to set up the art museum as an independent responsibility center, but there are too many small units. Therefore, the art museum is assigned to the president's office responsibility center, which is managed by the president's executive assistant.

17.3 DEFINING RESPONSIBILITY CENTER FINANCES

Once the organization has defined its responsibility centers, it needs to identify all of the direct revenues and costs associated with them. Responsibility centers may either be profit centers or cost centers. Profit centers generate income as well as expend costs. Their financial statements consist of revenue and expenses that yield a net income bottom line. The term *profit center* implies that such a unit will always be expected to generate more revenue than its spends. While overall the organization does need its revenue-generating units to produce surpluses to support those units that do not earn income directly, profit centers include units that produce some revenue but not enough to cover all of their expenses. The critical distinction is that a unit with a substantial source of revenue can manage both the revenue and expense sides of its budget to meet a net position target: If expenses are trending upward, the unit can either cut back on spending or try to boost revenues. The manager of this unit has more options and must be capable of more sophisticated analysis and projection.

Cost centers are units that generate no or little income and must be supported by income from other units or from the organization's general funds. In most cases, the key financial task of managers of these units will be to keep spending within their total budget. Cost centers can be turned into profit centers by creating internal recharge mechanisms in which the cost centers "sell" their services to profit centers through transfer pricing.

In establishing responsibility centers, the organization must make sure it has associated all costs with the right units. Some of these associations are obvious—the salaries for faculty and staff in Arts and Sciences become part of the A&S responsibility center. Other costs require more investigation to get them properly assigned. There may be staff funded centrally that serve a unit—that budget base should either be transferred to the responsibility center manager or the staff members should be reassigned. Some costs may have been pooled. A scholarship fund that has supported students in several schools needs to be split between schools so that each will get charged for the support that goes to its students. Some costs may require allocation formulas. The tuition for undeclared undergraduates needs to be allocated somehow between all schools that teach undergraduates, and Arts and Sciences should get credit for core liberal arts classes it delivers to students in other schools. Also, the organization will likely want to assign certain restricted funds to the managers of the programs supported by those funds so that the managers can make full use of restricted funds to relieve unrestricted funds wherever possible.

Once all of the direct costs have been associated with the right responsibility centers, the organization can establish financial targets. A critical decision for an organization moving to a responsibility center system will be whether it wants to establish break-even bottom goals for all profit-center responsibility centers by allocating all of the costs for administrative cost centers to those units. This process has the advantage of showing the full cost of providing each service or program and making explicit the requirement that revenue-generating units bring in enough income to support the organization's administrative and support requirements. Allocating costs requires that the organization come up with an allocation methodology. Methods for allocating overhead have been discussed in Chapter 5. The same issues apply here, including the decision as to the level of detail and specificity in calculating each unit's fair share.

Alternatively, organizations can choose not to allocate administrative costs, but can establish net income or contribution targets for revenue-generating units, and can establish deficit targets for administrative units. A unit will be targeted to hit a positive or deficit bottom line—all that matters is the variance from that target. The effect is the same as it would be if break-even budgets were created for all units through allocations. A negative variance is a negative variance. This method has the advantage of limiting a responsibility center's budget to those things the manager truly controls and avoiding the effort and cost of assigning administrative costs. Its disadvantages are that different revenue-generating units will have different contribution margin targets and some may feel they are being held to higher standards. Also, managers may be tempted to assume any surplus result is good performance, even if it falls short of the contribution expected and required by the organization.

As budgets are constructed for responsibility centers, central staff will need to put in place mechanisms for capturing and reporting data in the new structure. The accounting system may have a field that allows the organization to roll up any combination of accounts it chooses. Multiple levels of responsibility may complicate the reporting—for example, one vice president has several responsibility centers, or a responsibility center manager wants to subdivide the center into subsidiary centers. Some accounts may need to be restructured, such as an account for funds that supported multiple areas. Also, the accounting system may not be able to reflect allocations of shared staff costs or revenues. For any number of reasons, central staff may need to implement new methods of generating the required reports. These methods will range from spreadsheets containing data pulled from the accounting system to specialized analysis and reporting tools purchased to support the new system.

17.4 PERFORMANCE AGAINST TARGET

Managers who do better than their target in one year carry that surplus forward (or some part of it) into the future for spending or to cover deficits. Managers who do worse than their target carry the deficit forward as an IOU to the institution and must find ways to make up the deficit with surpluses. Carrying forward surpluses and deficits is a crucial element of RCB, because it is this feature which gives managers their strongest positive and negative incentives to manage the organization's finances prudently.

The ability to spend surpluses in future periods or the responsibility to cover deficits may be modified and may still have the desired effect. An organization may restrict the responsibility center manager from spending surpluses (which are one-time funds) on certain expenses, such as salaries, which are an ongoing obligation. Managers may be required to invest surpluses in endowments or other long-term assets to ensure that strong financial performance brings lasting benefits to the unit and the organization.

Responsibility center managers do not exercise complete freedom in their spending decisions within their unit. They must conform to all organizational policies on spending and accounting. They will be subject to any organizational policies on appointments. At a university, a school will still have to get provost and board approval for faculty appointments. Central offices retain responsibility for establishing and enforcing institution-wide policies and practices.

Responsibility center budgeting encourages managers to look for creative ways to make the most efficient use of resources and to maximize revenue. Managers finally have incentives to do the following:

- Develop new programs and exploit new revenue sources. Many traditional budgeting systems did not give program managers responsibility or credit for the revenues associated with their programs. Therefore, they had little incentive to try to develop new programs or think about ways to maximize revenue.
- Consolidate staff positions. Many traditional systems budget personnel on a position by position basis. If a unit ends a position, it loses those funds, even though units often find that they could get the job done less expensively with only one position if they could pay that position more.

- Reduce expenditures. Traditional systems include the "use it or lose it" provision in which funds unspent at the end of the year are returned to central administration. Thus, fiscal year-end shopping sprees occur as managers frantically try to spend their remaining money. A great effort in up-to-the-second tracking of account balances is required to know how much is left, an end-of-the-year crush of transactions occurs, and this situation often leads to irrational purchase decisions. An office may have a closet full of supplies that were purchased to use up funds. When managers can carry forward funds, their incentive to rush through purchases is greatly reduced and they gain an incentive to look for cost savings throughout the year.

- Maximize use of restricted funds. Traditional systems often managed restricted funds completely separately from unrestricted funds, assuming that they had purposes completely independent of the activity supported by unrestricted funds. Current thinking about restricted funds recognizes that managers usually have much more leeway in interpreting the purposes of gifts and can often find many expenditures that would satisfy the gifts' conditions.

17.5 CONTROL AND MANAGEMENT CONSIDERATIONS

(a) Supporting RCB

Responsibility center budgeting delegates much of the financial control to the responsibility center managers. Overall control on spending levels is reinforced by the incentives to spend at or better than target. Effective control requires more than the incentives in carrying forward surpluses and deficits. It is supported through:

- *Hiring.* Responsibility center managers must be chosen on the basis of an ability to understand and manage finances as well as other technical and managerial qualifications that may be relevant to the particular position. They must indicate a willingness to take financial management and policies seriously, and an understanding of the organization's financial situation and goals. It may also be necessary for the administrative offices of the responsibility center to include support staff who can assist the manager in handling the units' financial decisions and data. One approach taken by some organizations is to assign a staff member from central offices, such as Purchasing, the Controller, or Human Resources, to each responsibility center to support the manager, or to require that some support staff in these units report jointly to central offices.

- *Training.* Responsibility center managers and their staff need to receive training in financial management and in the organization's finance and accounting procedures and policies. An organization may want to give a unit responsibility center status only after its staff has gone through a training program certifying that they understand policies and procedures.
- *Communications.* Central finance staff must communicate with responsibility centers on the organization's financial concerns, and vehicles must be established to allow responsibility centers to communicate concerns, events, or trends in their units to central staff. Central staff may rely on responsibility center staff to conduct some of the financial analysis throughout the year in their areas, but this process must be coordinated so that the organization's leaders and board can continue to monitor overall financial performance.
- *Evaluation.* Performance against the budget target will constitute a significant factor in evaluating the performance of managers. The organization faces the danger that in spite of the incentives to come in below budget, managers will pay little attention to financial management and let other units or central administration bail them out. Failure to meet a target may also result from factors outside of a manager's control. The evaluation process should consider the responsibility center manager's compliance with spending and other policies—managers may be tempted to cut corners procedurally if the consequences will be felt by the organization as a whole and not by the unit itself. The performance evaluation must address whether the manager has made an adequate effort to manage finances, and it should reward those who take the task seriously (as well as those who experience good bottom line results).
- *Reappointment.* Failure to effectively manage the responsibility center budget should lead to a manager's removal from that role, which can take the form of termination or reassignment. An organization that retains a manager who persists in ignoring financial management will lose the credibility of its RCB program.

(b) Requirements for RCB

Responsibility center management is a very attractive option for organizations that are looking for a strategy to respond to a tough economic situation. Success with this approach requires:

- *Competent managers.* The responsibility center budgeting (RCB) approach assumes that managers have good ideas for maximizing revenue, saving money, and providing services. If this is not the case, the organization gains nothing from moving to RCB and only incurs risk. However, it can easily be argued that those skills are inherent aspects of managerial competency. If the organization's leaders feel nervous about delegating financial responsibility to the managers they have hired, they should hold off on RCB but should also think very seriously about how they choose managers.

- *Good data and reports.* Managers and central staff must have reports and data that allow them to see the responsibility center's finances and allow them to work from the same sources. The organization's accounting system may not be up to this task if the financial activity related to a responsibility center is split between too many accounts that do not roll up easily into a single report. The organization may need to create separate spreadsheets or templates for bringing the right data together, or may need to develop or purchase new software tools.

- *Shared planning.* Responsibility center managers and central staff and leadership need to work together in the planning process so that reasonable targets can be set that lead to overall financial equilibrium and so that initiatives taken by responsibility centers remain consistent with institutional strategies and goals.

- *Spending policies.* As already discussed, organizational policies must be clearly defined and documented so that responsibility centers can easily obtain guidance on how to stay within those policies. Mistakes within a responsibility center can create problems for the organization as whole.

- *Linkage between financial results and evaluation, pay, and appointment.* RCB requires that the organization establish a link between budget performance and evaluation, pay and appointment. The organization will need to decide how much weight to give financial performance—the more weight finances receive, the more attention they will get. One can go overboard and emphasize the budget to detriment of program delivery. The organization also needs to define financial performance in light of the total environment—if managers cannot totally control outcomes, they should get some credit for effort.

17.6 CONCLUSION

In recent years, more and more organizations have moved to some version of responsibility center management. In many cases, the responsibility center budgeting systems replace highly centralized systems in which central offices or leaders make discrete appropriations to departments by extense category. These traditional systems were criticized for fostering a sense of dependency and entitlement among managers, leaving them unaware of and uninterested in the organization's overall financial situation. Responsibility center budgeting gives managers more responsibility, accountability, and incentives for managing every aspect of their department or program's finances. Organizations that move to these systems hope to engage all of their managers in helping to create solutions for financial issues. In exchange, central staff and leadership may surrender some of their immediate control over decisions at an operating level, arguably to devote more attention to higher-level management decisions that ought to receive their focus.

PART FIVE

Tools

CHAPTER EIGHTEEN

Documents and Statements

18.1 INTRODUCTION

Each stage of the budget process requires forms to convey and collect information. Each organization will design these forms to fit its own processes and systems. Some will use electronic formats rather than paper. In this chapter, we provide examples of the typical forms and reports used in each stage of the budget process. Although the format may vary greatly between organizations, in most cases an organization requires some form or report that fills the function of the samples presented in this chapter.

18.2 BUDGET PREPARATION

If departmental budgets are based on previous years' budgets, central administration will need to issue statements of the starting budget base for each department. Departments can review the figures and raise questions if they disagree with the calculation of the budget base.

Often the budget base is integrated into a form that provides space for entry of the proposed budget. This form may include other information such as the previous year's actuals or current year-to-date results. See Exhibit 18.1. Many organizations issue subsidiary forms to collect proposals for salary increases and requests for capital, equipment, and other special expenditures. See Exhibits 18.2 and 18.3.

Exhibit 18.1 University of Okoboji Budget Proposal Worksheet

Account number	1-22100				
Name	MBA Program				
Manager	Alice Stewart				
Address	312 Baker				
Date generated	11/19/xx				
Description	Object Code	Current Budget	Guideline	Proposal	Comments
Fall tuition	1000	5,000,000	5,250,000	______	Attach enrollment/aid schedule
Spring tuition	1001	4,700,000	4,935,000	______	Attach enrollment/aid schedule
Summer session	1002	624,000	655,200	______	
Total revenues		10,324,000	10,840,200		
Faculty salaries	3000	4,890,000	5,036,700	xxxxxx	Use salary detail sheet
Professional salaries	3100	100,000	103,000	xxxxxx	Use salary detail sheet
Benefits pool charge	3400	1,247,500	1,284,925		
Total compensation		6,237,500	6,424,625		
Fall financial aid	4000	40,000	42,000	______	Attach enrollment/aid schedule
Spring financial aid	4100	36,000	37,800	______	Attach enrollment/aid schedule
Summer session financial aid	4200	4,000	4,200	______	
Total financial aid		80,000	84,000		
Office supplies	5000	82,000	82,820	______	
Lab supplies	5050	315,000	318,150	______	
Postage	5200	177,000	178,770	______	
Photocopying and duplicating	5250	80,000	80,800	______	
Telephones—long distance	5410	28,000	28,280	______	
Total operating expenses		682,000	688,820		

After these results have been compiled, the data will be used to issue budget summaries for review and approval by the organization's leaders and board. The budget summary may be accompanied by the additional forms that provide more detail for areas that leaders and the board want to review.

18.3 MONITORING

Each month the organization will need to issue statements of current activity for each account, including transaction and personnel details. Managers will review these reports to make sure the correct transactions have been posted to the account. The summary statement usually contains the

Exhibit 18.2 University of Okoboji Salary Proposal Worksheet

Account number	122100			
Name	MBA Program			
Manager	Alice Stewart			
Address	312 Baker			
Date generated	3/19/xx			

Position Number	Title	Incumbent	Current Salary	Proposed
221-1001	Administrative assistant	Jane Swiney	33,000	
221-1003	Associate director	James Throckmorton	36,000	
221-1004	Database administrator	Sara Smith	31,000	
			100,000	0

Exhibit 18.3 University of Okoboji Capital Request Form

Complete this form for requests for capital expenditures up to $25,000. Capital requests include requests for facilities alterations, furniture, equipment, and software that costs over $500, and all computer hardware, photocopiers, printers, and fax machines. Contact the Facilities Department for procedures on projects over $25,000.

Department: ______________________

Requested by: ______________________

Account number: ______________________

Location (building and room number): ______________________

Description of request/item: ______________________

____

Reason/use for acquisition/project: ______________________

____

Estimated cost: ____________ (attach further description of costs if needed)

Source for estimate: ____________

Date required: ____________

Submitted: ______________________ Date: ____________

Budget Manager

Approval: ______________________ Date: ____________

Vice President

budget, current month activity, and year-to-date total activity. Other information could include the budget for the period, encumbrances, and the remaining budget. See Exhibits 18.4, 18.5, and 18.6.

Periodically, the organization will want to assemble higher-level reports of financial activity and collect and present projections. A report might have to be issued for each account that shows the budget, activity to date, and provides a space for departments to fill in their projections. Detailed projections may be requested on key revenue source or expense types.

18.4 EVALUATION

At the end of the year, the organization should issue statements for each account showing budget, actual results, previous year's results, and pos-

Exhibit 18.4 University of Okoboji Account Results for August, xxxx

Account number 1-22100
Name MBA Program
Manager Alice Stewart
Address 312 Baker
Date generated 9/08/xx

Description	*Object Code*	*Budget*	*Current Month*	*Encumbrances*	*Total to Date*	*Percent Rec/Exp*
Fall tuition	1000	$5,000,000	$0			0.0
Spring tuition	1001	4,700,000	0			0.0
Summer session	1002	624,000	105,000		420,000	67.3
Total revenues		10,324,000	105,000	0	420,000	4.1
Faculty salaries	3000	4,890,000	225,000		450,000	9.2
Professional salaries	3100	100,000	8,333		16,733	16.7
Benefits pool charge	3400	1,247,500	58,333	0	116,683	9.4
Total compensation		6,237,500	291,667	0	583,417	9.4
Fall financial aid	4000	40,000	0		0	0.0
Spring financial aid	4100	36,000	0		0	0.0
Summer session financial aid	4200	4,000	500		1,500	37.5
Total financial aid		80,000	500	0	1,500	1.9
Office supplies	5000	82,000	2,000		2,500	3.0
Lab supplies	5050	315,000	12,000	2,000	26,000	8.3
Postage	5200	177,000	40,000		42,500	24.0
Photocopying and duplicating	5250	80,000	225		1,225	1.5
Telephones—long distance	5410	28,000	2,000		4,100	14.6
Total operating expenses		682,000	56,225	2,000	76,325	11.2
Total expenses		6,999,500	348,392	2,000	661,242	9.4
Net		$3,324,500	($243,392)	($2,000)	($241,242)	–7.3

Exhibit 18.5 University of Okoboji Transaction Detail for August, xxxx

Account Number	1-22100
Name	MBA Program
Manager	Alice Stewart
Address	312 Baker
Date generated	09/08/xx

Description	Object Code	Transaction Number	Date	Vendor	Description	Reference Document	Amount
Summer session		1002 CR1103	08/04/xx		Tuition receipts		55,000.00
		CR1104	08/18/xx		Tuition receipts		50,000.00
	Total						105,000.00
Faculty salaries		3000JV1121	08/01/xx		August payroll		225,000.00
	Total						
Professional salaries		3100JV1122	08/01/xx		August payroll		8,333.33
	Total						
Benefits pool charge		3400JV1123	08/01/xx		August payroll		58,333.33
	Total						
Summer session financial aid		4200JV1135	08/04/xx		Financial aid expense		500.00
	Total						
Office supplies		5000JV1125	08/01/xx	Main Street Office Supplies		PO303456	120.73
		TR1123	08/04/xx	Campus Bookstore	Bookstore charges	BR11275	46.15
		JV1129	08/08/xx	AMA Publications	AMA Journal	PO303433	75.00
		TR1131	08/11/xx	Printing Department	Photocopier paper	TR11411	250.00
		JV1131	08/11/xx	Babbit Furniture	Computer table	PO303459	425.00
		JV1132	08/11/xx	Babbit Furniture	File cabinets	PO303460	410.00
		JV1138	08/22/xx	Harvard Business Review Press	Time-based manufacturing video series	PO303421	242.80
		TR1134	08/23/xx	Campus Bookstore	Bookstore charges	BR11276	95.32
		JV1140	08/30/xx	InfoLand	LindoPro	PO303461	335.00
	Total						2,000.00

Exhibit 18.6 University of Okoboji Payroll Detail, August xxxx

Account number		1-22100			
Name		MBA Program			
Manager		Alice Stewart			
Address		312 Baker			
Date generated		08/01/xx			
Description	*Object Code*	*Date*	*Person*	*Title*	*Amount*
Faculty					
Salaries	3000	08/01/xx	Alfred Chandler	Professor	11,000.00
			Frederick Taylor	Professor	8,900.00
			Bennett Harrison	Professor	11,150.00
			Richard Daft	Professor	14,000.00
			Joan Woodward	Professor	11,000.00
			Evelyn Williams	Professor	13,000.00
			Giovanni Arrighi	Professor	10,500.00
			Amryta Sen	Associate Professor	8,200.00
			Gary Becker	Associate Professor	8,105.00
			Henryk Grossman	Associate Professor	7,700.00
			Merton Miller	Associate Professor	8,533.33
			Ronald Coase	Associate Professor	8,133.33
			Ernest Mandel	Associate Professor	7,700.00
			George Stigler	Associate Professor	7,880.00
			Kenneth Arrow	Associate Professor	7,933.33
			Leon McAuliffe	Assistant Professor	7,900.00
			Henry Maddox	Assistant Professor	6,800.00
			Allison Moorer	Assistant Professor	6,633.33
			Yang Yi	Assistant Professor	6,200.00
			William Black	Assistant Professor	6,233.33
			Thomas Duncan	Assistant Professor	6,100.00
			Rebecca Stout	Assistant Professor	5,885.00
			Abida Parveen	Assistant Professor	6,233.33
			Bascom Lunsford	Assistant Professor	6,400.00
			Ernest Stoneman	Assistant Professor	5,480.00
			Janet Wygal	Assistant Professor	5,900.00
			Mokkapati Rao	Assistant Professor	6,000.00
			Cecil Sharp	Assistant Professor	5,500.00
			Total		224,999.98
Professional					
Salaries	3100	08/01/xx	Jane Swiney	Administrative Assistant	2,750.00
			James Throckmorton	Associate Director	3,000.00
			Sara Smith	Database Administrator	2,583.33
			Total		8,333

sibly next year's budget. This report contains the detail information that will form the lowest level of variance analysis. The organization will also produce reports on an organization-wide level and at higher levels of summary that can be used to study the financial performance of the organization and its major parts. See Exhibit 18.7.

Exhibit 18.7 University of Okoboji Account Results for June, xxxx

Account number	1-22100					
Name	MBA Program					
Manager	Alice Stewart					
Address	312 Baker					
Date generated	07/18/xx					
Description	*Object Code*	*Current Budget*	*Current Month*	*Encum-brances*	*Total to Date*	*Variance*
Fall tuition	1000	$5,000,000			$5,210,000	$210,000
Spring tuition	1001	4,700,000			4,810,000	110,000
Summer session	1002	624,000	170,000		622,000	(2,000)
Total revenues		10,324,000	170,000	0	10,642,000	318,000
Faculty salaries	3000	4,890,000	225,000		5,030,115	(140,115)
Professional salaries	3100	100,000	8,333		103,000	(3,000)
Benefits pool charge	3400	1,247,500	58,333		1,283,279	(35,779)
Total compensation		6,237,500	291,667	0	6,416,394	(178,894)
Fall financial aid	4000	40,000	0		55,000	(15,000)
Spring financial aid	4100	36,000	0		50,000	(14,000)
Summer session financial aid	4200	4,000	2,500		4,200	(200)
Total financial aid		80,000	2,500	0	109,200	(29,200)
Office supplies	5000	82,000	17,000		84,000	(2,000)
Lab supplies	5050	315,000	54,000		310,000	5,000
Postage	5200	177,000	45,000		215,000	(38,000)
Photocopying and duplicating	5250	80,000	600		83,000	(3,000)
Telephones—long distance	5410	28,000	2,000		27,000	1,000
Total operating expenses		682,000	118,600	0	719,000	(37,000)
Total expenses		6,999,500	412,767	0	7,244,594	(245,094)
Net		$3,324,500	($242,767)	$0	$3,397,406	$72,906

18.5 CONCLUSION

Based on the samples in this chapter, an organization leader or budget manager should be able to design forms and reports to support budget preparation, monitoring, and year-end evaluation. Even with the advent of electronic means for collecting and disseminating information, it is necessary to bring this sort of information together in one place where it can be used by participants in the budget process.

CHAPTER NINETEEN

Automation

19.1 INTRODUCTION

Information technology can facilitate the budget process in a few primary areas:

- Modeling and guideline development
- Developing and processing proposals
- Analyzing results

There is a great deal of diversity in how information technology is used for budgeting and financial analysis. Some organizations make little use of automation and work with paper documents; others develop fairly complicated systems to support this process. The particular tools in use vary greatly from organization to organization.

19.2 MODELING AND GUIDELINE DEVELOPMENT

The budget process starts with the development of multiyear projections of the organization's finances. This information allows the organization to set guidelines for the budget proposals it will soon request. Most organizations will need some sort of computer model to project the organization's finances and test guidelines. The model can be a simple spreadsheet that mirrors the budget statement and allows the organization to test the net effect of different combinations of changes in revenues and expenses. Larger organizations need to consider different structures for their model and may look at using tools other than spreadsheets. Budget models need to be tailored to the financial conditions of the organization, so many organization have built their own budget model or had one custom designed for them.

19.3 PROPOSAL DEVELOPMENT AND PROCESSING

Automation can assist in several stages of developing proposals and processing them. The first step may be to calculate the budget base for each department and generate worksheets that will include that base and have room for departments to indicate their proposal. The program can also calculate the allowable increase pool so that departments and reviewers will know whether their proposals are within limits. These worksheets can be generated through a program that is part of the financial system, through the use of a reporting tool such as Focus, or by creating a separate budget system in Excel or another application.

Departments themselves may want a tool to help them develop their proposals. In some cases, the central administration is able to provide this capacity through spreadsheets or programs linked to the central system. Quite often when such a system is not provided, managers will create their own spreadsheets for developing and testing various proposals. The larger the unit and the more complicated its accounting structure, the more interest its manager will have in an automated tool for budget development.

Once proposals have been developed, they should be communicated to higher-level managers for review or approval, which can be accomplished with paper forms. However, eventually all of these proposals will have to be compiled to determine whether the proposals taken together meet the organization's overall requirements. Therefore, an electronic version of the budget proposals can save work for those reviewing and compiling them. This capability is particularly important if the organization has to do a reassessment in light of the net effect of all of the information. It may be necessary to determine how much additional revenue or lower spending is required to balance the budget, and possible solutions such as 1% higher prices. This assessment is much easier if the information has been compiled electronically.

Even organizations that do not provide a tool to assist managers in developing proposals may ask them to input their proposals into spreadsheets or a mainframe program so that they can be shared in electronic form and easily compiled. If a proposal development tool is available, it may be integrated with the tool used to compile proposals and to create the organizational budget.

The organization also needs to generate reports on its overall budget to take to its board for approval. Again, most organizations other than very small ones will want to generate these reports from automated sources to make sure that the math is correct and that all components of the budget proposals have been included.

Once approved, the budget amounts must be entered into the organization's accounting system. Some organizations will have integrated their software so that the tools that compile their proposals will also feed budget data into the accounting system. If those interfaces have not been built, the budgets may need to be entered manually into the system or into separate files that are uploaded to the accounting system.

All of these functions related to proposal development and processing can be handled through an integrated software application or through a combination of tools. Integrated tools may take more time and money to develop or acquire, but they will tend to reduce the potential for errors as data are transferred from one application to the next. Enterprise financial software may include budget development tools, but the budget module may not be well suited to the organization's budget process, requiring modifications to the off-the-shelf application and potentially delaying implementation.

19.4 FINANCIAL ANALYSIS

In order to monitor and analyze results, managers and central staff need to have access to up-to-date results on a regular basis and to transaction detail. Some systems allow users to access financial results on a real-time basis that includes all activity up to the time the system was accessed. More common are systems that provide data after the month has closed. Traditionally, managers received these reports in hard-copy form, but now they are increasingly getting access to this information on-line.

When current period information is available in hard copy only, or through look-up only on-line access (in which users can call up data to review it on screen or print, but cannot change or add to the content in any way), users may decide to input the data into their own systems for analysis and tracking. Common approaches include setting up a spreadsheet into which these data are input. Some users track transactions as they occur and then compare the centrally generated reports with the data in their local system. Usually those records differ because of timing differences in recording transactions centrally and locally, requiring an informal or formal reconciliation.

Allowing users to access the accounting system itself creates security and performance risks. Technology specialists have developed alternative approaches such as data warehousing, in which data are extracted from the system on a regular basis and copied to another system where users can access the information for analysis and reporting, but it is not fed back to the accounting system.

More sophisticated tools such as data warehousing and on-line analytical processing (OLAP) allow users to link current period data with previous periods, change the inclusion or display criteria to focus on some accounts or expense and revenue categories, or group information in different ways. The database may also include personnel and other data (such as enrollments at a university) that are necessary to thoroughly understand the raw financial figures. These tools are somewhat expensive and are most useful for central financial analysts or staff in large units, so they are found most often in large organizations. Other organizations will bring these data together as needed in spreadsheet or desktop databases.

19.5 CONCLUSION

Participants in budgeting for not-for-profit organizations should expect automation in the budget process to grow in the near future. Until recently, many of the tools available have been very expensive or badly suited to the needs of not-for-profit organizations. Organizations have more often built tools for themselves from readily available applications such as spreadsheets, limited by their expertise in using the application and the capacity of computers to process the tools strung together within these applications. New tools will make many more features available that are more affordable and user-friendly.

Glossary

Accrual accounting: A method of accounting for operating results whereby revenues are reported as earned in the period in which goods or services are delivered to the customer or client and in which expenses are matched with the period when the organization used the goods or services. For example, under accrual accounting an item that is paid in advance is not recognized as an expense until the goods or services purchased are consumed by the organization. Revenue is recorded as income at the time services are delivered to a customer, even if the organization receives the cash payment from the customer later. An accrual accounting system is designed to present a more accurate picture of economic events during a period than accounting on a cash basis, under which results might be distorted by the timing of disbursements or receipts.

Activity-based budgeting: A budgeting system in which funds are allocated on the basis of the cost required to achieve expected levels of outputs. An activity-based budgeting system requires that an organization undergo an activity-based costing study to identify its outputs (services or goods); the activities directly related to generating those outputs; and the other activities that support the organization's primary activities, as well as the types of costs consumed by those activities and the rate with which each unit of the activity consumes those costs.

Balance sheet: The statement of an organization's assets, liabilities, and fund balances at a given point in time. It is referred to in some organizations as the statement of financial position.

Benefits: Compensation other than pay for time worked. Benefits include programs such as health insurance, pensions, or life insurance that may be funded entirely or in part by the employer. In some cases a benefits program is funded by employee contributions in addition employer payments. Benefits can also take a form that does not involve a payment by the employer, such as a supplemental life insurance program in which employees pay the whole cost at low rates that the employer, by virtue of its size, has been able to negotiate with carriers.

Budget base: Under an incremental budgeting system, the initial set of expenses and revenues to which increase (or decrease) factors are applied to calculate the total funds and revenue targets for the next fiscal year.

Capital budget: An organization's planned funding and expenses related to the acquisition and disposal of assets from which it expects to receive benefits for a period greater than one year. Capital assets can include facilities, building systems, large-scale computer software, vehicles, furniture and fixtures, equipment, library books, works of art, and stage sets.

Capitalization: In *accrual accounting,* an entry that offsets the operating expense related to a capital acquisition so that the multiyear cost of a capital item does not appear on the operating statement in the expenditure for its acquisition, but through depreciation entries that represent its use.

Capital project: A project involving the purchase, construction, or creation of a capital asset.

Carry forwards: Unused funds from a department or program's budget in one year that the department or program is allowed to use in subsequent years in addition to its normal funding allocation. Surpluses (unused spending authority) and deficits (excess spending) may be carried forward. Carrying forward a deficit usually reduces the department or program's funds in subsequent years.

Cash budget: An organization's planned cash receipts and disbursements for a particular period of time.

Chart of accounts: A structured system that defines the fund groups, and asset, liability, revenue, and expense types that will be used to categorize all financial transactions. The chart of accounts typically includes a numeric system that establishes hierarchical relationships of funds and assets, liability, income and expense codes, titles and definitions for each fund and code, and rules for their use.

Classification system: A system that defines the jobs in an organization, groups them, and assigns them to pay ranges.

Contingency: Funds to be used for discretionary or emergency purposes, and that are not allocated for a specific purpose at the time the budget is established.

Control: A system put in place by an organization's board, management, and other personnel to provide reasonable assurance regarding the effectiveness and efficiency of operations, reliability of financial reporting, and compliance with applicable laws and regulations. A control system consists of the overall control environment, risk assessment, control activities (such as reviews, reconciliations, information processing edits, physical controls, segregation of duties, and policies and procedures), and communication and monitoring.

Cost allocation: The process of associating costs with or assigning them to departments, activities, or programs (cost objects). Some costs may be directly identified with a department, activity, or program, such as the salaries for personnel assigned to a department. Other costs have an indirect relationship to the ultimate cost objects and are allocated according to activity levels, formulas, or some other method.

Cyclicality: A repeating pattern exhibited by time series data. A cyclical pattern may vary in its magnitude and temporal length.

Depreciation: In *accrual accounting*, an expense charged against operating results that represents the value of that portion of an asset's useful life estimated to be expended during the accounting period. Depreciation entries are based on a schedule developed at the time an asset is acquired that estimates the asset's annual decrease in value.

Endowment: Organizational assets held on a long-term basis whose use is limited to the income or a portion of the income earned by those assets. True endowments are established by stipulation of the donor of the asset and restricted to use as endowment on a permanent basis or for a specified time period. An organization's board may also set aside funds and treat them like an endowment, making a long-term investment of the asset and limiting use to income earned; these are often called quasi-endowment funds.

Financial equilibrium: A condition achieved when an organization's current and future revenues and cash receipts are projected to be sufficient to cover its projected operating costs and cash requirements and to sustain its long-term capacity to fulfill its organizational mission.

Fiscal year: A 12-month period that an organization designates as its year for accounting, reporting, and other business purposes. Common practices are to begin the fiscal year on January 1 or July 1, but any starting date can be chosen as long as it is applied consistently from year to year and there is a good business reason for choosing that period.

Fixed cost: Costs that do not change in response to changes in the levels of a specific activity. A cost that may be fixed in relation to one activity may be variable in relation to another. A not-for-profit organization typically defines fixed costs as those that do not vary in relation to changes in the volume of services it delivers.

Fund accounting: An accounting system under which funds are segregated according to donor restrictions and board designations. Fund types commonly in use include current unrestricted funds, current or temporarily restricted funds, endowment funds, and plan funds. Use of fund accounting is limited to not-for-profit organizations.

Fund balances: The difference between the total assets and total liabilities of a not-for-profit organization, or of particular funds within an organization.

Incremental budgeting: A budgeting system in which the budget for the next year is based on the current year's budget. The current year's budget serves as a budget base that is increased or decreased by some amount or rate to arrive at a new budget. Different increase factors may be applied to different revenue and expense elements (such as salaries, equipment, etc.).

Markets: A framework within which owners of property rights can make contact with each other and trade something for which they can jointly determine the price.

Object codes: Within an organization's chart of accounts, the codes used to identify specific types of transactions.

Operating budget. The organization's plan for revenues and expenses related to current period operating activity. Current period operating activity consists of revenues for services delivered and expenses for services consumed in the time period covered by the budget.

Operating statement: An organization's statement of its cumulative current operating revenues and expenses during a particular time period. The operating statement is one of the three basic statements used in financial accounting (the other two being the *balance sheet* and *statement of cash flows*). Organizations use different names for this statement, including income statement, statement of activities, statement of changes in unrestricted net assets, and statement of current funds revenues, expenditures, and other changes.

Program budgets: The budget for a discrete program within an organization. The program may be defined according to organizational characteristics (e.g., the activities and associated revenue and costs of a single department or director) or funding source (e.g., activities and costs funded from a particular grant).

Project budgets: The budget for a particular project, including all costs directly associated with the project or assigned to it: it may also identify the source of funds for the project. Project budgets are most frequently developed for capital projects, but they are also used for special projects within an organization's operations (e.g., a major fund-raising event).

Reconciliation: The process of checking a figure or set of figures from one source against figures from another source that are expected to have the same values or exhibit a predicted degree of difference.

Responsibility center budgeting: A system under which an organization's operating budget is divided into responsibility centers that include all of the activities and units that make up discrete programmatic areas and are controlled by one manager. The manager of a responsibility center is responsible for meeting a targeted net result after all revenues and expenses for all accounts under his or her control are aggregated. The manager is free to make trade-offs between accounts and revenue and expense object codes (possibly with some policy restrictions) to achieve the best combination of financial efficiency and program effectiveness.

Restricted funds: Funds whose use is restricted to certain purposes by the donor.

Risk: The degree of uncertainty about future results. In financial transactions, investments that carry more risk are expected to pay a risk premium as compensation for the greater possibility that returns may be worse than expected.

Scarcity: A concept from economics that when demand for any particular good or service exceeds the supply, mechanisms to optimize the use of resources and the consumption of what is produced become necessary. The concept is important to budgeting because it implies that there will always be competition within an organization for resources, and therefore, that every organization needs a method for making choices between conflicting demands.

Seasonality: A pattern that repeats itself at a fixed temporal interval. A phenomenon can exhibit seasonality that corresponds to points in the course of a year, quarter, month, week, or any other unit of time. Seasonal patterns can occur in conjunction with trend patterns so that the seasonal fluctuations appear as rates of deviation from the trend line.

Statement of cash flows: An organization's statement of its cumulative cash receipts and disbursements during a particular time period.

Statement of Financial Accounting Standards 116: The Financial Accounting Standards Board statement governing not-for-profit organizations' accounting for contributions. SFAS 116 declares that all contributions should be recorded as revenue in the period in which they are received or pledged.

Statement of Financial Accounting Standards 117: The Financial Accounting Standards Board statement governing the external financial statements of not-for-profit organizations. SFAS 117 established new standards for external financial reporting, including the replacement of the fund structure traditionally used by not-for-profit organizations with a new structure for reporting net assets according to three classes: unrestricted, temporarily restricted, and permanently restricted.

Step functions: Any phenomenon in which a dependent variable exhibits a discontinuous rate of change in response to changes in another factor. In step functions, the dependent variable moves to its next increment of value not with each change in value of the driver or independent variable, but only when the driver reaches a certain level.

Trend: A consistent rate of growth or decline exhibited over time by a phenomenon.

Unrestricted funds: Funds that an organization receives without restriction as to their use.

Useful life: The estimated amount of time a capital asset is expected to be in service, used as the basis for its *depreciation.* The useful life of an asset for accounting purposes is usually based on industry standards applied to broad categories of assets rather than an analytically based projection of the amount of service for a specific item. For example, many accountants apply a useful life of five years to vehicles based on the assumption that, on average, after five years of use a vehicle will be unusable or will require excessive maintenance costs.

Variable costs: Costs that increase or decrease in relation to some activity factor, such as sales or participation rates.

Variances: The mathematical difference between two values for the same expense and/or revenue factor within the same set of fund groups, account groups, departments, or programs. Variances can be calculated for the differences between any combination of budgets, projections, and actual results for various time periods.

Volatility: The degree to which a phenomenon exhibits wide, difficult-to-predict swings in values over time. A phenomenon can exhibit volatility relative to a median point or a trend line.

Zero-based budgeting: A budgeting system in which an organization builds up its budget from scratch, starting with a projection of revenues and service levels that serves as the basis for determining the need for resources by the organization. In a zero-based budgeting system, every element within each of the organization's budgets must be justified each year. Zero-based budgeting contrasts with *incremental budgeting*, in which the organization's future budget is based on the current budget levels.

Bibliography

BUDGETING AND ACCOUNTING

Anthony, Robert N., and David W. Young, *Management Control in Nonprofit Organizations*, 6th ed. (Homewood: Richard D. Irwin, 1998).

Blazek, Jody, *Financial Planning for Nonprofit Organizations* (New York: Wiley, 1996).

Finney, Robert G., *Basics of Budgeting* (New York: American Management Association, 1994).

Garner, C. William, *Accounting and Budgeting in Public and Nonprofit Organizations* (San Francisco: Jossey–Bass, 1991).

Herbst, Anthony, *The Handbook of Capital Investing: Analyses and Strategies for Investment in Capital Assets* (New York: Harper, 1990).

Horngren, Charles T., and George Foster, *Cost Accounting: A Managerial Emphasis*, 7th ed. (Englewood Cliffs: Prentice Hall, 1991).

Johnson, Hazel J., *Strategic Capital Budgeting: Developing and Implementing the Corporate Capital Allocation Program* (Chicago: Probus, 1994).

Rachlin, Robert, and H.W. Allen Sweeny, editors, *Handbook of Budgeting*, 4th ed. (New York: Wiley, 1998).

Shim, Jae K., and Joel G. Siegel, *Financial Management for Nonprofits* (New York: McGraw Hill, 1997).

FORECASTING

Fogarty, Donald W., John H. Blackstone, Jr., and Thomas R. Hoffman, *Production and Inventory Management*, 2nd ed. (Cincinnati: South–Western, 1991).

Nahimas, Stephen, *Production and Operations Analysis* (Homewood: Irwin, 1989).

SPECIAL TOPICS IN BUDGETING

Cooper, Robin, and Robert S. Kaplan, "The Promise—and Peril—of Integrated Cost Systems," *Harvard Business Review*, July–August 1998, Volume 76, Number 4, pp. 109–119.

Phyrr, Peter A., *Zero-Base Budgeting: A Practical Management Tool for Evaluating Expenses* (New York: Wiley, 1973).

Whalen, Edward, *Responsibility Center Budgeting: An Approach to Decentralized Management for Institutions of Higher Education* (Bloomington: Indiana University Press, 1991).

STRATEGY

Allison, Michael, and Jude Kaye, *Strategic Planning for Nonprofit Organizations: A Practical Guide and Workbook* (New York: Wiley, 1997).

Brinckerhoff, Peter G., *Mission-Based Management: Leading Your Not-For-Profit Into the 21st Century* (New York: Wiley, 1998).

Bryson, John M., *Strategic Planning for Public and Nonprofit Organizations: A Guide to Strengthening and Sustaining Organizational Achievement* (San Francisco: Jossey–Bass, 1988).

Eadie, Douglas C., *Changing by Design: A Practical Approach to Leading Innovation in Nonprofit Organizations* (San Francisco: Jossey–Bass, 1997).

Fahey, Liam, and Robert M. Randall, *The Portable MBA in Strategy* (New York: Wiley, 1994).

Porter, Michael E., *Competitive Advantage: Creating and Sustaining Superior Performance* (New York: Free Press, 1985).

Steckel, Richard, Robin Simons, and Peter Lengsfelder, *Filthy Rich and Other Nonprofit Fantasies: Changing the Way Nonprofits Do Business in the 90s* (Berkeley: Ten Speed Press, 1989).

Index